Human Relations and Your Career

Third Edition

DAVID W. JOHNSON

University of Minnesota

D1399491

PRENTICE HALL, Englewood Cliffs, New Jersey 07632

Library of Congress Cataloging-in-Publication Data

Johnson, David W.
   Human relations and your career / David W. Johnson.
      p. cm.
    Includes index.
  ISBN 0–13–446253–X
    1. Career development. 2. Interpersonal relations. 3. Work
  groups. I. Title.
  HF5381.J56 1991
  650.1′3—dc20   90–14222
                                CIP

This book is dedicated to my father and grandfather, who taught me the meaning of work, and to the many employers and coworkers who taught me how to survive on the job.

Editorial/production supervision
  and interior design: *Mary Kathryn Leclercq*
Cover design: *Ray Lundgren Graphics, Ltd.*
Prepress buyer: *Debbie Kesar*
Manufacturing buyer: *Mary Ann Gloriande*

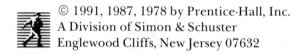
Printed in the United States of America
10 9 8 7 6 5 4 3 2 1

ISBN   0-13-446253-X

Prentice-Hall International (UK) Limited, *London*
Prentice-Hall of Australia Pty. Limited, *Sydney*
Prentice-Hall Canada Inc., *Toronto*
Prentice-Hall Hispanoamericana, S. A., *Mexico*
Prentice-Hall of India Private Limited, *New Delhi*
Prentice-Hall of Japan, Inc., *Tokyo*
Simon & Schuster Asia Pte. Ltd., *Singapore*
Editora Prentice-Hall do Brasil, Ltda., *Rio de Janeiro*

Contents

Preface

Human Relations and Your Career is designed to teach the interpersonal and group skills needed to be successful. A major complaint of employers is that many people lack the skills in getting along, cooperating, communicating, and managing conflicts with fellow employees. In most career training programs, not enough attention is paid to the cooperative skills needed to build productive and satisfying relationships on the job. No matter what a person's job is, no matter how his or her career is developing, the interpersonal and group skills needed to work cooperatively with others are essential. There is no substitute for working effectively with other people. Persons who cannot cooperate, communicate, help make high quality decisions, and resolve conflicts constructively are not selected for retention and promotion.

 Human Relations and Your Career introduces readers to the (a) theory and research findings needed to understand how to interact effectively with fellow employees and (b) the skills required to apply that knowledge in practical situations. Expertise in working with other people is based on an integration of such knowledge and skills. This is more than a book reviewing current knowledge in the area of interpersonal and small group skills, and it is more than a book of skill-building exercises. The theory and exercises are integrated into an inquiry or experiential approach to learning. Just as "the truth will make you free," **throughout one's life, choices, opportunities, and successes are created by (a) knowledge of social skills and (b) mastery of the skills required to apply that knowledge in practical situations.**

This book is designed so that readers can learn practical interpersonal skills through structured experiences as well as through reading the text material. Exercises in each chapter provide experiences involving the attitudes and skills relevant to working effectively with other persons.

The purposes of this book, therefore, are to (a) provide a clear conceptualization of the interpersonal and group skills needed to be a competent employee, (b) provide educational experiences, exercises, and simulations to help readers learn and practice these skills, and (c) help readers understand **when** the use of specific skills is appropriate.

Acknowledgments

I wish to thank many people for their help in writing this book. Judy Bartlett has been of invaluable help. I owe much to the psychologists who have influenced my theorizing and to the colleagues with whom I have conducted various types of experiential learning sessions. Whenever possible I have acknowledged the sources of the exercises that are not original in this book, but a few are so commonly used that the originators are not traceable. I wish to thank the vocational educators who read the manuscript and commented on it: John M. Neimann, Indiana Vocational Technical College; John Adamski II, Indiana Vocational Technical College; and Sandra Wolfe, DeKalb Technical Institute; and the students who did likewise. Special thanks go to my wife, Linda Mulholland Johnson, who contributed her support to the development and writing of this book. Finally, I wish to thank the artists, Nancy Waller and Tom Grummett, who drew the cartoon illustrations. All the photographs (with a few exceptions) were taken by me.

David W. Johnson

1

What This Book Is About and How to Use It

Each chapter in this book begins with a Questionnaire. Its purpose is to explain the main terms and concepts of the chapter. (The answers are given on the right side of the page.) To do the Questionnaire, cover the answer column with a strip of cardboard or paper. Working with a partner, read the first question and come to an agreement about your answer. Then, move the strip of cardboard down to uncover the correct answer. Check your answer to each question before going on to the next one.

After completing the Questionnaire that follows, you should be able to define and give examples of:

- Organization
- Cooperation
- Technical job survival skills
- Interpersonal job survival skills
- Learning from experience
- Feedback

Now turn the page, cover the answers, and begin.

QUESTIONNAIRE: Main Concepts in Chapter 1

1. All work takes place within organizations. An *organization* is a planned group that is formed to achieve a set of goals. General Motors is an organization because it consists of a group of people organized to achieve the goal of making products for a profit. When several people join together to form a window-washing company, they are forming an _____.

   organization

2. A business is a group of pepole who have _____ themselves to produce and sell a certain product or service.

   organized

3. All organizations are based on cooperation among their members. Two or more people are *cooperating* when they act together to achieve desired goals. Within Ford Motor Company, workers cooperate to build cars. _____ is two or more people acting together to achieve desired goals.

   Cooperation

4. An example of *cooperation* would be when one person scrubs a window and another person dries it. Or, when one person unpacks a store's merchandise and places it on shelves and another person takes the merchandise off the shelves and sells it to customers, the two persons are _____ in running a store.

   cooperating

5. When several people form a business, they have created an _____ based on _____ among the persons employed by the business.

   organization
   cooperation

6. To survive on the job, a person needs organizational skills. *Organizational skills* include arriving on time, rarely missing work, following through on assigned tasks, and having good work habits. If workers have good work habits and follow through on assigned tasks, they have _____ _____.

   organizational skills

7. To survive on the job, a person needs technical skills. *Technical skills* include repairing a car, programming a computer, and giving a haircut. They are the skills needed to do the technical aspects of a job. If a person hired to repair television sets is skilled at doing it, then that person has the _____ skills needed for the job.

   technical

8. To survive on the job, a person needs interpersonal skills. *Interpersonal skills* include cooperating with

coworkers, communicating skillfully, and resolving conflicts productively. If a worker is able to form good relationships with fellow employees and constructively resolve any conflicts that come up on the job, that person has good _____ skills.

interpersonal

9. Everyone learns from experience. *Learning from experience* involves having an experience, thinking about it, and making conclusions about how to improve a given behavior next time. When you lose your temper, yell at a customer, think it over, and decide not to do it again in the future, you are learning from your _____.

experience

10. In order to learn skills, you need feedback on how well you are doing something. To get *feedback,* have someone observe you practice a skill and tell you how well you are performing that skill so that you can improve. When you ask coworkers to observe your communication skills and to tell you their observations, you are asking for _____.

feedback

Surviving on the Job

○   ○   ○

"In an industrial organization it's group effort that counts. There's really no room for stars in an industrial organization. You need talented people, but they can't do it alone. They have to have help."

John F. Donnelly, President, Donnelly Mirrors

○   ○   ○

John is an excellent computer programmer. He likes computers, and computers seem to like him. He works very fast and is really good at his job. At his last job, he never missed a day of work in six months and was always on time. He worked overtime whenever he was asked. But he could not get along with his fellow employees. He argued, complained, fought, criticized, and generally upset everyone he interacted with. After six months with the company, he was fired. He did not survive on the job because he could not get along with other people.

A basic requirement for getting a job, being successful at your work, and progressing in your career, is the ability to work effectively with others. Your job survival depends on how well you can relate to fellow employees, suppliers, and customers. The question all employers have in mind when they interview each job applicant is, "Can this person get along with other people?" Having the technical skills needed for the job is not enough. Your ability to get along with fellow employees can spell the difference between success and failure on the job.

This is a book about working with other people. It will give you a clear understanding of what interpersonal skills are needed on the job, and it will provide experiences aimed at helping you learn and practice these skills. Having these skills will influence whether or not you can survive on the job.

The work most people do for pay usually takes place in an organization. An *organization* is a network of interpersonal relationships structured to achieve goals. Factories, stores, and gas stations are all examples of organizations. Their goal is to make a profit. Some organizations, such as General Motors, are very large and employ tens of thousands of people. Other organizations, such as family restaurants, are small and may employ only ten or twelve people. Whatever the size, an organization begins when people join together to make a product or give a service. They decide what kinds of jobs are needed in order for their organization to be a success, and they decide who will do each of the jobs. When the jobs are put together, the organization exists. If everyone works hard and all are able to work together well, the organization will be successful—which means making a profit, expanding, and hiring more employees.

Edythe, Keith, and Dale, for example, decide to form an organization which they name Edythe's Car Repair. To earn a profit they must advertise, buy parts and tools, keep records of money collected and paid out, and do the repair work. Dale becomes the buyer and purchases the parts and tools on time so that the mechanics can do their job. Keith advertises to attract customers and also does the bookkeeping to make sure adequate money is being collected to pay for the new parts and tools. Edythe repairs the cars. By doing their jobs well and cooperating with each other, they ensure the success of their company and thereby ensure the success of their careers. Each could not run the whole company by himself.* In an organization, individual efforts do not lead to individual success. A company can go bankrupt no matter how hard any one individual works. It is their joint efforts, the combining of their unique and different skills and competencies, that make success possible.

Career Cycle: Employability, Job Success, and Career Progression

Career success depends on moving through the cycle of:

1. Getting a job.
2. Succeeding at your job (getting raises and recognition).
3. Leaving a job (for a better one).

To be employable, to be successful at your work, and to progress within your chosen career you must have three types of competencies:

*Male and female pronouns are used at random throughout this book.

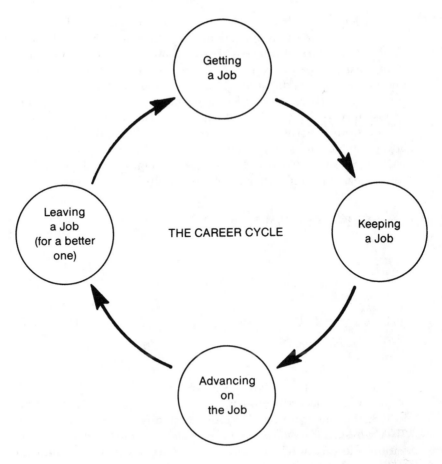

1. **Interpersonal skills,** such as cooperating, communicating, and resolving conflicts.
2. **Organizational skills,** such as:
   a. Reliability—arriving on time, not missing work, and not making mistakes.
   b. Responsibility—following through on assigned tasks, taking an interest in your work, having good work habits, and being self-disciplined, responsible, loyal to the company, and honest in your dealings with it.
3. **Technical skills,** such as the skills involved in being an accountant, computer programmer, restaurant manager, or secretary.

Employability is your ability to obtain a job. Employability depends on your having the basic interpersonal, organizational, and technical skills needed to do so. *Job success* is the recognition and rewards you receive for being competent and effective at your work. Job success depends on your mastering and demonstrating the basic interpersonal, organizational, and technical skills needed to (1) be perceived as competent, and (2) be liked and appreciated by coworkers, subordinates, and superiors within the company.

When you apply for a job you present yourself as having the necessary technical training and interpersonal and organizational skills to be a productive employee. Being hired for a specific job, however, does not mean that you will be doing that job for the rest of your life. You may be promoted or recruited by another company, depending on the opportunities available and your job performance. *Career progression* is advancing to positions that require greater responsibility for leadership and expertise. Career progression depends on your demonstrating the interpersonal, organizational, and technical skills needed to advance to positions that require more technical expertise and more expertise in motivating, supervising, and leading fellow employees. Progressing in one's chosen career is the long-term goal of most adults in our society.

Technical Skills Are Not Enough

○   ○   ○

"I will pay more for the ability to deal with people than for any other ability under the sun."

John D. Rockefeller

○   ○   ○

If you have the technical skills necessary, you will be successful at the job. Right? Wrong, according to a number of recent government and private reports. In 1982 the Center for Public Resources published *Basic Skills in the U.S. Workforce: The Contrasting Perceptions of Business, Labor, and Public Education.* This study was a nationwide survey of businesses and industries that had annual 1980 sales of greater than $100 million and that employed at least 500 employees. Also included were major labor unions and public educational institutions in all parts of the country. Businesses, labor unions, and schools were in agreement that collab-

orative skills were important in employment retention. Being fired for lacking technical skills was not reported frequently. Being fired for poor job attitudes, poor and disruptive interpersonal relationships, and inappropriate behavior and dress accounted for 90 percent of terminations. The survey shows that for career advancement, interpersonal, technical, and organizational skills are needed.

There is a basic set of academic skills, behavioral patterns, and attitudes toward work that forms the minimum requirement for success in the work force. The President's Committee for Economic Development (1985) conducted a nationwide survey of large and small companies and found that specific occupational skills are less crucial for entry-level employment than are interpersonal skills. Interpersonal skills were identified by both large and small companies as being the key factor for entry-level success and for advancement on the job. The survey found that for entry-level positions, employers are looking for young people who demonstrate a set of attitudes, abilities, and behaviors associated with the ability to work as part of a team. These include being able to communicate well; having a sense of responsibility, self-discipline, and pride; striving to do well; being able to set priorities; and showing enthusiasm. Employers also put a strong value on the ability to continue to learn and the ability to solve problems and make decisions.

These surveys indicate that you must come to the workplace with the competencies, skills, attitudes, and behaviors that are associated with effectively cooperating with coworkers and wanting to do a good job. Teamwork, communication, coordinating your behavior with that of others, and divisions of labor characterize most work settings. *The most important skills for getting a job, being successful in your work, and progressing in your career are the interpersonal skills needed for cooperating with your fellow employees.* If you are not interpersonally skilled, responsible, dependable, and willing to learn, technical abilities are of little value. Once these requirements are met, problem solving and technical skills become important for advancement on the job.

○   ○   ○

There was no identification with the job. No saying, "I am a mechanic." . . . They were already trying not to have any thoughts about their work on the job. In their own way they were . . . living with technology without really having anything to do with it. Or rather, they had something to do with it, but their own selves were outside of it, detached, removed. . . . There is no manual that deals with the real business of motorcycle maintenance, the most important aspect of all. Caring about what you are doing is considered either unimportant or taken for granted.

ROBERT M. PIRSIG

Zen and the Art of Motorcycle Maintenance

○   ○   ○

Technical and scientific knowledge are of no use if you cannot work effectively with other people. It does no good to complete a training program if you cannot work effectively with other people and contribute what you know to joint efforts. The industrial strategy of Japan is a good illustration. Japanese management has been quoted as stating that the success of the Japanese industrial system is not based on the fact that their workers are more intelligent than are the workers of other countries, but rather is based on the fact that their workers are better able to work cooperatively and in harmony with each other.

Other People: You Can't Work Without Them

○　　○　　○

"Coming together is a beginning;
Keeping together is progress;
Working together is success."

Henry Ford

○　　○　　○

No matter what your career, you cannot avoid other people. Some careers (such as mechanic, bookkeeper, and computer technician) involve working with machines and paper for the most part. Other careers (such as beautician, nurse, and receptionist) involve working with people. But every career requires you to work with others for at least some of the time. To do your work, to achieve company and personal goals, you have to interact with other people—coworkers, supervisors, suppliers, and customers. To survive on the job, you have to be able to build and keep good relationships.

These "other people" are a key aspect of your success on the job. They can help you do a good job, or, sometimes they can make you do a bad job. Other people make your work interesting, challenging, rewarding, and meaningful. If you like your fellow employees and they like you, going to work each day will be something you look forward to. But if you dislike your coworkers and they dislike you, it will be difficult to make yourself go to work each day.

An important aspect of career progression is to **build coalitions** with ambitious and competent individuals to advance each other's careers. The relationships formed within training programs and at entry-level jobs can have important consequences for your career success. To ensure that your career progresses, and that you have opportunities to be promoted within the company you work for, form a **network** with hard-working, ambitious, and competent colleagues who are likely to be successful. Everyone who is part of such a social network has a better chance to succeed than isolated individuals who try to make it as loners. It is especially advantageous to network with a competent superior. If you want to progress in your career quickly, for example, be indispensable to your boss. When she gets promoted, she will take you with her.

Organizational Skills: How To Be Successful At Work

There are a number of organization skills that will significantly increase your career success.

1. **Be reliable.** Arrive at work on time, do not miss work, and do not make mistakes in what you do.
2. **Be responsible.** Follow through on assigned tasks, take an interest in your work, have good work habits, and be self-disciplined, loyal to your company, and honest in your dealings with it.
3. **Add value to your work.** Constantly strive to improve the quality of the service or product you provide. Your job security and advancement rest on "adding value" to what you are doing. Reduce waste, improve quality, be creative. You can add value to your work by being creative in thinking of new ways to market and sell the products or services your company provides, use new technology to make differing products or provide new services, or invent new technologies related to what your company does.

4. **Strive for personal excellence.** Take pride in the quality of your work. Be the best that you can be. Be intolerant of mistakes, sloppy work, and negativism. Give positive energy to the people you work with by being cheerful, optimistic, positive.

5. **Improve your work process.** What you do should be constantly changing as you think through how to do it better. In a well-known printing company, the model is "change is job security." The company eats and breathes change. Employees are expected to take training courses and then take more training courses, to learn how to do their job better and then to learn even more, to teach what they know to others and to continue to teach. Most training courses are given on the job and in the company's own school house. This train-train, learn-learn, teach-teach philosophy pervades the actions of teams who run six-million dollar printing machines. Each team makes decisions about how to improve the quality of its work. At the end of the year, no printing press is supposed to look the same as it did at the beginning of the year, because it has by then been modified a thousand tiny times by a thousand people (all members of press teams) who have been educated and are continually educated. Everybody is expected to improve everything. Workers are expected to become smarter each year in order to make the company better each year. In this company, **job security is based on a person's ability to make the company better continually.**

6. **Add to and expand your job-related knowledge and skills.** Seek new training constantly. Take advantage of any opportunity your company presents for further training. Continue your formal education at night and on weekends. The notion that school begins at age 6 and ends at age 18 or 22 is passe. Education will continue throughout your lifetime. Those who survive and prosper will be upgrading their skills and creating new contributions to their company continually. Think five years ahead, not five minutes. Prepare for the future of your company as well as for the present. Prepare for *your* future career as well as for your present one. General math, reading, and writing skills help. In most modern companies, employees need **at least** 10th-grade math skills, 9th-grade reading and composition skills, and even bilingualism. Technology is changing so rapidly that continual upgrading of technical competencies is required as well.

7. **Make friends throughout the company.** Network. Things get done more by friendship than by authority. Cultivate and maintain relationships in all departments.

8. **Be a team player.** Help others succeed. Make your boss and coworkers look good.

9. **Learn how to work with everyone.** Give up all prejudices, stereotypes, and biases. The world is a very heterogeneous place. There are all kinds of people. Sometime in your lifetime you will probably work with each kind. Accept all cultures and backgrounds. Look at how well people do their job, not what ethnic group they are from.

Build Character through Work Habits

○   ○   ○

*"Into the hands of every individual is given a marvelous power for good or evil—
the silent, unconscious, unseen influence of his life. This is simply the constant
radiation of what man really is, not what he pretends to be."*

William George Jordan

○   ○   ○

Stephen Covey (1989) conducted an in-depth analysis of the success literature
published in the United States since 1776. He read hundreds of books, articles,
and essays in fields such as self-improvement, popular psychology, and self-help.
He noticed a startling pattern emerging. Almost all literature from 1776 to about
1926 focused on the **character ethic** as the foundation of success. Shortly after
World War I, the basic view of success changed to the **image ethic.**

The **character ethic** views success as coming from integrity, industry, in the attempt to make a contribution to other people and the world, fidelity, courage, humility, patience, fairness, in the realization of potential through growth and development, and by following the Golden Rule. Benjamin Franklin provides an example; his autobiography is the story of one person's effort to integrate certain principles and habits deep within his nature. The character ethic teaches that there are basic principles of effective living, and that you can only experience true success and enduring happiness as you learn and integrate these principles into your basic character. As Oliver Wendell Holmes said, "What lies behind us and what lies before us are tiny matters compared to what lies within us."

The **image ethic** views success as coming from creating the right impression, using power and persuasion for quick fixes, and using interpersonal band-aids and aspirin to relieve symptoms. Individuals sell an image of themselves to others. All situations are assumed to be short-term and, therefore, lasting relationships are unimportant. You cannot shortcut growth and development. No amount of positive thinking will make you a professional tennis player or great pianist. You have to sweat on the practice field before you can perform on the playing field. You have to dedicate your life to gaining expertise in your chosen endeavors to become outstanding.

Your character gives life to your interpersonal and organizational skills. Your character provides the foundation on which interpersonal and organizational skills are based. They are of little use without character. In the long-run, if you use "image" techniques to get other people to do what you want, while your character is flawed by duplicity and insincerity, then you cannot be successful. Your duplicity will breed distrust and all your interpersonal charisma and skills will be perceived as manipulative.

Eventually, if there is not deep integrity and fundamental character strength, the challenges of life will cause true motives to surface and human relationship failure will replace short-term success. As Emerson said, "What you are shouts so loudly in my ears I cannot hear what you say." In the last analysis, what we are communicates far more eloquently than anything we say or do.

Your character is a composite of your habits. As Covey (1989) said, "Sow a thought, reap an action; sow an action, reap a habit; sow a habit, reap a character; sow a character, reap a destiny." As Horance Mann, the great educator, once said, "Habits are like a cable. We weave a strand of it every day and soon it cannot be broken." **Habits** are the intersection of knowledge, skill, and desire. Knowledge is the theoretical paradigm, the **what** to do and **why.** Skill is the **how to do.** And desire is the motivation, the **want to do.** In order to make something a habit in our lives, we have to have all three, and that takes sweat and effort. As Thomas Paine once said, "That which we obtain too easily, we esteem too lightly. It is dearness only which gives everything its value. Heaven knows how to put a proper price on its goods."

Surviving a Difficult Boss

At many times people feel they cannot survive working for a difficult boss. When you feel that way, remember Victor Frankl. Frankl was a psychiatrist who was imprisoned in the death camps of Nazi Germany for being a Jew. His parents, his brother, and his wife were either sent to the gas ovens or died in the camps. Except for his sister, his entire family perished. Frankl himself suffered torture and innumerable indignities so repugnant to our sense of decency that we shudder to repeat them. He never knew from one moment to the next if his path would lead into the ovens or if he would be among the "saved" who had to remove the bodies or shovel out the ashes of those killed. One day, naked and alone in a small room, he became aware of what he later called "the last of the human freedoms"—a freedom so basic that even his Nazi captors could not take it away. That freedom was the ability to decide within himself how external events were going to affect him. Between what the Nazis did to his body and his response, he had the freedom to choose what his response would be. To exercise that freedom Frankl would first detach and look at himself as an outsider. He would project himself into different circumstances, such as lecturing to his students after his release from the death camps, describing the lessons he was learning during his torture sessions. He would then consciously choose how he was going to react. He ended up by believing that he had more freedom, more internal power to exercise his options, than his Nazi captors. He became an inspiration to those around him, even to some of the guards. He helped others find meaning in their suffering and dignity in their prison existence. The moral is, never let a bad boss or coworker make you feel miserable. Imitate Victor Frankl and decide for yourself how you will react to another's treatment of you.

School Can Provide Distorted Views of Work

Much of what you learn in school may be worthless in the real world. School teaches you some lessons about work that turn out to be wrong for survival on the job, so be prepared for some shocks. First, school may have taught you that success comes from passing objective tests on your own. School rarely requires students to lead or direct others or even to work cooperatively with others. Second, school may create an impression that if you attend class and do minimal work, a promotion is due every year. That is not the case in most jobs. Third, success in schoolwork comes from focusing on books and lectures; students can get top grades without ever talking with a professor or a classmate. Education is structured to produce technically competent (more or less), though socially naive people. When you put a person who has learned individually for 12 to 16 years into a job that requires leadership, what usually happens is quite predictable. The person does well on the technical aspect of the job but does poorly in getting the team to function at its full potential. When confronted with a less than optimal evaluation, such people often react defensively and angrily.

Fourth, attendance in class, coming to school on time, and not missing a day of school, are not emphasized as important in many schools. A student who is allowed to graduate with numerous unexcused absences, regular patterns of tardiness, and a history of uncompleted assignments will make a poor employee. Fifth, in many schools there is an attitude that it is up to the teacher to motivate the students, making sure they get to class and are treated fairly. On the job you are expected to take responsibility for your own motivation and work performance. Sixth, the implicit message about "work" that gets drummed into students' heads from kindergarten through graduate school is that schoolwork (a student's job) means performing some task or tasks largely by oneself, even though other people are often present. Because the needed tools are supplied, the goals and rules are clearly specified, and the grading of performance is "objective," securing cooperation from others is not seen as an important issue. It is even discouraged as "cheating" at times. From kindergarten through graduate school, one can get excellent performance appraisals and yearly promotions, and yet learn virtually nothing about leading others.

In the real world of work, things are altogether different. The heart of most jobs, especially the higher-paying, more interesting jobs, is getting others to cooperate, leading others, coping with complex power and influence issues, and helping solve people's problems in working with each other. Paying attention to superiors, colleagues, and subordinates, knowing what their concerns and pressures are, and knowing what they wish to achieve are important aspects of the social sensitivity on the job. Understanding coworkers and being sensitive to their needs and moods is a vital job survival skill. Finally, learning how to develop a power base is important. To get things done you need a power base to help you influence others. A power base comes from knowledge about the company and its customers; having a good reputation within the company; having a good track record of being responsible, reliable, and productive; and having clear-cut achievements.

Millions of technical, professional, and managerial jobs today require much more than technical competence and professional expertise. They also require leadership. That means you will have to get things done by influencing a large and diverse group of people (bosses, subordinates, peers, customers, and others), despite the lack of formal control over them, and despite their general disinterest in cooperating.

Getting a group of people you do not control to march in some needed direction is rarely easy. When they are a diverse group—in background, pespective, and priorities—it is even harder. Yet this is precisely the kind of leadership skill that many jobs demand, even of relatively low-level employees in project management, secretarial, and other positions. The number of people who can handle these jobs effectively is far less than the number these jobs demand.

To learn to be a leader you need to be exposed to experiences in school that teach you a willingness to lead; the ability to motivate others to achieve goals; the ability to negotiate, represent, and mediate; the ability to get decisions implemented; the ability to exercise authority; the ability to develop credibility; and a number of other interpersonal skills. Education should address the behaviors and skills that give individuals the capacity to lead.

Some people pick up the lessons of the workplace the hard way, through experience. Others never learn, and become bitter and unsuccessful.

Job Survival Skills: The Focus of This Book

"This person has the technical skills for the job, but can she get along?" This question is in the mind of every employer who interviews you for a position. It is in the mind of every boss who is deciding whether to promote you. It has already been answered by the supervisor who is about to fire you. Your ability to relate to co-workers, customers, superiors, and suppliers can spell the difference between success and failure on the job. A number of interpersonal and small group skills are essential to employability, surviving on the job, and career progression. The first set of skills focuses on your goals, assets, and credentials. All work relationships begin with you as a person. Your needs and goals, skills and abilities, past training and education, self-awareness, ability to control and express your feelings, and your sense of who you are as a person—all affect your job relationships. So first of all you need a sense of who you are as a person—where you are going in life, why you are working, what your skills and abilities are. If you are aware of your goals and needs, you will be able to combine them with the goals and needs of your organization and fellow employees. In Chapter 2, therefore, we focus on the awareness of your needs, goals, credentials, and assets. Other aspects of you as a person are covered in succeeding chapters.

The second set of interpersonal skills are the helping, sharing, combining, and leadership skills you need to work as part of a cooperative team. Your career will be based on cooperating with other people to achieve an organization's goals. The overall goals of the organization are achieved by coordinating your efforts with the efforts of other employees. This requires leadership. Leadership is providing the actions needed to help an organization achieve its goals and keep good working relationships among members. Cooperative skills are discussed in Chapter 3, and leadership is discussed in Chapter 4.

Communication is an important part of any relationship or organization. On the job, you communicate with many different people, including your boss. Work cannot take place without communication. Communication consists of *sending* messages so they can be understood. It also consists of *receiving* messages so the sender knows you understand what he or she is trying to communicate. An especially difficult aspect of communicating is for the sender and the receiver to understand each other's feelings. You need skills in sending and receiving messages containing statements about feelings, and you need to be able to control and manage your feelings. Communication skills are discussed in Chapters 5, 6, and 7.

Teams of workers are expected to improve the quality of the product or service they are providing and the efficiency with which it is produced or given continually. Employee teams, therefore, will be involved in making important decisions. The fourth set of interpersonal skills then involves the skills needed to present the "best case" for alternative solutions to problems identified by the team and challenge the thinking of teammates as decisions are being made. Being

Interpersonal Competencies and Skills

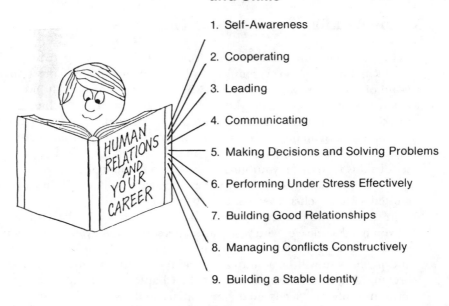

1. Self-Awareness
2. Cooperating
3. Leading
4. Communicating
5. Making Decisions and Solving Problems
6. Performing Under Stress Effectively
7. Building Good Relationships
8. Managing Conflicts Constructively
9. Building a Stable Identity

OVERVIEW OF THE BOOK

part of a decision-making group involves preparing a position to be presnted to the team, challenging the thinking of teammates, building a synthesis based on the best thinking of all team members, and appreciating differences among persons. This is discussed in Chapter 8.

Conflicts will take place on the job no matter how hard you try to avoid them. You and your boss, and you and your coworkers will have disagreements. How you manage your conflicts with fellow employees, customers, and suppliers is of great importance to your career. An extremely important set of interpersonal skills are those involved in making sure conflicts benefit your career, rather than hurt it. Depending on how you manage conflicts, they can be positive and help you solve problems, or they can be negative and make problems worse. The skills for managing conflicts are discussed in Chapters 9 and 10.

Chapters 11 and 12 review the basic material covered in the book. They deal with building a stable identity and applying *your* interpersonal skills in your own career.

Job success does not automatically happen when you have high technical skills, or when you are reliable and responsible. Job success depends on getting along with other people. The more successful you are in relating to your fellow employees, customers, and suppliers, the more successful your career will be. These skills will also help you at home, school, and anywhere else you interact with other people.

This book provides structured exercises and games to teach you interpersonal skills. In the rest of this chapter, we shall review how to learn from your experiences in the exercises and games, and cover how to learn these interpersonal skills.

Learning from Experience: The Method of This Book

We all learn from our experiences. For example, by touching a hot stove, we learn to avoid heated objects. By dating, we learn about male-female relationships. By being in a family, we learn about family life. From my six-month-old-son, I learned what it feels like to have my finger dented by a kid with only two teeth. Every day we have experiences we learn from. Many things about relating to other people can only be learned through experience. For example, seeing a movie about love is not the same as experiencing love. Hearing a lecture about what to say to an angry boss is not the same as facing an angry boss. We all learn best from our experiences.

To learn interpersonal skills, you need to understand what the skills are and when they should be used, and you need to actually practice the skills. The best way to do this is to learn from structured experiences. This book is written so that you can learn interpersonal skills through experiences as well as through reading. Each chapter has a series of exercises that provide experiences on the attitudes and skills you need to work effectively with other people. Each chapter also includes material on how to get along with other people. Learning from your experiences follows a pattern:

1. Having an actual personal experience.
2. Thinking about the experience and the effectiveness of your behavior.
3. Making conclusions about how to improve your behavior next time.
4. Trying out the new behaviors in a new personal experience.

Let's illustrate this with an example. I once sneaked into my older sister's room and read her diary. Unfortunately, I was caught in the act. I immediately tried to put the blame on my sister for leaving her diary in plain sight underneath her clothes in a dresser drawer. I was then unfairly beaten, kicked, and scratched! Thinking about my experience, I concluded that putting the blame on my older sister caused the beating. The next day, I was caught looking for the diary. Testing my theory, I immediately stated that my looking for the diary was not my sister's fault. Rather, it was my own nature that led me into such an unthinkable action. I was then unfairly beaten, kicked, and scratched! Thinking about my experience, I concluded that people who tried to read their older sister's diary did not live past the age of ten. I then acted on my personal theory by never trying to find the diary again. This is learning from experience!

You will experience each interpersonal skill discussed in this book. To learn such skills, you need to involve yourself actively in the games and exercises and try to draw as many conclusions as possible from your experiences. The exercises are structured so that you can experiment with your behavior, try things out, see what works, build skills, and build your own personal theory about how to work with other people. The reading material is usually presented *after* the exercises, so that you can think about your experiences *before* you read about how most people reacted to the same or similar situations.

Learning from your experiences is especially useful when you want to learn skills. No one wants to ride in an airplane with a pilot who has read a book on how to fly but has never actually experienced flying a plane. Reading about how to communicate is not enough to make you skillful in communicating with others. You need to practice, to experience good communication skills. In the next section, we shall review how interpersonal skills are learned.

How Skills Are Learned

No one is born with interpersonal skills and they do not magically appear some night while you are asleep. You have to learn them. And you cannot count on other people having them—you have to master them. Job survival skills are learned just as any other skill such as playing the piano or basketball is learned. All skills are acquired through the following steps:

1. *Understand why the skill is important and how it will be of value to you.* To learn a skill, you must first see the need for it.
2. *Understand what the skill is and what you have to do to master it.* To learn a skill, you

must have a clear idea of what the skill is; you must know how to act in order to perform it. Often it is helpful to have someone who already has mastered the skill go through it several times while he describes it step by step.

3. *Find situations in which to practice the skill.* To master a skill, you have to practice it again and again. Try practicing the skill for a short time each day for several days until you are sure you have mastered it completely.

4. *Get someone to watch you and tell you how well you are performing the skill.* This is called *getting feedback.* Getting feedback is necessary for correcting mistakes in learning a skill, for identifying problems you are having. Through feedback, you find out how much progress you are making in mastering the skill. Feedback lets you compare how well you are doing with how well you want to do.

5. *Keep practicing!* In learning most skills, there is a period of slow learning, then a period of fast improvement, then a period in which performance remains about the same (a plateau), then another period of fast improvement, then another plateau, and so forth. Plateaus are quite common in skill learning; you just have to stick with it until the next period of fast improvement begins.

6. *Load your practice toward success.* Set up practice units that you can master easily. It always helps to feel like a success as you practice a skill.

7. *Get friends to encourage you to use the skill.* Your friends can help you learn by encouraging you. The more encouragement you get, the easier it will be for you to practice the skill.

8. *Practice until it feels natural.* The more you use a skill, the more natural it feels. While learning a skill, you may feel self-conscious and awkward. Practicing a skill is like role playing—it does not feel like *real* behavior. But you should not let this awkwardness stop you from mastering the skill. Ever trying learning to type by only doing it when it feels natural? It is through role playing and drill that all skills are learned. If you keep practicing, the awkwardness will pass. Soon you will become comfortable in using the skill and it will be part of you.

How to Do the Exercises

To do the exercises in this book, your class will usually work in groups of six students; you will be in the same group throughout the course. The other members of your group are the people you need to cooperate with in order to learn the interpersonal skills covered in this book. In a sense, they are your coworkers. The success you have in working with your fellow group members may indicate how successfully you will work with other people during your career. The better the members of your group work together, the more each of you will learn.

Group Warm-up

A group works better when each member has some idea of how the other members are feeling. This helps you know how best to work with each other during the exercise. It gives you a chance to practice being open with your feelings, and puts you in contact with the other group members (whom you haven't seen since the last session). It helps you to get to know the other group members better. Knowing how others feel may help you be more understanding and also more accepting of what they do and say.

Before doing an exercise, each group will warm up in the following way: First, draw numbers to see who will begin; then go around the group clockwise. Each person should tell how he is feeling at that moment, and briefly say what he thinks is causing that feeling. This should be done in a few words or a couple of sentences. When a member seems particularly worried or upset, the group may wish to offer a few words of support to that person.

Closing

At the end of the exercise, each member of the group in turn tells what she learned from the exercise and how she plans to use that knowledge in the near future.

EXERCISE 1.1   **Getting to Know Who's Who**

PURPOSE

The first step in working with other people is to get to know them. The second step is to let them get to know you. The purpose of this exercise, therefore, is to give you a way to get to know the other members in your group and let them get to know you.

PROCEDURE

1. Working alone, write your first name in the center of a 3 × 5 index card. Write it large enough so other people can read it at some distance. In the *upper left-hand corner*, write the names of three places: where you were born, your favorite place, and a place where something significant happened to you. In the *upper right-hand corner*, write three of your favorite activities. These may be sports, hobbies, pastimes, jobs, or other ways you enjoy spending your time. In the *lower left-hand corner*, write three adjectives that describe your personality. In the *lower right-hand corner*, describe something you are looking forward to, something you are excited about doing in the future—for example, a family vacation or a new job.
2. Pin the card on the front of your shirt or blouse.
3. Break into pairs within your group. Discuss each other's cards for

about six minutes. Then form into new pairs, and again discuss each other's cards for about six minutes. Repeat this process until you have met all the other members in your group.

4. If you finish early, discuss what you have learned about each other.

5. Keep your name tags and wear them for a couple of sessions until you know everyone's name in your group.

Indiana	Mountain climbing
British Columbia	Falling in love
New York City	Working
DAVE	
Intense	Going down the
Fun-loving	Colorado River on
Hard-working	a raft

EXERCISE 1.2   **Who Has Done What***

PURPOSE

The purpose of this exercise is to find out something about the work experiences of the members of your group.

PROCEDURE

Answer the following questions in your group:

1. List the current jobs of the members of your group.
2. List all previous jobs of the members of your group.
3. What job involved the most hours worked a day by a group member?
4. What job demanded the most physical strength by a group member?
5. What was the easiest job a group member has held?
6. What was the most unusual job a group member has held?
7. A mysterious stranger has offered your group a hundred extra years of life, provided that you agree to work all that time at the same job. Assuming you accept the offer, what job would your group choose, and why?

*Remember to do the group warm-up before starting the exercise (see page 20).

2

Choosing Career Goals

After completing the Questionnaire that follows, you should be able to define and give examples of

- Goals
- Opportunities
- Credentials
- Assets

The answers are given on the right side of the page. Work with a partner and keep the answers covered until you have agreed on your response. Remember to check each answer before going on to the next item, as explained on page 1.

QUESTIONNAIRE: Main Concepts in Chapter 2

1. A *goal* is a desired future state of affairs. When a person is working toward creating a desired future state of affairs, he or she is working to achieve a _____.

   goal

2. Becoming a carpenter is an example of a career _____.

   goal

3. Becoming rich is an example of a financial _____.

   goal

4. An *opportunity* is a favorable chance to achieve your goals. When you are looking for a job as a mechanic and you stop at a local car dealer and learn that one of their mechanics has just quit, you are face to face with an _____.

   opportunity

5. A *credential* is a certification of your competence and reliability. It indicates to employers that you have mastered certain skills and abilities. When a potential employer asks for proof that you have been adequately trained for the job you are applying for, he is asking for your _____.

   credentials

6. A high school diploma indicates to employers that you can read, write, and do arithmetic at a high school level. It is an example of a _____.

   credential

7. An *asset* is a desirable or a valuable thing to have. When you have a personal quality that employers find desirable, you have an _____.

   asset

8. Any past achievement, skill or ability, or personal quality, such as appearance, manners, motivation, or health, that helps you get a job is an _____.

   asset

9. A career _____ directs your efforts toward a desired future state of affairs. To achieve your career goals, you have to have the _____ to do so. Your career opportunities depend on your _____ and _____.

   goal
   opportunity
   credentials
   assets

10. You have to be able to tell potential employers about your _____ and _____ in order to get the _____ to achieve your career _____.

    credentials
    assets
    opportunity
    goals

11. In order to know what _____ to seek out, you must know what your career _____ are.

    opportunities
    goals

12. If you do *not* have the _____ and _____ credentials
to qualify for an _____, you will have to assets
change your career _____. opportunity
goals

13. Long-term career planning requires setting career goals
_____, and getting the _____ and credentials
_____ to qualify for the right _____. assets
opportunity

A Fable with a Sad End*

Once upon a time, a young rabbit decided to go out into the world and seek his fortune. His parents gave him $30, wished him well, and he began his search. Before he had traveled very far, he met a pack rat.

"Hey, little rabbit, where are you going?" asked the pack rat.

"I'm seeking my fortune," replied the young rabbit.

"You're in luck," said the pack rat. "I have here a suit of beautiful clothes that I will sell to you for only $10. Then you can go seeking your fortune looking prosperous and stylish!"

"Say, that's fantastic!" replied the young rabbit, who immediately bought the clothes, put them on, and continued his search for his fortune. Soon he met a deer.

"Hey, little rabbit, where are you going?" asked the deer.

"I'm seeking my fortune," replied the young rabbit.

"You're in great luck," said the deer. "For only $10, I will sell you this motorcycle so you can go seeking your fortune at great and exciting speeds!"

"Say, that's fantastic!" replied the young rabbit, who immediately bought the motorcycle and went zooming across the countryside. Soon he met a coyote.

"Hey, little rabbit, where are you going?" asked the coyote.

*Based on a fable in Mager (1962).

"I'm seeking my fortune," replied the young rabbit.

"You're in great luck!" said the coyote. "For a measly $10, I will let you take this shortcut," said the coyote, pointing to his open mouth, "and you'll save yourself years of time!"

"Say, that's fantastic!" replied the young rabbit. And paying his last $10 he put his head into the coyote's mouth, and was immediately devoured.

The moral of this story is: If you don't know where you're going, you are likely to end up somewhere you don't want to be!*

Career Goals: Seeking Your Fortune

Your career begins with your goals. To seek your fortune, you must know where you are going and how you will get there. And you have to know why you are seeking your fortune. Goals will help you do all three of these things. A *goal* is a desired state of future affairs—something you want in your future. Your career goals may be to be a successful accountant or a rich businessperson. Your career goals provide a sense of direction (Where am I going?). They are guides for action (How do I get there?) and explanations for why you are working (Why am I doing this?). The clearer your goals, the clearer you will be about where you are going, how you get there, and why you are doing what you are doing.

Your career goals will include long-term goals, medium-range goals, and short-term goals. Being an executive secretary is an example of a long-range goal; finishing business school is an example of a medium-range goal; going to typing class tomorrow is an example of a short-range goal. Without goals, you will have no sense of direction, no guide for action, no reason for working.

Whatever your career goals are, they can be achieved only if other people cooperate with you. When you get a job, your organization will expect you to commit yourself to its goals. You accept the job because by helping achieve your organization's goals you will also be achieving your own goals. Your coworkers will all be expected to be committed to the organization's goals. They will also be convinced that their goals will be best achieved by achieving the organization's goals. For example, if their goal is to get a high salary and the organization's goal is to make a profit, hard work by the employees can achieve both sets of goals. If the employees do not work hard, the organization will not make money and the employees' salaries will be low. Thus the work of the employees helps achieve both their goals and the organization's goals. In your career, you will work hard to achieve the organization's goals in order to achieve your goals.

The organization's goals and your goals can only be achieved if most employees take their work seriously. If you work hard but no one else does, then the organization will not be successful, and you, in turn, will not be successful. You have to depend on your coworkers to help achieve the organization's goals, and they have to depend on you. Your success and their success are tied together. It is only by cooperating to achieve the organization's goals that both you and your coworkers will be successful.

*A well-known text by psychologist David Campbell is entitled *If You Don't Know Where You're Going, You'll Probably End Up Somewhere Else.*

Matching your goals to the goals of the organization and coworkers is one of the most important aspects of working. To do so, you must be intensely aware of your career goals.

How Can I Increase My Choices?

What most people want out of life, more than anything else, is to be able to make choices (Campbell, 1974). The worst possible life is a life without choices. It is depressing and discouraging to have no hope for new things, to have no chance to change your job if you want to, to be unable to do anything else. In contrast, the best possible life is a life with choices. It is encouraging and satisfying to be able to change your life when you feel like it, to have many choices all through your life.

○   ○   ○

It affects me. It gives you that feeling: Oh hell, what's the use? I've got to get out of this. Suddenly you look in the mirror, and you find out you're not twenty-one any more. You're fifty-five. Many people have said to me, "Why didn't you get out of it long ago?" I never really had enough money to get out. I was stuck, more or less.

Doc Pritchard, Hotel Room Clerk
in STUDS TERKEL, *Working*

○   ○   ○

One way of looking at your career is as a long, never-ending path stretching out ahead of you (Campbell, 1974). For some people, there are no career choices: There is only one path open and it cannot be changed later in life. Such a person may be a secretary forever. For other people, there are many career choices: They have many paths open to them, and they can change careers when they wish to. Such a person can choose to be an accountant, a lawyer, a college professor, a teacher, a mechanic, a computer programmer, and so on.

Each career has a gate that you have to open before you can follow it. The gate will open only if you have the right credentials and assets. *Your credentials and assets are keys for opening career opportunities and choices.*

Your **credentials** certify your ability and reliability. They indicate to employers that you have mastered certain skills and abilities. They also may indicate that you have a positive attitude and are willing to work hard to achieve your goals. Your credentials are your proof that you have been adequately trained for the job you are applying for. They may be a high school diploma, a graduation certificate from a vocational training program, your grade-point average in high school or standing in your vocational training program, or your college diploma. Whatever they are, your credentials are your keys to career opportunities.

Your **assets** are your valuable and desirable qualities. Assets are personal qualities that employers find desirable. Your assets include your skills and abilities, your intelligence, your past achievements, your personal appearance and

manners, your health, and your motivation to do good work. Whatever they are, your assets are your keys to career opportunities.

Credentials and assets are important. They open the gates to career opportunities and choices. Each career has a gate, which will open for you only if you have the keys—the right credentials and assets.

To have choices, you must create opportunities for yourself. You create opportunities mainly by earning credentials and building assets. Even if you do not know for sure what career you wish to pursue, you can do some things in the short run that will give you more choices when the long run gets here. For example, you can earn more credentials and build more assets.

You will have to work hard building credentials and increasing your assets. As someone said (Campbell, 1974), "People who want milk should not seat themselves on a stool in the middle of a field in hopes that the cow will back up to them."

Credentials and assets are not gained overnight. They are obtained gradually. You will gradually accumulate them over years of studying, training, and job experience. Earning credentials and assets takes patience and endurance.

Some people, because of the family they are born into or because of their parent's career, have more opportunities than others. If your parents own a farm, you may have a better opportunity to be a farmer than someone whose parents live in the city. If your parents are rich, you may have more opportunities than someone whose parents are poor. But everyone has some opportunities, and everyone can create opportunities for herself.

Some careers you can enter at any time during your life. Any time you want to, if you have the time and money, you can enter a training program in computer programming and learn the skills needed. But other careers cannot be entered unless you begin early. To become a great guitar player usually requires learning how to play the guitar at an early age and continual practice. Other careers cannot be entered until you are old enough. To be president of the United States, you

have to be thirty-five years old. The way you live your life now will affect your career choices in the future.

It takes planning to get the credentials and assets you need for future career choices. *You have to plant the seeds now to get a harvest later.* Opportunities do not appear through magic or luck. They have to be planned for, earned, and sought after. You seek your fortune, you get new opportunities, and you find choices by building your credentials and assets gradually over a period of years.

Living with Tomorrow in Mind

Your career begins with your goals. To achieve your career goals, you have to have opportunities, which depend on your credentials and assets. A person with lots of opportunities will be more successful in achieving his career goals than will a person with few opportunities.

Your career goals may have to be changed constantly. If you do not have the credentials and assets to get the needed opportunities, there is no sense in holding on to the goals. For example, your goal may be to be a medical doctor. But if you quit high school, you will have to give up that career goal. You may wish to be a carpenter. But if you are never trained to be a carpenter, you will have to give up that career goal. The credentials you earn and the assets you develop determine your opportunities, which, in turn, determine whether or not you will achieve your career goals. As you get certain credentials and not others, as you develop some assets and not others, and as you take advantage of some opportunities and not others, you will have to revise your career goals. Every choice you make will result in a revision of your career goals.

Reviewing Your Credentials and Assets

Your credentials and assets are your keys to career opportunities and choices. To begin planning how you can improve your credentials and assets, it may be helpful to review what they are currently. Your **credentials** include your past education and job experience. Your **assets** include your talents, skills, abilities, achievements, intelligence, appearance, manners, and health. The two exercises that follow are aimed at helping you summarize your current credentials and assets and at planning how to increase them in the future. Such keys to career opportunities and choices will affect your career goals. Your career goals will be matched with the goals of the organization, job, and coworkers you will be involved with in the future. Becoming a nurse, for example, depends on having such credentials as a high school diploma, high grades in science classes, and admission into a nursing training program. It also depends on such assets as skills in relating to other people, the physical strength and health needed, and the motivation to complete nursing training. If the needed credentials and assets are not available, then the career goal is not realistic.

GROUND RULES FOR GROUP DISCUSSIONS

In all group discussions during this course, you and your fellow group members should follow three basic rules. These rules must be clearly understood by both students and teachers.

1. *A student always has the right to pass.* Whenever you feel you cannot do what the exercise asks, you can politely tell the other group members that you pass. They will respect your feelings. This does not mean that whenever you do not want to

work you can simply drop out of the group. It means that if you feel the exercise would be too upsetting, you can ask the group to excuse you temporarily.

2. *Any statement a student makes must be accepted by the members of the group.* No one may ridicule or pass judgment on a fellow member's contribution to the discussion. During an exercise, a member of your group may state a thought or feeling that you do not understand. It is important that you never make a judgment as to whether the statement is right or wrong. Judgments make it difficult for members to participate in group discussions. Work hard to accept the statement as what the person is thinking or feeling at that time. Being accepting is very important in helping the group members learn from the exercises.

3. *Students must participate as actively as possible in the exercise activities.* Being involved in the exercises is essential for both your learning and the learning of the other group members. Being silent or absent means that you will not benefit from the exercise. It also means that you are hurting the other group members by not helping them learn. Try to listen carefully, accept what the other members say, and ask questions or make comments that will help them learn.

EXERCISE 2.1   **Your Credentials**

PURPOSE

Your major credentials are your past education and your past job experience. The purpose of this exercise is for you to review your credentials and plan what new credentials you hope to obtain. You will first write down some information about your credentials. Then in your groups you will discuss your credentials and the credentials of the other group members.

PROCEDURE

1. Working alone, on a sheet of paper complete the ten unfinished sentences in List A about your past education and training. Then write out the answers to the questions about your past work experience (List B). Take twenty minutes to do this.

2. In your group, draw numbers to choose who is to begin. The first person then reviews her credentials with the group. Other members ask any questions about her credentials they wish to. Then the person on the right of the first person reviews his credentials with the group. Repeat the procedure until all group members have reviewed their credentials with the group. Take twenty-five minutes to do this.

3. Go around the group once more, letting each member state briefly (in one minute or less) what credentials he or she is now working on obtaining.

4. Think about and discuss the following questions in your group: Are there any differences in the credentials being sought by the males and females in the group? Why do such differences exist?

List A: Your Education and Training

The most important credentials you have are your education and training. Most careers require certain levels and types of education as keys. Write a description of your education and training by completing the following sentences.

1. The amount of education and training I now have is . . .
2. The school subjects I enjoyed most were . . .
3. The reasons I enjoyed them are . . .
4. The school subjects I enjoyed least were . . .
5. The reasons I didn't like them were . . .
6. The school subjects I did the best work in and received the highest grades in were . . .
7. The school subjects I did the worst work in and received the lowest grades in were . . .
8. The thing I liked about my favorite teachers were . . .
9. The things offered free at school that I have taken advantage of are . . .
10. The educational and training credentials I hope to obtain are . . .

List B: Your Past Work Experience

When did you start to work? What were the first jobs you held outside the home? Many people do not start work until they are graduated from high school. Other people start to work at young ages. I started shoveling snow, raking leaves, and selling Christmas cards and garden products when I was eight. Before I graduated from college, I worked nine years as a janitor. I also had held the jobs of paper boy, farm laborer, auctioneer helper, dishwasher, pots-and-pans washer, busboy, waiter, salad chef, secretary, newspaper reporter, tutor, archery instructor, and camp bugler. Answer the following questions:

1. When did you take your first job?
2. What are all the jobs you have had in your past? (List them.)
3. Put a star next to the jobs that were hard work.
4. Put a check next to the jobs that you would not want to do again.
5. Circle the jobs that were fun.
6. What job experience do you hope to get in the near future?

Education and Training

Education and training are important credentials because they help you create new assets. Having a good education and training means you have learned useful skills and developed abilities. Education and training often lead to interesting and useful experiences. You will meet many of your friends in school and training programs. What you learn in school and in a training program may increase your motivation to do good work on the job. Education and training increase your career opportunities and choices more than any other type of credential.

In planning your career, you need to plan what education and training you are going to obtain. The three guidelines that follow may help you plan your future education and training (Campbell, 1974):

1. Study something you enjoy. If you are not sure what that is, give yourself a few years to try different areas out. Take both basic and applied courses and pick courses that will build your assets. Do not worry if you have not yet found an area that excites you. Many people take several years trying new and different areas before they find the one they like best.

2. Go to the best school or training program you can afford and can get into. You usually get better education and training at a good school. And at good schools you meet capable and stimulating people who may encourage or inspire you to develop your assets as fully as possible. The reputation of your school and training program affects your career opportunities. Employers will be impressed by the reputation of your school.

3. Do as well as you possibly can. The better your grades, the more opportunities open to you. It is even more important to have good grades than it is to go to a good school. Persons who can work hard enough to get good grades in school tend to work hard enough to be a success on the job. People who expect to succeed in school expect to succeed on the job.

Job Experiences

Another important credential is your job experience. You can plan your experiences so you gain the most from them. Do not just let them happen to you. If you are unsure what you want your career to be, try out as many different job experiences as possible. On each of your jobs, do your best. Good recommendations from previous employers are worthwhile credentials to have. Finally, develop as many job-related skills as possible. Every job you have will hopefully build your assets as well as your credentials.

EXERCISE **Your Assets**
2.2

PURPOSE

Just as important as your credentials are your assets. Your assets include your past achievements, your skills and abilities, your appearance and manners, your intelligence, and your health. To set realistic career goals, it is important to know your assets. To plan for a future career often means planning how to develop new assets. The purpose of this exercise is to review your current assets.

Your Achievements: If You've Done It, Be Proud of It!

People do things they are proud of. Sometimes these success experiences are things everyone else knows about; sometimes they are things that only you know about. Everyone has had many achievements every year of his life. An achievement might be a good grade in a class that is difficult for you, not losing your temper for a week, or doing a job extra well. In reviewing your assets, it is important to review the successes and achievements you are proud of. Past achievements and successes are used to build future achievements and successes.

PROCEDURE

1. Working alone, list the achievements and successes you are proud of. Take only your own feelings into account and include your entire past life. (If you have less than ten items on your list, you are not trying hard enough.)
2. In your group, have each member describe her past successes and achievements, and why she feels good about them. Help each member be as specific and complete as possible.
3. Discuss how each member can use her accomplishments to obtain the credentials and opportunities needed for her planned career.

Being Honest

Are you embarrassed about talking with others about your past successes? Some of us have been taught that we must be humble—that it is a sin or social error to say positive things about ourselves. Perhaps it will help you to be honest with the other members of your group to realize that being humble does not mean that you should "put yourself down" or hide your abilities and talents. Being honest with yourself and other people includes recognizing the skills and abilities you have. Your psychological health, furthermore, is affected by your awareness of your assets and your use of them to manage the problems of living. Do not be embarrassed about the truth—do not be afraid to name all your personal achievements, skills, abilities, and positive qualities. They are things a future employer will be very interested in hearing about. It is very important that you know and be able to discuss your past achievements and successes, and the abilities and qualities you have that led to those achievements. Don't be shy, be honest!

**EXERCISE
2.3**   **Your Skills and Abilities**

PURPOSE

Everyone has certain skills and abilities he or she is proud of. These are important in opening new paths. Your abilities and skills might include musical, mathematical, mechanical, or athletic talent; drawing; a good sense of humor; molding clay; or writing. Some skills and abilities are more helpful in opening career opportunities than others. You might want to ask yourself the following questions:

1. Is the skill required as part of some occupation?
2. Will other people pay you to teach them the skill?
3. Will the skill be useful throughout life, or will you outgrow it?
4. Will the skill help you gain new experiences and achievements?
5. Do you like using the skill?

The purpose of this exercise is to spotlight your skills. Whatever they are, remember Campbell's (1974) famous saying: "If you've got it, use it!"

PROCEDURE

1. Working alone, list your skills and abilities (if you have less than ten, you are not really trying!).
2. In your group, have each member describe his or her abilities and skills. Help each person be as complete and specific as possible.
3. Discuss how each member can use her skills and abilities to achieve her career goals.

If You've Got It, Use It, or You'll Lose It!

Having skills and abilities is not enough. You must be willing to use them, to keep them sharp. If you don't use them, they become rusty. Some people seem to have lots of skills and abilities. With them, it's "easy come, easy go." They take their skills and abilities for granted and never bother to develop them. Then one day they wake up and find that they no longer have the skills and abilities they now need. Other people seem to have very few skills and abilities. With them, it's "If I manage to struggle and develop it, I'm going to keep using it to make sure I keep it!" They do not take their skills and abilities for granted. Because they worked to develop them, they try to keep them sharp.

You can lose your skills and abilities. It's easy. All you have to do is to take them for granted and never use them. You must be willing to exercise them. You must be willing to seek out good coaching to improve them. And you must be willing to practice and practice. Whatever skills and abilities you have, you need to work to keep them, improve them, and perfect them. But plan for gradual improvement, not spectacular leaps. And remember another famous saying by Campbell: "If you have it, use it, or you will lose it!"

Look Like a Million Dollars, Not Ten Cents!

Like it or not, your appearance and manners are going to have some impact on your career opportunities. Employers often pay great attention to appearance and manners in job interviews. Your coworkers and customers will also pay attention to the way you look and act. Psychological research has proved firmly that attractive people are liked and thought well of. Thus a well-dressed and well-behaved person has more career opportunities open to him than do poorly dressed and poorly behaved persons. You may think this is unfair—after all, beauty is only skin deep. But "Sometimes skin deep is deep enough!" (Campbell, 1974)

"But I can't do anything about my looks or behavior! I'm just me!" you might say. Not true! You can take what you have and make the best of it. You can study how persons in the career you want dress, and dress similarly. You can learn exceptional manners, and you can keep your appearance attractive by staying slim and healthy. Your appearance and your behavior can be important assets, so take advantage of them where you can. Looking neat, clean, healthy, and appropriately dressed, and behaving in a respectful and courteous manner can never hurt your career!

Knowing Where You Want to Go

Your career goals point out where you want to go, what you want to become, and what you hope to gain by working. This part of the chapter focuses on your own career goals and plans. These goals and plans must be realistic. A career goal is realistic if:

1. You have the credentials and assets needed to unlock the opportunity to begin the career (i.e. you cannot plan to become a college professor if you drop out of college).

2. You can obtain the credentials and assets needed to unlock the opportunity to begin the career.

Earlier in the chapter we reviewed your credentials and assets. They determine what opportunities are open to you. Your opportunities determine, to a large extent, how realistic your career goals are. Without the right credentials and assets, you will not have the opportunities you want. For example, I once wanted to be a professional singer. Unfortunately, I have a mediocre voice. Because I did not have the abilities needed, I have to give up that career goal and switch to another one. Everyone has to be realistic about what career he will pursue. Trying to follow a career for which you do not have the credentials and assets needed is like trying to ride a dead horse—it just will not get you where you want to go.

Besides being realistic, career goals have to be flexible. Your goals have to fit in with the goals of the organization that hires you. If you want to get a lot of different experiences with computers but your employer wants you to do the same thing day after day, you will either have to modify your career goals for a while or else look for a different job, or both. Your career goals also have to fit in with the goals of your fellow employees. If you want to work hard, but your fellow employees want to do as little work as possible, you will either have to modify your career goals for a while or else look for a different job, or both. Your goals, the organization's goals, and the goals of your fellow employees all have to overlap if things are to go well on the job.

Your career goals will always be personal—they are *your* goals for *your* life. But you cannot ignore the importance of other people in helping you reach them. If you do not use your skills in building and keeping good relationships on the job, you will find it hard to achieve your career goals.

Finally, it is important to remember that the choices you make now in pursuing career goals should leave some flexibility for the future. Many people change their careers. You may someday wish to change your career; what you want to be and what you want to gain from working may change. It is always wise to get extra credentials and assets, to help you change your career if you ever decide to do so.

EXERCISE   Your Career Plans
2.4

PURPOSE

Most people go through several changes in career plans as they grow up. The author is no exception. When I was in kindergarten I wanted to be a cowboy or a farmer. When I was in grade school I wanted to be an explorer or medical missionary. In junior high I wanted to be an archaeologist. In high school I wanted to be a hobo. In college, at first I wanted to be an advertising executive or a writer; later on I wanted to be a psychologist. I had a hard time making up my mind what I really wanted to do. In this exercise you will draw up lists of your career goals—past and present—and then discuss them with your group.

PROCEDURE

1. Working alone, complete the following sentences:
   a. When I was in grade school, I wanted to be a . . .
   b. When I was in junior high school I wanted to be a . . .
   c. Last year I wanted to be a . . .
   d. My parents always wanted me to be a . . .
2. Working alone,
   a. Make a list of the different careers you would like to try sometime.
   b. For each career, list the credentials you think you would need in order to be able to follow the career.
   c. For each career, list the assets (as far as you know) you would need in order to be able to follow the career.
3. In your group, draw numbers to see who is to go first. Each member of the group will review his career plans. Help each group member find out what excites him about each proposed career.

EXERCISE 2.5   **Career Interviews**

PURPOSE

Many people work at several different careers in their lives. You will probably have several different careers before you retire. The purpose of this exercise is to increase your awareness of how careers sometimes change during a person's life, and how you might change careers during your life.

PROCEDURE

1. Working alone, pick out two people you know who are over forty years old. Interview them about their career history. Start with their first *full-time* job and work up to their present job. Describe each full-time job they have had and report why they changed their careers as they got older.
2. Now imagine you have just retired and someone has asked to do a career interview with you. What do you think it might be like? What will your first full-time job be? What will your second career be? What will your third career be? How many careers will you have between now and retirement? What will they be?

3. In your group, discuss the two career interviews you have done and your reactions to each one. After each member has discussed his interviews, see what conclusions you can make about the career histories of the people who are currently forty years old or older.

4. In your group, discuss your imagined career interviews. State the careers you hope to have before you retire. Help the other group members think about the careers they will have between now and retirement as well.

EXERCISE 2.6   **Your Personal Career Needs**

PURPOSE

What do you seek to gain from working? Is it money, freedom from your parents, fame, fun, or personal satisfaction? The purpose of this lesson is to give you the chance to reflect on what you need and want from your career.

PROCEDURE

1. Working alone, write as many short answers as you can to the question, "What do I want from my career?"

2. In your group, take the answers of each member, and then decide on a group list. The group list can include new items that no one mentioned in their individual list, and it can omit individual items which the rest of the group does not value. An example of a group list is shown on the opposite page.

3. Have each member make a copy of the group list. Then, individually, rank order the items as they apply to you: In the Importance column, put number "1‘ next to the need that you value most, put "2" next to the need that is second most important to you, and so forth.

4. Still working alone, fold your sheet of paper so that you cannot see the ranking you have just finished. Now, in the Opportunity column, rank order each item on the list again, this time in terms of chances for meeting the need in your job or career. Put "1" by the item that you are most likely to get in your job or career, "2" by the item that is second most available, and so forth.

5. In your group, discuss your rankings. Use the following questions to help guide your discussion:
   a. How alike or different are your two rankings?
   b. How alike or different are the rankings of the group as a whole?
   c. What can you learn by comparing the rankings?

PURPOSE

People have always dreamed of a career that meets all their personal needs. But this dream can never come true. There are always tradeoffs in any career. You have to give up getting some of the things you want or need in order to get others. In any organization, there is a constant tension between the needs of the organization and the needs of each employee. One reason for this tension is that no two employees have exactly the same needs. Another reason is that many employees may need something that is limited in supply—such as money, power, or office space—and, therefore, when one employee gets what she wants, another employee does not. The purpose of this lesson is to compare your own needs with the needs of the organization you work for or intend to work for.

Importance	fold here	EXAMPLE OF A GROUP LIST Needs	Opportunity
_____		High salary	_____
_____		Prestige, respect from other people	_____
_____		Sense of personal achievement	_____
_____		Freedom, control over my own life and activities	_____
_____		Helping other people, contributing to a better world	_____
_____		Variety, change, and absence of routine	_____
_____		Leadership, control over other people's activities, making important decisions, responsibility	_____
_____		Making new friends, being with people I like	_____
_____		Lots of leisure time, short hours, and long vacations	_____
_____		Challenge, learning new skills, improving myself	_____
_____		Being part of an organization that is accomplishing things	_____
_____		Early entry into the job, little or no training needed to get and hold the job	_____
_____		Doing something I like and I am interested in	_____
_____		Good chance to get ahead and be promoted	_____

PROCEDURE

1. In your group, list as many specific things as you can that organizations want from their employees. The list might include such things as:

High-quality work	Responsibility
Personal development of employees	Loyalty to the company
	Employee satisfaction
Commitment to the organization's goals	Reliability
	Appreciation for everything the company is doing for the employees
Ability to work cooperatively with others	

2. Compare your list of organization needs with the lists of personal needs made by each member in the previous exercise. Discuss these questions:

   a. What are the conflicts or areas of disagreement between the organizational needs and your personal needs?

   b. How alike and different are the organizational needs and the individual needs of group members?

   c. What major conflicts do you expect between your needs and the needs of the organization you work for or intend working for?

   d. How will you manage your career so that most of your individual needs will be met?

3. What have you learned from this exercise?

EXERCISE 2.8 **Career Determination by Coworkers, Opportunities, and Yourself**

PURPOSE

Your present career activities are affected by the way your fellow employees or fellow students act, the chances you have to build toward the career you want, and your own characteristics as a worker. The purpose of this exercise is to give you a chance to discuss these three aspects of your present career activities.

PROCEDURE

1. Most career activities involve interacting with other people. What benefits do you get from working with other people? Look at the following list of possibilities. Working by yourself, rank them in order of most important, "1," to least important, "10." If other benefits that are important to you are not included in this list, you may add them.

   The benefits I receive from working with other people are that they:

   _____ keep me company.

   _____ provide me with someone to talk to.

   _____ are possible future friends.

   _____ give me personal support.

   _____ recognize the value of what I do.

   _____ give me someone to measure myself against.

_____ distract me from my work.

_____ help protect me from the boss.

_____ are interesting, I learn all kinds of things from them.

_____ are people to joke around and goof off with.

2. In your group, discuss the rankings of each member and then make a group ranking. Try to come to an understanding as to why each member ranked as he did and why the group as a whole ranked as it did.

3. What are the opportunities you now have that will help you build the future you want? Working alone, rate your chances (excellent, good, poor, nil, or not relevant) of:

_____ finishing a good career training program.

_____ getting a good grade in this course.

_____ entering a career training program.

_____ finishing high school.

_____ entering college.

_____ choosing among several jobs.

_____ being promoted on present job.

_____ other (describe).

4. In your group, discuss the opportunities of each member and the extent to which each member is taking advantage of opportunities in building toward his desired career.

5. Working alone, list ten words or phrases that describe yourself as an employee.

6. Working alone, how would you rate yourself (low, medium, high) on the following employability skills?

_____ responsible.

_____ reliable or dependable.

_____ cooperative.

_____ can take directions.

_____ can give directions to others.

_____ feel satisfaction from doing my work.

_____ give an honest day's work for an honest day's pay.

_____ can provide leadership when it is needed.

_____ can communicate in skillful and effective ways.

_____ can build positive and open relationships with fellow employees.

_____ can manage conflicts constructively with coworkers, boss, and customers.

_____ can work well with people from different backgrounds.

_____ can manage my feelings constructively.

_____ have an identity and a sense of purpose in life that includes my career.

_____ other (describe).

7. In your group, compare the descriptions each of you has made as a worker. Are they similar to each other? How would other group members change your description? What are important qualities for a worker to have in order to get and hold a job and to be successful at a career?

○　　○　　○

I never did get along very well with the other people in the office. They took everything so seriously. I wanted to enjoy myself at work. I never cared much about details. I'd argue a lot when people would find small mistakes in my work. It got so bad that I finally quit. We just didn't seem to want the same things from the work.

Sam Donaldson, Office Manager
in STUDS TERKEL, *Working*

○　　○　　○

Where to Go from Here

Who you work with is determined by what job you get, which in turn is determined by your goals, assets, and credentials. And once you are on the job your needs and goals, skills and abilities, and past training and education all affect your relationships with fellow employees. Your work relationships begin with who you

are as a person, what you are like, what your past has been like, and what you want to become and achieve. All your personal qualities will affect your relationships on the job. Being clear about who you are and what you are like is the first step in building a relationship. Developing interpersonal skills is the second step. But before we begin building the skills needed to develop and keep good relationships at work, we will briefly review what work is, why you have to do it, and how fellow employees affect your work life. This will make it clear why good relationships on the job are so important.

Some Major Points

1. Your career begins with your goals. You have to make sure you know where you are going, or else you are likely to end up somewhere else.
2. To unlock career opportunities, you need credentials and assets. By acquiring them, you plant the seeds for a future harvest. By exercising and using them, you ensure that they don't waste away. And by being open and honest about them you ensure that employers know about them.
3. It is important for your career that you have some choices. Don't put all your career eggs in one basket.
4. Be future-oriented. There *is* a tomorrow. Be realistic about your career goals and keep them flexible. You will change, so plan your life so change is possible.
5. Don't forget other people. You can't have a successful career without the involvement and support of others.

Making Personal Decisions

To get a job, to be successful at your work, and to leave one job for a better one, there are countless decisions to be made. Within any job, you will be part of a team that will need to make group decisions. Your fellow employees will ask your advice concerning decisions they face. Day in and day out, numerous decisions have to be made and implemented. Decision making typically involves considering possible alternatives and choosing one. The purpose of decision making is to choose a well-considered, well-understood, realistic action toward goals you wish to achieve—a choice you will not regret. To make a *good decision* implies that you are certain as to which of several courses of action is most desirable for achieving your goals. Most important decisions are such that you cannot know what the long-term results will be. If you decide to change jobs, for example, you cannot know for certain whether you will be better off in five years. If you enter one training program rather than another, you cannot be certain whether you will be better off years later. If you decide to marry so-and-so now, you cannot be certain whether a better spouse might be found sometime in the future. So when you accept one opportunity, you never know whether a better opportunity might present itself later on. Because the results of most decisions are unknown, making decisions can be difficult and cause considerable stress.

In the rest of this chapter we will discuss (1) the general nature of career decisions, (2) the five basic patterns of decision making that may be used when you are confronted with a decision, and (3) the steps to be used when a reasoned and high-quality decision is needed. The process will be applied to career decisions.

Making Career Decisions

How many times have you been asked, "What are you going to be when you grow up?" People probably began asking you that question as soon as you had learned to talk. Years ago it was an easy question to answer. A son was expected to follow in his father's footsteps, entering the same career as his father. A few careers were open to women, but in general a daughter was expected to get married and raise a family. Today, however, society frees individuals from the expectation that they will follow in their parents' footsteps. This freedom of choice is confusing and frightening to many people, because the word *career* implies a lifelong commitment to a certain type of work. Fortunately, most people now have the opportunity to change their occupations at many points in their lives.

The decision about what to be "when we grow up" is an important and difficult one for most individuals. It begins early in life, when children *fantasize* about various occupations and role play at various jobs. Children assume they can be whatever they want to be. At times they may "be" a doctor, movie star, police officer, astronaut, or president. Between ages 11 and 17, individuals enter the *tentative* stage of career decision making. They begin to examine their interests, abilities, attitudes, and values, and search for occupations that will best fit them. Different occupations are thought about as individuals realize that they will soon have to enter one occupation or another. After the age of 17, there is a *realistic* narrowing of choices. Individuals look at the rewards offered by different jobs and weigh these against the training required for the job and the effort required in the occupation. The opportunities available are faced and a career choice is made based on a compromise of interests, training, and opportunity.

"Here I am," states a middle-aged man, "stuck with a miserable career chosen for me by an uninformed 19-year-old boy." In making a career choice it is important to remember that there is no one "right" job for any of us. Many different occupations could fulfill each of our needs. We need to find *a* job that will be satisfying, not *the* job. As we grow older, our needs and desires change. No decision is irreversible. An occupation we might like in our 20's may not be what we want to do in our 40's. We will be faced with decisions about our career throughout our lives.

Aids to Decision Making

There are a number of aids to making an informed decision about a career. Guidance counselors are trained to identify your interests, values, attitudes, and abilities. They will then discuss the wide variety of jobs that are available and help you identify the types of jobs that may be a "good fit" with who you are. Counselors may suggest that you take tests aimed at identifying your abilities and interests. *Ability tests* measure your reasoning, memory, mechanical, mathematical, and psychomotor abilities. *Interest tests* compare your interests with those of successful people in a wide variety of occupations. The assumption behind these tests is that a person is more likely to be happy if his or her basic interests are similar to those of people already in the field. Armed with the results of the tests and with a record of your background, the counselor interviews you. In the interview, the counselor further pinpoints your values and ambitions, discusses a number of different occupations, and outlines what is required to enter each. Parents can often be helpful in providing advice and information about various careers. Internships and summer jobs give valuable experience to help you find out your job likes and dislikes.

Five Basic Patterns of Decision Making

Roger is very happy at his job. He is service manager of a small automotive dealership. Roger does his job well and is respected by his coworkers. He knows that he may someday become general manager of the dealership. Unexpectedly, Mr. Jones, the manager of a much larger dealership, phones Roger and asks him to lunch. Over lunch Mr. Jones offers Roger the job of service manager, at a much higher salary than he is presently making. Since it is a larger company, Roger would supervise more people and would have more responsibility. But his chances for a promotion might be less, and his coworkers might not be as supportive. He must make a decision. Here are five alternative ways he can react to the offer:

1. Turn down the job offer immediately, stating that he is happy with his current job.
2. Accept the job offer immediately, and hand in his resignation right after lunch.
3. Give an evasive answer such as, "Maybe, after I think about it a while."
4. Panic and think to himself, "I can't just sit here eating my lunch—I have to tell him yes or no immediately or else he will think I'm a wimp!"
5. Calmly say, "Let me think it over for a few days. I would like to visit your dealership, talk to a few of your employees, find out what fringe benefits you offer employees, and assess my future with your company."

If Robert turns down Mr. Jones's job offer, he may never get another chance to work for a large company. But if he accepts the job offer he may be stuck with the position of service manager and never have an opportunity to manage an entire dealership. Although he needs the additional money the new job would pay, would he feel as secure and comfortable in a new place? "How do I decide?" he wonders.

When you are confronted with this kind of choice, there are five basic patterns of decision making (Janis and Mann, 1977). For each pattern you ask yourself a basic question and, depending on the answer, you experience high, low, or moderate stress and choose a strategy of decision making. The first four patterns you want to avoid under most conditions; the fifth you want to implement whenever possible. Let's discuss each of the five patterns in turn.

1. **Complacent Choice of the Status Quo.** The question you ask yourself is, "Are the consequences serious if I do not change?" If the answer is no, you experience little stress, and have no conflicts in adhering to your present course of action. If the answer is yes, you may complacently decide to continue whatever you have been doing, ignoring any information about the risk of losses if you do so. In either case, there is an incomplete search for new information, incomplete appraisals of alternatives, and incomplete planning for contingencies. You may have a nonrational resistance to change, clinging to tradition, being inert and maintaining habits, being overdependent on authority, having illusions of powerlessness, or be insecure about the consequences of the change for yourself. Familiar problems are often preferable to unknown new possibilities. Many people keep undesirable jobs or refuse to look for employment elsewhere because they are afraid of the unknown.

2. **Uncritical Change.** The question you ask yourself is, "Are the consequences serious if I do change?" If the answer is no, you experience low stress, and have no conflicts about changing. Or the answer may be yes, and yet you may uncritically adopt whichever new course of action is most highly recommended or seems best to you at the time. You do not think much about the decision. There is an incomplete search for new information, incomplete appraisal of alternatives, and incomplete planning for contingencies. Some people seem to have no regrets and never seem to look backward. Change is easy because there is little commitment to the present and little chance of feeling guilt or regret if the decision turns out to be a bad one.

3. **Defensive Evasion.** The question you ask yourself is, "Is it realistic to hope to find a better solution?" If the answer is no, you experience high stress, and defensively avoid a search for more information, appraisal of alternatives, and planning for contingencies. Even if the answer is yes, you may be reluctant to make a decision. You are beset by conflict, doubts, and worry, and struggle with *incongruous longings, antipathies, and loyalties.* You escape the conflict—at least temporarily—by *procrastinating,* shifting responsibility to someone else, or constructing wishful rationalizations to bolster the least objectionable alternative, remaining selectively inattentive to corrective information. You believe you are "damned if you do and damned if you don't." You believe there are serious risks involved both in staying with the current course of action *and* in moving to a new course of action. Either way you are pessimistic.

4. **Panicky Decision Making.** The question you ask yourself is, "Is there sufficient time to search for new information and deliberate about its meaning?" If the answer is no, you experience high stress, and feel pressure to make the

BALANCE SHEET FOR DECISION MAKING

	advantages/gains	disadvantages/losses
1. Gains and losses for you		
2. Gains and losses for significant others		
3. Impact on your self-approval or self-disapproval		
4. Approval or disapproval by significant others		

Adapted from Janis and Mann (1977).

decision immediately. Fear and anxiety about the consequences of the decision cause you to search frantically for a way out of the dilemma. Impulsively, you seize on a hastily contrived solution that seems to promise immediate relief, overlooking the full range of consequences of your choice. There is an incomplete search for information, incomplete appraisal, and lack of planning. Your reasoning may be characterized by a high degree of emotionality, reduced memory span, and simplistic, repetitive thinking. You may have a reduced time perspective, which leads you to place a higher value on immediate goals and less rigorous evaluation of alternatives and their consequences. In its most extreme form, hypervigilance is referred to as "panic."

5. **Alert Decision Making.** The question you ask is, "Is there sufficient time to obtain and evaluate additional information?" If the answer is yes, you search painstakingly for relevant information, consider it, and think about alternatives carefully before making a choice. A moderate level of stress is experienced, and you engage in a thorough search for relevant information, a thorough consideration of each alternative, and thorough planning. You are confident about your ability to make a good decision and believe there is adequate time to do so.

Alert Decision Making

People often make poor decisions, not because they do not think of the proper alternatives, but because they do a poor job of evaluating and choosing among the alternatives they consider. Systematic evaluation of each alternative and analysis of the advantages and disadvantages of each alternative before making a final decision is the most important factor in alert decision making (Mann and Janis, 1983). Each alternative should be systematically evaluated on the basis of four factors:

1. The real and definite gains and losses for you.
2. The real and definite gains and losses for significant others.
3. The impact of the choice on your self-approval or self-disapproval: Will you feel proud or ashamed if you choose the alternative?
4. The approval or disapproval of you by significant others: Will persons important to you think you made the right decision?

When you make a decision, prepare a balance sheet on each alternative course of action you are considering, and then compare the balance sheets and rank the alternatives from "most desirable" to "least desirable."

Procedure for Selecting the Best Decision

When making personal decisions there is a basic procedure to follow. The procedure is prescriptive in that it specifies what you should strive to do in order to avoid making regrettable errors in selecting a course of action.

1. **Awareness Stage.** You are confronted with a challenge to your current course of action. This may occur when you near the end of high school and face the need to decide whether to seek a job or enter a training program. Or it may occur when you have an opportunity to apply for a new job. During the awareness stage you realize you have to make a decision.
2. **Search.** You begin to search for alternative courses of action that have some

promise of achieving your goals. You may seek the advice of friends and family, or perhaps a professional counselor. All the alternatives you can find are identified.

3. **Information Seeking and Appraisal or Thinking Through.** You consider the advantages and disadvantages of each alternative course of action. Dependable information relevant to the expected outcomes of each alternative is sought. Facts and forecasts are obtained from a wide variety of sources. The positive and negative consequences of all known alternative courses of action, including those previously rejected, are reconsidered. Some worrying may be productive during this stage. A tentative decision is reached.

4. **Trial Balloons.** You consider how to implement your tentative decision and convey your intentions to family, friends, business associates, members of other reference groups, and casual acquaintances. Their possible approval or disapproval is considered and the decision is reviewed in light of their reactions. Seeking out individuals who may disagree with your decision and argue against it is often helpful during this stage. You have a second chance to make the decision after considering the views of significant others and opposing arguments.

5. **Choice and Follow Through.** You finalize and implement your decision. A sense of competence and satisfaction is experienced. Any negative consequences are tolerated because you are confident you made the best decision you could under the circumstances.

The Two Basic Errors in Decision Making

Many people faced with important decisions tend to make two major errors. The first is delaying a decision. Vacillation, procrastination, and indecisiveness may cause a person to postpone carrying out the essential tasks of search, appraisal, and choice. The second error is premature closure, whereby you commit yourself impulsively without going through the stages requisite for arriving at a sound choice. Premature closure is terminating the decisional dilemma without generating all the alternatives and without seeking or appraising the available information about the outcomes to be expected for the limited set of alternatives under consideration. There is undoubtedly much room for improvement in the information-seeking and appraisal activities of most people.

Work: A Definition

What is work? Is being employed by a local hospital work? Is cleaning your room or apartment work? Is looking after your younger brother a form of work? Think of all the phrases and words that describe work. Write them down. What sort of definition of work do you end up with?

The report of a Special Task Force, submitted to the United States Secretary

of Health, Education, and Welfare in 1972 and entitled *Work in America,* defines *work* as "an activity that produces something of value for other people." There are four important aspects of this definition. First, it implies that work has a goal of producing goods or services that other people need and want. The goods might be food or cars. The services might be haircuts or house repairs. Second, the definition implies that the purpose of working is to increase the quality of both your life and the lives of other people. You work at a certain job because other people need and want the product or service, not just because you like doing it. For example, you may want to make washboards, but if no one wants to buy a washboard you will soon go broke and have to find another type of job.

The third aspect of the definition of work is that work requires physical and psychological energy. You expend this energy to produce the goods and services. When you work, you use energy to achieve a goal. Finally, if you are working, you cannot be resting or playing at the same time. There is some sacrifice of leisure when you work. Leisure activities are postponed until the work is finished.

It's OK for Other People, but Do I Have To?

When I was young, I lived on a farm. My grandfather was always insisting that I work. Plow the fields, plant the crops, feed the pigs, milk the cows, repair the tractor! All day long (and half the night), my grandfather was always telling me to do one job or another! It's a wonder I lived through it! Every time my grandfather gave me a job, I would say the same thing. "Why me?" "Why do I have to work?" Somehow, my grandfather never gave an answer to that question that I could understand. I wanted work to be a choice, not a requirement. Here are some answers to that question that may or may not make sense to you.

Answer Number One is that you work to survive. Work is the means to earn a living. You work to sustain yourself—to buy the food, clothing, health care, and shelter you need to survive. Liking your work has nothing to do with the necessity of providing for your survival. A farmer does not farm because he loves hard physical labor, sunstroke, mud up to his ears, and being kicked by his cows. Of course not! He farms because he needs to produce food to survive. A carpenter does not build a house because he loves to work in the rain and hit his thumb with a hammer over and over again. He does it because he wants to sell the house for enough money to pay his bills so that his family has the food, clothing, health care, and shelter they need.

Work is part of family and community survival. It is part of the survival of our society. We are all better off when we join together and combine our efforts. We work to provide food for our children so they will work to provide us food when we are old, and we work to provide food for the sick so they will work to provide us food when we are sick. Being a member of a family, community, and society requires that you work to contribute to the productivity and survival of the group. Work is a social obligation to your family, community, and society.

Historically, work has often been related to being a father or mother. Before a community will allow a person to be a parent, it feels he or she should become a worker and a potential provider. The assumption is that before you become a mother or a father you should first prove you can provide the food, shelter, health care, and clothing needed to raise a child.

Work has always been a place to meet people, talk, and form relationships. People who do not work often feel isolated, lonely, unwanted, and unappreciated. Working with other people is a natural part of building and keeping friendships and relationships.

You gain your independence through work. When you were a child, other people worked to provide you with food, clothing, health care, and shelter. You were dependent on your parents. Becoming an adult means becoming financially independent through working—taking care of yourself, meeting your own needs, and contributing to the survival of your community and society. When you were a child, other people supported you as an investment in the future. They expect you to repay them by contributing to the support of the family, community, and society when you become an independent adult.

There are also psychological benefits from working. How you define yourself as a person is influenced greatly by your career. Your sense of purpose and meaning in life is influenced by your career. Your feelings of being part of a joint effort and community are affected by your career. Your sense of self-worth is affected by your career.

Finally, work helps you build a rhythm in your life. It provides a regularity, the basic patterns of day, week, month, and year. Your life will be organized around your job. The rhythm of your life will be provided by the hours you work and the hours you do not work.

If none of these reasons for working make sense to you, then maybe you can think of others that do. If you can think of no reason why you should work, you may want to remember one of Campbell's (1974) famous statements: "*Those in this*

world who do not work, either by choice or by circumstances, do not amount to much. Usually, they don't even like themselves."

You Can't Avoid It!

Things have really changed in the last 10,000 years. Today, work is not a matter of choice, it is a fact of life. Ten thousand years ago, you could work when you felt like it. Most hunters and gatherers had much more freedom from work than you will ever have. For better or worse, a career is not an option for those who want one. A career is a necessity for every member of a family, community, and society.

Some people are disappointed when they do not have fun at work. Of course, you *can* have a lot of fun with your coworkers, and you *can* enjoy your job. But the purpose of work is not to be entertained, stimulated, or titillated. The purpose of work is to produce something of value for yourself and other people. Enjoyment is, unfortunately, not the main reason why people work. Most work involves some monotony, boredom, strain, anxiety, and the feeling that every day is just like every other day. Even without enjoying your work, you can take pride and satisfaction from doing a good job, and you can enjoy the company of your coworkers. Applying the skills discussed in this book will increase the enjoyment you get from working greatly. You can interact with your coworkers in ways that bring you enjoyment. And, of course, you can maximize the enjoyment of your work by choosing your job wisely.

Work: Meaningful or Meaningless?

What makes work meaningful or meaningless? Is it the work itself? Or is it the person doing the work? Your career is a search for daily meaning as well as for daily bread. It is a search for recognition as well as for cash. Everyone has a hunger for a sense of pride and meaning in a career.

○   ○   ○

Man's concern about a meaning in life is the truest expression of being human.

VICTOR FRANKL

○   ○   ○

What is the difference between Mike Lefevre, a steel worker, and Carl Bates, a stonemason? As quoted in Studs Terkel's book, *Working*, Mike Lefevre said, "It's the nonrecognition by other people which makes my work so meaningless." Carl Bates said, "I take a lot of pride in [my work] and I do get . . . a lot of praise or whatever you want to call it. . . . I think I'm pretty well recognized." Is it the difference in the *type* of work they do that makes these two men feel so differently about their work? Or is it the difference in their attitude toward their work that makes them feel so differently about it?

Some jobs are more interesting than others. But every job has a lot of routine and repetition that can be boring. What is one person's burdensome toil is another person's labor of love. The meaning you receive from work is up to you. You can make your work meaningful, or you can make it meaningless.

How does a person make his work meaningful? Is it really possible? Listen to a waitress named Delores Dante (Terkel, 1972): "When I put the plate down, you don't hear a sound. When I pick up a glass, I want it to be just right. When someone says, 'How come you're just a waitress?' I say, 'Don't you think you deserve being served by me?' . . . To be a waitress, it's an art. . . . I tell everyone I'm a waitress and I'm proud." Does Delores Dante make her work meaningful? Or is she just kidding herself?

Recent surveys have found that most people in the United States find their work meaningful. Probably most people in human history have found their work meaningful. What are the attitudes that have helped them do this? One religious view of work is as follows: Since there is a God, and since God put people on earth to do "His" work, when a person works he is following God's will. How can a person be unhappy with his work when it is what God wants him to do? Millions of people have lived their lives with this attitude.

Another view of work focuses on its contribution to our society. Everyone's work helps the society to continue. Everyone's work helps the values of our society to survive. By doing your work, you are part of the overall economic system of our society. By helping the economic system succeed, you are helping your society. Millions of people have lived their lives with this attitude.

A third view of work focuses on its contribution to other people in your community. Financially, materially, and psychologically, your work helps you, your family, your friends, and everyone in your community. Everyone's work is important to other people in his community. Being a garbage collector, for example, helps almost every person in your community. A garbage collector can feel a lot of pride from helping his neighbors and friends. Whatever your work, it helps your neighbors, friends, and fellow members of your community.

Finally, your work is part of a cooperative effort to provide a product or service. You are part of a joint effort. Other people could not do their work if you did not do yours, and vice versa. There is a great deal of meaning in such cooperation.

THINK ABOUT IT

Will working less for more pay make your work more meaningful? Is a short task more meaningful than a long task? Does the amount of pay determine how meaningful a job is? Does the status of a job define how meaningful the work is? What does make work meaningful? Write down what you think.

How you think about your work and how your friends and coworkers think about your work affect how meaningful it is to you. When your friends and coworkers value your work and give you recognition for doing a good job, then you will take pride in your work and find it meaningful.

That means it is important how you choose your friends. We use our friends as guides for our own actions and are influenced by what our friends think. If our friends find our careers meaningful, we will tend to find our careers meaningful. If our friends value what we do, so will we. Choosing your friends carefully is one way of influencing yourself. By putting ourselves in close contact with people who value our work, we are more likely to find our work meaningful. If we put ourselves in close contact with people who hate their work and view working as selling out to the establishment, we are more likely to find our work meaningless. Birds of a feather do flock together. Choose carefully what birds you want to flock with.

○　○　○

Take hold of your lives. Most of the things that distress you, you can avoid; most of the things that dominate you, you can overthrow. You do as you will with them.

PLATO

○　○　○

It is also possible to build supportive relationships with coworkers. You can be part of a group at work that gives recognition to, and appreciation for each other's work efforts. Research indicates that people who are skilled in building cooperative relationships on the job enjoy their work more, are more productive, and find more meaning in their work. The same is true for life in general. Our relationships with other people make life worthwhile and meaningful. Interpersonal skills are essential for building the type of relationships that make both working and living meaningful.

Twelve Ways to Get Yourself Fired

The United States Department of Labor has identified twelve examples of poor work habits that often cause people to lose their jobs:

1. Being continually careless with your work so that a lot of time and effort by other employees is required to correct errors.
2. Being unwilling to follow company rules.
3. Acting lazy on the job.
4. Being absent and late for work frequently without any good reason.
5. Being a troublemaker, causing friction among the workers, and showing continual resistance to cooperation.
6. Spending a lot of time reading the sport pages, making personal phone calls, and organizing weekly parties and betting pools.
7. Relying on others for everything, not starting work until you are told, and not doing anything unless you absolutely must.
8. Making no effort to learn about your job or the industry.
9. "Bad mouthing" your company at every opportunity.
10. Not carrying out your work as directed.
11. Showing little interest in your work and not helping others with their work.
12. Misleading customers and telling a few "white lies" about your company and your boss.

How to Avoid Job Burnout

You went into your job with enthusiasm, ambition, optimism, and even exuberance. Unless you are careful, however, you may end up feeling disgruntled, used up, disenchanted; at worst, you may feel that your work life has become hollow and meaningless. Even the best job becomes wearisome after a while. Now and then a resurgence of energy occurs when your efforts and competencies are recognized, such as when you receive promotions, new assignments, favorable job reviews, and raises. Most of the time, however, a job consists of the day-in-and-day-out accumulation of small accomplishments that you expect will set you up for those rewards and exciting changes. Long-term, your career progression may depend on staying enthusiastic about your job and keeping job burnout from creeping up on you.

If you are feeling bored and blasé about your job, here are ten recommended antidotes:

1. **Collaborate more with associates.** Team up with a coworker on a project or get together with a group to work on achieving a task. Especially if your work makes you feel isolated, this is a constructive way to get some companionship on the job.

2. **Set up a project for yourself that really means something to you.** Emphasize the part of the job you really like. Find a project that both fits into your employer's plans and reconnects you with the reason you entered your field in the first place. Job satisfaction increases when your job fits your unique personality, both in terms of your life values and the maximum use of your greatest talents and abilities. Most people cannot get enough of the work they are physically, mentally, and spiritually in tune with.

3. **Take new initiative in communicating with your boss.** Feeling unrecognized by your supervisor can take some of the glow off an otherwise very rewarding job. Communicate with your boss. Do not expect the boss to read your mind. Let your boss know how things are going, where the problems are, what your achievements have been, what your short- and long-term objectives are. The better your boss knows you, the more your boss will value what you do and your contribution to the success of the company. Usually, *to be visible is to be valued*. Hold up your end of communication between your supervisor and yourself and chances are (assuming you do not make unwelcome demands on your boss's time), your boss will increasingly view you as conscientious and your work as more valuable.

   At some point you might make a straightforward approach to your supervisor and ask for an assessment of your achievements. Don't blame your boss if you have not been getting any feedback. Just say you'd like to make sure your efforts are on course and to find out what your boss thinks of what you have done so far. If you have really been knocking yourself out on the job, the praise should be loud and strong.

4. **Repair a bad relationship.** In every job, some fellow employees are a pain in the neck. Sometimes an associate simply takes a dislike to you and shows antagonism while standing in the way of your work goals and career objectives. Or maybe a coworker has a talent for making your day overcast. In such a situation, remember Abraham Lincoln's advice: "The way to defeat an enemy is to make him your friend." All your agonizing about another person's behavior does not help; it can only make you feel more helpless. The way to end such a situation is to make the other person your friend or at least a friendly colleague. Stretch yourself; be generous. Express goodwill. Find common ground. Find joint projects. When the person becomes less

disagreeable to you, you can then proudly enter this repaired relationship on your list of "things I have accomplished that keep me sane."

5. **Give some work away.** Sometimes it's good for you to delegate some of your work or to relax your perfectionism. Letting go of part of what is driving you crazy is one of the easiest cures for burnout.

6. **Let yourself laugh and play now and then.** Technically, this kind of timeout is called *executive recreation*. Find incidents during the day to laugh about with colleagues. Find ways to share fun, to express humor, to brighten both your day and that of your associates. When executive recess is over, you can easily make up for any time out—in fact, you will be more productive because you will be refreshed and relaxed.

    Laughter is just plain good for you. And it should be taken seriously. Hearty laughter results in both personal and interpersonal benefits. Chapter 12 has a full discussion of the importance of humor in avoiding job burnout and other psychological and physical problems.

7. **Seek out others with positive energy and avoid coworkers who express negativity.** Don't spend time with disgruntled coworkers who complain about how miserable they are. Sour exchanges rarely accomplish anything except to make you feel worse. The truth is, enthusiasm loves company. Be positive and cheerful. Encourage others to be enthusiastic about their jobs. And seek out others whose outlook and behavior are positive.

8. **Take care of your body.** Do not let the demands of your job come between you and your fitness. Eat right. Exercise regularly. Get enough sleep. You can not feel good about your job (or anything else, for that matter) if you are feeling physically unfit and under par.

9. **Have something else important to do with your life.** People who have commitments that claim their time and attention outside of their jobs have a better perspective on their work lives than those whose noses are always to the grindstone. Even a wonderful job cannot be expected to provide the entire meaning for one's life. We pass this way just once and we have only one chance to make a difference. What we do for the company might well be a significant part of the difference we make, but often as not, what we do on our own time adds at least as much to the meaning of our life. *You can enjoy a job more when it makes possible doing other things you enjoy.*

10. **Improve your relationships outside of your job.** When you have solid friendships and a love relationship, everything in your life tends to seem better.

What to Do When a Coworker Slacks Off

If you are a conscientious worker, you probably will carry more than your fair share of committee tasks or office duties. When a colleague shirks responsibility, do not suffer in silence—but do not whine either. Take control of the situation without losing your cool. The following three-point approach is your best hope of solving the problem.

1. **Do not complain to your boss.** You are expected to deal with such problems, not burden your boss with them. Complaints, no matter how justified, can make you appear to be weak under pressure.

2. **Approach the slacker in a calm, nonblaming manner.** Stress team spirit. You might say, "I am finding myself a bit swamped. Let's split the typing on this report so *we* can get it out on time." Sit down and agree on a fair work distribution. Do not accuse. Just assume she will want to pitch in. Let a few days go by. If she does not cooperate, repeat your request. It will be harder for her to ignore your concerns the second time.

3. **Take the lead on joint projects, and blow your own horn.** Give your boss weekly reports clarifying your contributions. Say, for example, "I want to let you know how the telephone campaign is coming along. Out of the 60 calls you suggested we make, I have completed 40, with some exciting responses. At this rate, with Jane's help, I will be done by the end of next week." If you take credit for your work, you will not be taken for granted.

SUMMARY AND REVIEW: Chapters 1 and 2

Setting Learning Contracts

At the end of each section in this book, you will set a *learning contract* with your group. This contract should summarize the most important things you have learned from the exercises in this section and should include a plan as to how you will use what you have learned.

In Section I, the exercises focused on identifying your credentials and assets and on reviewing your career plans and goals. We also focused on the importance of interpersonal skills on the job, the nature of work, and the meaning of work. It is time to sum up, with your group's help, what you have learned from this section and to plan how you can use what you have learned.

Be as specific as you can in stating what you have learned and how you will apply it. The following procedure is to be used in setting your learning contract with the group.

Procedure

1. Working alone, make a list of the most important things you learned about yourself, your credentials and assets, your career plans and goals, and the career opportunities you want. List at least five things you have learned about yourself.

2. Select the five most important things you have learned about yourself. For each one, plan an action you can take in the next two weeks to apply that learning. For example, if you learned that you do not know which careers meet your needs and interests, you might plan to see a career counselor,

LEARNING CONTRACT	
MAJOR LEARNINGS	ACTION PLANS

Date _____ Date of Progress Report Meeting _____

Student's Signature _____

Signatures of Other Group Members

_____

_____

_____

_____

_____

_____

_____

LEARNING CONTRACT PROGRESS REPORT

Student's Name _____ Section _____

DAY AND DATE	DESCRIPTION OF TASKS AND ACTIVITIES PERFORMED	SUCCESS EXPERIENCED	PROBLEMS ENCOUNTERED

Comments

from whom you can find out more about available careers. In making your action plans, be specific and practical. Do not try to do too much—but do not try to do too little, either.

3. Copy the Learning Contract form on page 59. Fill it out, but do not sign it.

4. In your group, draw numbers to see who is going to go first. The member selected reviews her learnings and action plans with the group. The group helps the member clarify any vague items, add to her list, and improve her action plans by concrete suggestions for implementing goals.

5. The member's learning contract is modified until both she and the rest of the group are satisfied with it. She then signs the contract, and then the rest of the group signs the contract. The member is now committed to the group to carry out her action plans.

6. The whole process is repeated until every member of the group has completed and signed a learning contract with the group.

7. The instructor will set a date—about two weeks from signing the contract—for the group to review each member's progress in completing his acion plans.

8. Working alone, keep a record of your progress in implementing your action plans. Copy and fill out the Learning Contract Progress Report on page 60. Use it when you give a progress report to your group.

9. In the progress review session, you will report to your group the day and date of the actions taken, describe what you did, what success you had, and what problems you encountered.

3

Cooperating with Others

After completing the Questionnaire that follows, you should be able to define and give examples of:

- Cooperation
- Competition
- Individualism
- Division of labor
- Coordination

The answers are given on the right side of the page. Work with a partner and keep the answers covered until you have agreed on your response. Remember to check each answer before going on to the next item, as explained on page 1.

QUESTIONNAIRE: Main Concepts in Chapter 3

1. When two or more people act together to achieve desired goals, they are engaging in *cooperation*. Maria and Jimenez are doing an inventory together. Their joint effort is an example of _____.

   cooperation

2. *Competition* is trying to achieve a goal better or faster than someone else. When Manuel tries to get a better sales record than Frank, he is in _____ with Frank.

   competition

3. *Individualism* is trying to achieve a goal that is unrelated to anyone else's goals. When you engage in an activity such as reading or watching television, your effort is an example of _____.

   individualism

4. There are three approaches to achieving goals: on your own, or _____; together with others, or _____; and working against others, or _____.

   individually
   cooperatively
   competitively

5. Cooperative efforts often entail a *division of labor*. When different persons do different parts of the whole task, they engage in a _____ of labor.

   division

6. Assembly-line production in automobile plants was made possible by _____ ____ _____.

   division of labor

7. When several persons do different parts of one task, their work has to be *coordinated*. The work of several people is coordinated when it is put in the proper order. Putting the work of several people in the right order is known as _____.

   coordination

8. Luis orders computer cards and puts them in the store room. Linda takes a supply to the keypunch department. Tai keypunches information onto the cards. Joanne writes a computer program to organize the data. Kazuko has the computer analyze the data. The work of these five persons is _____.

   coordinated

9. Efforts to achieve goals within organizations are almost always _____. Cooperative work almost always involves a _____ ____ _____. When a task is divided into parts, the work of different people has to be _____.

   cooperative
   division of labor

   coordinated

A Fable

Aesop, in about 550 BC, told the story of the bundle of sticks. A father wearied of his sons quarreling despite how often he asked them not to. One day when the quarreling was especially divisive, he asked one of his sons to bring him a bundle of sticks. Handing the bundle to each of his sons in turn, he asked them to try to break it. Although each one tried with all his strength, none was able to do so. The father then untied the bundle and gave the sticks to his sons to break one by one. This they did very easily. "My sons," said the father, "do you not see how certain it is that if you agree with each other and help each other, it will be impossible for your enemies to injure you? But if you are divided among yourselves, you will be no stronger than a single stick in that bundle." The moral of the tale is, **in unity is strength.**

Groups In Business And Industry

○   ○   ○

"Take care of each other. Share your energies with the group. No one must feel alone, cut off, for that is when you do not make it."

Willi Unsoeld, Mountain Climber

○   ○   ○

The productivity of United States business and industry has been falling. The implementation of more effective work teams are one means available to reverse this trend. During the first half of this century, the United States was without question the world leader in manufacturing, had developed new technologies, and translated them into products that were available nowhere else in the world. Today, the United States ranks fourth behind Europe, Japan, and Russia in manufacturing research, third in the consumption of machine tools, and fifth in the production of machine tools (NCMS, 1989). The share of the world automotive market has dropped from 76 percent to 24 percent, machine tools from 100 percent to 35 percent, and color TV's from 90 percent to 10 percent. At one time 27 United States companies produced TV's—now only one does.

To halt the decline of the United States manufacturing industries, companies are turning to the high productivity generated by small groups. Teams are central to increasing productivity. Teamwork, for example, is an integral part of the "HP Way," Hewlett-Packard Company's philosophy and style of doing business revolves around teams. While recognition is based on individual contribution, the company emphasizes working together in teams and sharing rewards. IBM is often quoted as saying, "If you can't work as part of a team, you can't work for IBM." Ford Industries, facing serious production and morale problems in the early 1980's, formed **problem-solving groups** to deal with shop floor problems, **interface groups** to work on problems that cut across work groups, **opportunity teams** to oversee implementation of new technology and facilities improvements,

special project teams to manage specific events such as auto shows, **linking teams** to deal with issues that require input from several shifts and departments, **launch teams** to coordinate across process and design needed to launch a successful new project, **vendor quality teams** to develop ongoing communication with suppliers both inside and outside the company, and **resource committees** to provide consulting and training on request (Banas, 1988). In almost every Ford plant, employees at all levels meet weekly in groups with their supervisors to deal with problems connected with production, quality, and the work environment. After rumors of bankruptcy in the early 1980's, Ford has made a dramatic comeback through the use of teams. Quality improved and sales of newly designed cars helped the company achieve record profits in the late 1980's. Ford is convinced that the quality of work they need to compete in the global economy requires high participation by workers. In the "excellent" companies, work is conducted in a variety of teams. A knowledge of group dynamics is thus central to running each company.

From the military to the Fortune 500, employers are emphasizing a core of new basic skills in their workers. Many of these skills, such as interpersonal and team skills as well as skills involved in continuous learning, would not have been considered either basic or even necessary only a short time ago. But the days are gone when a command of the three Rs would be enough to get and keep a job. Teamwork is the backbone of the future. Operating as a team, where each member brings to bear the maximum strength required to move the organization toward its goals, is essential for success. Today there is a whole range of new skills that employers want in the people they hire.

○　　○　　○

What is your view of work and why? Work is (a) labor, (b) craft, (c) art, or (d) philosophy.

○　　○　　○

Self-Managing Teams

○　　○　　○

The greatest rewards come only from the greatest commitment.

Arlene Blum, leader, American Women's Himalayan Expedition

○　　○　　○

Imagine you are the president of small manufacturing firm in the Midwest. You pay your workers $9 to $15 an hour. Your competition in Mexico pays work-ers $.80 an hour. Your employees literally have to work "smarter" if the company is to stay in business. What do you do? Here is a solution implemented by a person who was actually in this position:

1. Have employees work in teams that are responsible for improving both the quality of the product and the process by which the product is produced on a consistent basis.

2. Improve the basic skills of all employees to 9th-grade reading and writing and 10th-grade math. All employees are strongly encouraged to take night classes at the work site to improve their basic academic skills.

3. Develop a culture of learning and a norm of continuous improvement within the work teams so that workers are focused on improving the quality of the goods and services provided.

Workers then (a) rebuild, debug, and improve their own machines and procedures and (b) learn from their customers and each other continuously in order to fine tune and adapt their product or service to the needs of the customer. Both are aimed at innovating and adapting quickly.

Today, your job will probably not be defined narrowly so that only a low level of skills is needed. And you will certainly not perform the same thing over and over again. Your job will change all the time in many ways. The reason is that changes in the world economy have changed the nature of work as we know it.

Any new product or service, and any new technology, can be duplicated easily anywhere in the world. In today's manufacturing world, any new technical breakthrough can be quickly copied all over the world. In the new global economy, nearly everyone has access to new breakthroughs and the machines and money to turn them into standardized products at about the same time and in roughly the same terms. Competitive advantage no longer lies in one-time technological breakthroughs. Workers in South Korea, Taiwan, or Mexico, for instance, can churn out products just as well as American workers and for far lower wages. What cannot be copied, duplicated, or stolen is the employees' ability to learn and adapt and respond to market needs. Competitive advantage lies in keeping a technology by elaborating on it continually, developing variations and small improvements, so that particular needs of individual markets are met better. Companies compete on the basis of how quickly and well they can transform ideas into better products incrementally. This depends on the functioning of workers in teams within an organizational culture of learning.

Work force productivity results from (a) a **culture of learning** in which skilled labor (that's you) comes up with ideas to improve production and quality and (b) the widespread use of cooperative work teams. This means you have to master the skills for working as part of a cooperative team, at least a knowledge of 9th-grade reading and writing and 10th-grade math, and an overall technical and scientific competence related to your work. The culture of learning is aimed towards:

1. Continuous improvement of the machines and procedures you use to do your job: You need the skills to consistently redesign the machines and procedures you use to improve the quality of the services you provide or the product you make.

2. Continuous learning from your customers and your coworkers in order to

fine tune and adapt the services or product's you provide to the needs of the customer. If your company is going to adapt and respond quickly to customer's needs, you and your coworkers need to learn what your customers need and adapt quickly.

Quality, flexibility, and continuous improvements and innovations are the keys to success. In manufacturing firms, production will be handed over to small teams of skilled workers (which include you) who make incremental improvements in products and services. Products and services must change continually; they can become obsolete within one year. **Where before companies sold a "product" or "service," they now sell a "process."** The new basics of business are (a) world-class quality and service, (b) enhanced responsiveness to small markets through greatly increased flexibility, and (c) continuous, short-cycle innovation and improvement aimed at creating new markets for both new and apparently mature products and services. To be productive, a business has to respond quickly to multiple demands and needs. In essence, any worker who has contact with a customer is part of a "customer action team" whose purpose is to adapt continually the product or service provided to the changing needs of the customer.

The keys to today's and tomorrow's manufacturing are the team and the workers' commitment to continuous improvement. Procter and Gamble, for example, is using a participative work system in which employees must perform a broad range of tasks, including operating and maintaining equipment and carrying out administrative functions. Frequently, employees must perform their own quality control inspections. Participation in goal setting, budgeting, and other processes formerly viewed as the exclusive domain of management is also expected of workers. Employees work in largely self-directed teams, and problem solving and decision making are important parts of the job. Tasks will be nonroutine, placing greater demands on you to be able to think critically and respond to changes in the environment with reasoned judgment. To flourish, companies will need involved and committed workers, who are self-directed and creative thinkers, who continually seek to upgrade their knowledge and skills, who rapidly improve products and services, and who are willing to move from job to job. Teamwork makes this possible because the employees usually are "cross-trained" to perform all tasks. They can fill in for absent coworkers and respond quickly to changes in models and production runs. They can make short production runs to create and service small, individual markets. They can teach knowledge and skills to each other. They can monitor members' actions and ensure high quality of work and products.

In essence, education will continue throughout your life. While in the past people have tended to think of education as occurring from kindergarten to graduation from high scool or college, in the future education will be viewed as continual throughout one's career. Knowledge and skills will be updated and expanded continually in order to increase expertise and ensure that what you do "adds value" to the product or service provided by the company you work for. You will take part in this continual learning process throughout your career.

Types of Teams

○   ○   ○

Productivity through people.

Singapore Management Philosophy

○   ○   ○

The Minnesota Timberwolves faced their first year as an NBA professional team with an emphasis on playing as a team. A game such as basketball requires elaborate teamwork if played with any degree of expertise. Each play must be practiced again and again until the athletes function as a single unit, and desire for personal success must be transformed into a desire for group success. Practices are designed to foster team spirit, formulate group goals, identify weaknesses in team play, build a desire for group success, and strive for better and better cooperation and integration.

Just as athletes must learn how to pool their individual abilities and energies to maximize the team's performance, employees must learn to coordinate their efforts with those of the other group members. A **team** is a set of interpersonal relationships structured to achieve established goals. The productivity of teams is not a simple function of team members' technical competencies and task abilities. Group goals must be set, work patterns structured and practiced, a desire for team success must be built, and a sense of group identity developed. While technical superstars are a great asset, unless all members pursue team success over their own personal stardom, the team suffers. There is no place for "lone rangers" on a team, whether the team is a family, in a business, or in any other organization. Individual members must learn how to coordinate their actions, identify any strains and stresses in working together, and improve the integration of their efforts continually. The action research procedure that is the foundation of organizational development is also the foundation of team development. **Team building** emphasizes the analysis of work procedures and activities to improve productivity, relationships among members, the social competence of members, and the ability of the team to adapt to changing conditions and demands.

Teamwork is known by many different names in business and industry. It has been called *employee involvement* (EI), *worker participation,* and *labor-management "jointness."* Within business and industry, teams are not only viewed as positive, they are also viewed as inevitable. There are many different ways that work teams may be used within organizations. Three of the most common types are:

1. **Problem-solving teams** are teams consisting of 5 to 12 volunteers, hourly and salaried, drawn from different areas of a department. Problem-solving teams meet one to two hours a week to discuss ways of improving quality, efficiency, and work environment. They are "off-line" discussion groups that have no power to reorganize work or enlarge the role of workers in the production process. Problem-solving teams have been found to reduce costs and improve product quality, but have little effect on how work is organized or how managers behave. Consequently, they tend to fade away. They were first implemented on a small scale in the 1920s and 1930s and, based on Japanese Quality Circles, adopted more widely in the late 1970s.

2. **Special-Purpose Teams** are teams whose duties include such things as designing and introducing work reforms and new technology, meeting with suppliers and customers, and linking separate functions. In organizations that have unions, special-purpose teams have been used to facilitate collaboration between labor and management on operational decisions at all levels. Special-purpose teams are involved in work decisions at ever-higher levels, creating an atmosphere for quality and productivity improvements. The teams create a foundation for self-managing work teams. Special-purpose teams have been implemented in the 1980s as the next step after problem-solving teams. They are still spreading, especially in companies with unions.

3. **Self-Managing Teams** are teams of 5 to 15 employees who produce an entire product instead of subunits. Team members learn all tasks and rotate from job to job. The teams take over managerial duties, including work and vacation scheduling, the ordering of supplies and materials, and the hiring of new members. Self-managing teams can increase productivity 30 percent or more and substantially raise quality. They fundamentally change the way work is organized, giving employees control over their jobs, wiping out tiers of managers, and tearing down bureaucratic barriers between departments. A "flatter" organization results. Self-managing teams have been used by a few companies in the 1960s and 1970s and have rapidly spread in the mid- to late 1980s. They appear to be the wave of the future.

There is some doubt as to whether many companies understand how deep the change in organizational functioning must be—how they should really "go after it." Using self-managing teams and providing continuous training of employees has to become the primary consideration.

Structuring Working Relationships Among Workers

The Plains Indian People, known to whites as the Cheyenne, Crow, and Sioux, are truly the Painted Arrow, the Little Black Eagle, and the Brother People. They follow the Medicine Wheel Way. The Medicine Wheel is pictured in Figure 3.1. Each of the stones within the Medicine Wheel represents one of the many things in the Universe. All things are organized within the Medicine Wheel and all things are equal within it. All things within the Medicine Wheel know of their harmony with every other thing, except for humans. Finding harmony involves recognizing the uniqueness of each person and their unity within the Medicine Wheel.

The Medicine Wheel Way states that each person is unique in all ways but one. There is only one thing that all people possess equally, and that is loneliness. No two people on the face of this earth are alike in any one thing except for their loneliness. And the only way we can overcome our loneliness is by "touching" others. The Medicine Wheel Way begins with touching others. Touching others means to be to each other a gift, as is the buffalo. Touching others means nourishing each other, that we all may grow. Through touching others we find our place within the universe and to be in harmony with all other things within the universe. We touch others by joining a team and seeing the unity of all members. We are all separate and unique individuals. We are all part of a larger harmony working with each other.

The Plains Indians are not the only ones who believe in unique individuals seeking harmony within a team. Personal productivity in most cases cannot take place without team productivity. **It often takes a team to get extraordinary things done.** There are three ways that relationships among team members may be structured: competitively, individualistically, or cooperatively.

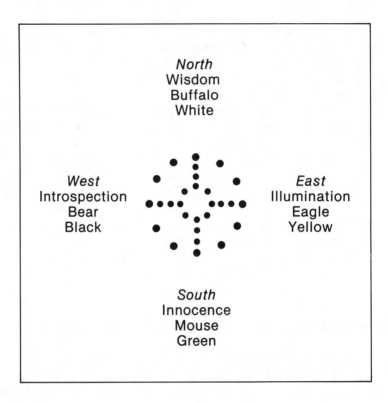

Figure 3.1 The Medicine Wheel

Members of a team can **compete** to see who is best. Team members can be ranked from best to worst and paid accordingly. Within a sales team, for example, the person who sells the most could receive a bonus of $500, the second best salesperson $300, and the third best salesperson $100. The rest receive no bonus. When a sales team is paid competitively, members become very concerned about making sales personally. They tend to hoard "leads" and hide potential new accounts from each other. No sale at all is preferable to having a team-mate make the sale. The more one person sells, the less likely it is that others will receive a bonus. Other examples include piecework and merit pay systems. In the **Lincoln Electric Company,** for example, workers are paid on a piecework basis, and given a yearly bonus that is determined by how many merit points an employee has as compared to others. A competitive structure tends to promote a few "superstars" and many, many others who never reach that plateau. Employees tend to dislike each other and have considerable hostility towards their superiors and the company as a whole. At Lincoln Electric, for example, one long-time employee stated, "You don't have a friend at Lincoln Electric!" Everyone was out to make themselves look good at their coworkers' expense. In addition, all workers tended to be rated average or above; any worker who was rated below average was considered a failure by the supervisor.

Members of a team can work **individualistically** to achieve up to a preset criteria for excellence and be paid accordingly. When a sales staff is paid individualistically, members become focused on reaching a preset sales quota. A sales person will receive $500 for selling over $5,000 of products, $300 for selling over $3,000 of products, and $100 for $1,000 of products. Everyone can succeed or everyone can fail. The efforts of members are independent so that how many sales one person makes has no positive or negative influence on the success of others. Employees tend to become "Lone Rangers" who are out to do well on their own with little or no concern for their coworkers. An example is **Konico Business Machines,** whose employees can earn points with each sale that are redeemable for merchandise and free trips.

Team members can work **cooperatively** to maximize the productivity of the team. Team members can be paid equally on the basis of overall team performance. Team members each receive a $500 bonus if the total sales of all members reach $50,000, $300 bonus if their total sales reach $30,000 and a $100 bonus if the team's total sales reach $10,000. When a sales team works cooperatively, they combine their efforts to maximize the sales of all members. Success depends not only on how many sales one member makes but also on the sales of all other team members. The more successful one's teammates are, the more successful you become. Members become very concerned about helping each other do well. Leads and potential new accounts are given away. Helping a team-mate make a sale is as good as making the sale oneself. Cooperation builds the sense that, "We are all for one and one for all." Working in a team then, is similar to hockey or basketball where "assists" are recorded.

EXERCISE 3.1   **Broken Squares Puzzle***

PURPOSE

What is cooperation like? What is competition like? How does it feel to cooperate or compete with other persons? Each of us have had lots of experience cooperating and competing. The purpose of this exercise is to explore the results of cooperation and competition in solving a group problem. Your group will be given a problem to solve. You may try to solve it either cooperatively or competitively.

PROCEDURE

1. In your group, decide who is going to be the observer. The other members are participants. The exercise consists of completing a group task involving a puzzle.

2. Each person is to read his set of instructions printed below. The participants read the Instructions for Participants. The observer reads the Instructions for Observers. The instructor gives each participant

*Instructions for teachers in preparing the puzzle pieces are given in Appendix B.

an envelope containing puzzle pieces. Do not open the envelopes until the instructor gives the signal to do so. The instructor reviews the instructions so that everyone understands the rules.

3. The instructor gives the signal to begin. The groups are to work until they have solved the problem or until twenty-five minutes have gone by.

4. The instructor collects the observation sheets. She then records the information in the Results Table (see page 75).

5. Each group discusses the following questions:
   a. What actions helped the group solve the problem?
   b. What actions hurt the group's efforts to solve the problem?
   c. What did members feel during the efforts to solve the problem?
   d. If you were to do this problem again, what would you do differently?

6. Each group writes down their conclusions as to how cooperation and competition affected their success in solving the problem.

7. The instructor presents the observations summarized in the Results Table.

8. The groups share their conclusions and the major points from their discussion in a class discussion of the exercise.

Instructions for Participants

Each participant is given an envelope containing the puzzle pieces. When the instructor gives the signal to begin, the task of your group is to form five squares of equal size. The task is considered complete when everyone has made a perfect square. All five squares of the group must be exactly the same size. Here are the specific rules you must follow:

1. No talking, pointing, or any other kind of communication among the five participants is allowed.

2. No student may ask another student for a puzzle piece. No student may in any way signal that another student is to give him a puzzle piece.

3. Students may *give* puzzle pieces to other students.

4. Students may not simply throw their puzzle pieces into the center for others to take: They must hand the pieces directly to a person.

5. The observer is to enforce these rules.

Instructions for Observers

Your job is to be part observer, part recorder, and part rule enforcer. Observe the participants as they attempt to solve the puzzle. Do your best to enforce the rules. Then, as accurately as possible, record your observations of the items listed below. The information you record will be used for discussing the results of the exercise.

1. Did the group complete the tasks?___(Yes)___(No).
2. How long did it take the group to complete the task: ___minutes, ___seconds.
3. Number of times a group member took a puzzle piece from another member:___.
4. Number of times a group member gave a puzzle piece to another member: ___.
5. How many members finished their squares and then just sat back and watched the rest of the group?___.
6. Were there any critical turning points at which cooperation or competition increased in the group?
7. What behaviors in the group show cooperativeness or competitiveness?

		RESULTS TABLE FOR BROKEN SQUARES PUZZLE				
	Group 1	Group 2	Group 3	Group 4	Group 5	Group 6
Did the group complete the task?						
Time for task completion						
Number of times a member gave away a puzzle piece						
Number of times a member took away a puzzle piece						
Number of members who just sat back and watched the others						
Examples of cooperative behaviors						
Examples of competitive behaviors						

**EXERCISE
3.2**   **Triangles Puzzle***

PURPOSE

Some people prefer to work by themselves rather than in groups. A member in your group may be a person who would rather work alone. What is the advantage of working together? Does it really make any difference in your success in solving problems? The purpose of this exercise is to compare the success in solving a problem of persons working by themselves and persons working in a small group.

PROCEDURE

1. The instructor will hand out to each student a diagram of a triangle with several triangles inside it. Working alone, you are to count the number of triangles in the diagram. Your job is to find as many triangles as you can. Write your answer on a sheet of paper. Keep your eyes on your own paper. You will have up to 15 minutes to complete the task.

2. Now, working as a group, count the number of triangles in the diagram. Make sure that every group member agrees with the group's answer. Write the group answer down on a sheet of paper. You have twenty minutes to complete this task.

3. The instructor will collect both your individual answers and your group answers.

4. In your group, discuss the following questions:
    a. How did it feel to do the task individually?
    b. What were your feelings while you were doing the task as a group?
    c. How did the individual answers compare with the group answer?
    d. What were the advantages of working as a group?
    e. What were the disadvantages of working as a group?
    f. Would you rather work on similar problems as a group or individually?

5. The instructor will present the answers of the entire class on the board. You will then discuss your group's results with the class as a whole.

*Teacher's instructions are given in Appendix B.

Cooperation At Work

○   ○   ○

Two are better than one, because they have a good reward for their toil. For if they fall, one will lift up his brother; but woe to him who is alone when he falls and has not another to lift him up . . . And though a man might prevail against one who is alone, two will withstand him. A threefold cord is not quickly broken.

Ecclesiastes 4:9–12

○   ○   ○

I once worked as a waiter in a restaurant. One of the other waiters, named Ralph, was always competing with everyone else. Ralph would come over to a fellow waiter and say, "I've waited on more people than you have." "I give better service than you do." "I'm getting more tips than you are." "Let's see who can serve the next table the fastest!" "Do you want me to show you how to fold those napkins so they look right?" **Working with Ralph was a drag.** Everything became a contest to see who was best. Ralph would even ask the cooks and the busboys who they liked the best! There was nothing he couldn't turn into competition.

Contrast Ralph's behavior with that of another waiter, named Bill. Bill was always trying to be cooperative. Bill would come over and say, "Anything I can do to help?" "I'm free for a few minutes, let me fold some napkins for you." "I have a plan about dividing up the dining room that would allow us to wait on people more efficiently." "You look like you're really tired today; want me to take over some of your tables?" "Meet Sam, who just started working here. I thought we could help Sam get to know how the boss likes to have things done around here." **Bill was great to work with.** He would help fellow employees, and they would help him. His attitude was "How do we work together better? How do we do our job better? How can we have more fun doing it?" There was nothing that Bill could not turn into cooperation.

On every job, you will find some beautiful people who see the need for cooperating. On every job, you will find some people who insist on competing. And there are usually some people who just want to be left alone. The basic nature of work, however, is always cooperative. People work together because they can do things better cooperatively than if they all worked alone.

Consider the two exercises you just did. What were your group's conclusions after participating in these exercises? Here are some conclusions arrived at by other groups:

1. Groups accomplish more working cooperatively than do members trying to do the task by themselves.

2. In the Broken Squares Puzzle, if one member completed his square and did not help the other members complete theirs, the group could not finish the task.

3. In the Broken Squares Puzzle, although one member could not figure out how to put the squares together so that everyone had a completed square, other members could.

4. In the Triangles Puzzle exercise, a person working alone was able to find only the obvious triangles, but the group working together was able to find the nonobvious ones.

5. In the Triangles Puzzle exercise, the group was able to find a way to proceed in finding triangles that was better than the procedures used by most of the members when they were working alone.

It is hard to lose with cooperation. There have been hundreds and hundreds of studies comparing cooperation with competitive and individualistic efforts. Cooperation has been found to result in (Johnson and Johnson, 1989):

1. Greater individual achievement and higher group productivity.
2. More positive, caring, committed, and supportive relationships among members.
3. Greater psychological adjustment, social competencies, and self-esteem.

These three outcomes are interrelated (see Figure 3.2). The more individuals work together to get the job done, the more they care about each other. The more they care about each other, the harder they will work to get the job done. The more individuals work together, the greater their social competencies and psychological health. The healthier individuals are psychologically, the more energy they have to devote to their work. The more caring and committed the relationships among team members, the healthier individuals are psychologically. The greater the members' psychological health is, the better able they are to form caring and committed relationships with teammates. In addition, cooperation adds to employee morale. Compared to competing and working individually, cooperation usually results in employees having more positive attitudes about their jobs and the organization they work for. Cooperation increases employee commitment to do a good job and the amount of satisfaction employees receive from completing their work. The positive results derived from cooperative efforts, however, do not happen automatically. Team efforts are made cooperative by the careful structuring of five essential components: *positive interdependence, face-to-face interaction, individual accountability, interpersonal and small group skills,* and *group processing* (Johnson & Johnson, 1989a).

Positive Interdependence

○   ○   ○

"All for one and one for all."

Alexandre Dumas

○   ○   ○

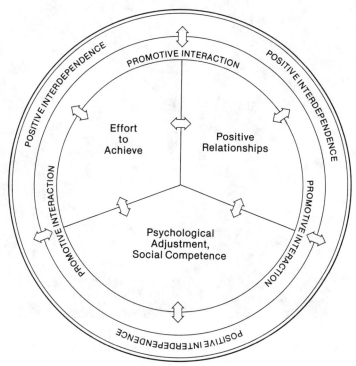

Figure 3.2 Outcomes of Cooperation. Source: Johnson and Johnson (1989a). Reprinted with permission.

Within a football game, the quarterback who throws the pass and the receiver who catches the pass are interdependent. The success of one depends on the success of the other; it takes two to complete a pass. One player cannot succeed without the other. Both have to perform competently if their mutual success is to be assured. They sink or swim together.

The first requirement for any team is that members believe that they "sink or swim together." Team members are both responsible for their own productivity and for the productivity of teammates. The technical term for that dual responsibility is positive interdependence. **Positive interdependence** exists when members perceive that they are linked with groupmates in a way that they cannot succeed unless their groupmates do (and vice versa) and/or that they must coordinate their efforts with the efforts of their groupmates to complete a task. Each member's work benefits all other members. As a result, team members (a) work together to get the job done, (b) share resources, (c) support and assist each other, and (d) celebrate joint success. When positive interdependence is clearly understood, it highlights that each member's efforts are required and indispensable for group success (i.e., there can be no "free-rides") and each member makes a unique contribution to the joint effort because of his or her resources and/or role and task responsibilities. Poor teams have no overall goal—individual members work toward personal goals that have little or no relation to the goals of others. **Good**

teams are characterized by mutual goals and positive interdependence. **We,** not **me,** has to dominate.

In order to make your work teams cooperative, two sets of actions are required. **First,** you need to observe the actions of group members while you participate and diagnose the extent to which members are committed to mutual goals and each other's success. You tell if positive interdependence is present by observing whether all members (a) care about each other's success, (b) are involved in and contribute to team discussions and activities, and (c) take responsibility for their own and others' performances. **Second,** you need to take action to increase the positive interdependence within the team. This is done by reminding members of the team's goals and objectives, asking members to contribute, highlighting the team's mutual fate (we all gain or lose on the basis of the overall performance of the team), formulating a better division of labor, highlighting the unique resources that each member contributes to the team effort, and by striving for consensus in all team decisions.

How can employees improve their cooperation on the job? The following provide some guidelines:

1. Each person must understand the overall task to be accomplished.

2. Each person must share the cooperative goal of achieving the task as a group.

3. Each person must see how he can contribute to the accomplishment of the task.

4. Each person must be aware of the potential contributions of the other group members to the accomplishment of the task.

5. Group members must interact, give and receive help, share ideas and information, and encourage each other to acomplish the task.

6. Group members must be aware that a division of labor is possible. Different persons can make different contributions to accomplishing the task.

Cooperation is absolutely essential for an organization to achieve its goals. When you are hired for a job, your cooperation with fellow employees is an absolute requirement. Above all else, you must be able to cooperate with your fellow employees and your boss to survive on the job.

Face-To-Face Interaction

○　　○　　○

United we stand, divided we fall.

Watchword of the American Revolution

○　　○　　○

The second essential component of cooperation is *face-to-face interaction* among team members. Within teams, members need the opportunity to promote each other's success by helping, assisting, supporting, and encouraging each other's efforts. First, there are cognitive activities and interpersonal dynamics that only occur when students get involved in explaining to each other how the answers to assignments are derived. This includes explaining how to solve problems orally, discussing the nature of the concepts being learned, teaching one's knowledge to classmates, and connecting present to past learning. Second, it is within face-to-face interaction that the opportunity for a wide variety of social influences and patterns emerge. Helping and assisting take place. Accountability to peers, ability to influence each other's reasoning and conclusions, social modeling, social support, and interpersonal rewards all increase as the face-to-face interaction among group members increase. Third, the verbal and nonverbal responses of other group members provide important information concerning a student's performance. Direct face-to-face interaction has a number of effects. **First,** there are cognitive insights and understandings that can only come from explaining one's conclusions and views to others. **Second,** it is within face-to-face interaction that the opportunity for a wide variety of social influences and patterns emerge. **Third,** the verbal and nonverbal responses of other group members provide important feedback concerning each other's performance.

Fourth, it is the interaction involved in completing the work that allows team members to get to know each other as persons, which in turn forms the basis for caring and committed relationships among members. People who share the same goals are likely to come to care about one another on more than just a work level. The more team members care about each other, the harder they will work to ensure team success. Extraordinary accomplishments result from team members getting personally involved with the task and with each other. What results is personal encouragement. The word **encouragement** has its root in the Latin word **cor,** which means "heart." When you encourage someone, you give them heart. Encouragement, help, assistance, and support means more when it comes from a person who cares about you and whom you care about.

Individual Accountability

○   ○   ○

The purpose of a cooperative group is to make each member a stronger individual in their own right.

Johnson and Johnson (1989)

○   ○   ○

Among the early settlers of Massachusetts, there was a saying, "If you do not work, you do not eat." The third essential component of a productive team is for members to be individually accountable for their share of the work. **Individual accountability** exists when the contributions each team member makes to the overall team effort are assessed and the results are given back to the group and the individual. It minimizes the likelihood of any member loafing and getting a free ride. To ensure that each team member is individually accountable to do their share of the work:

1. Assess how much effort each member is contributing to the group's work.
2. Provide feedback to the team and individual members.
3. Help the team avoid redundant efforts by members.
4. Ensure that every member is responsible for the final outcome.
5. Highlight and clarify the responsibilities of each member.

Small Group And Interpersonal Skills

○   ○   ○

If you want one year of prosperity, grow grain.
If you want ten years of prosperity, grow trees.
If you want one hundred years of prosperity, grow people.

Chinese Proverb

○   ○   ○

To be a contributing team member, you need to master and appropriately use interpersonal and small group skills. Placing socially unskilled individuals on a team and telling them to collaborate does not guarantee that they are able to do so effectively. Many individuals have never been required to work as part of teams and, therefore, lack the needed cooperative skills for doing so. Other individuals may be skilled socially but not be motivated to provide the leadership, decision making, trust-building, communication, and conflict-management skills needed to make the team productive. Teams cannot function effectively if members do not have and use the needed interpersonal and small group skills.

Group Processing

○　　○　　○

The honor of one is the honor of all.
The hurt of one is the hurt of all.

Creek Indian Creed

○　　○　　○

No one learns from experience unless they stop and reflect on it. The fifth component of a productive team is ensuring that the team members regularly discuss how well they are (a) achieving their goals and (b) maintaining effective working relationships. During processing sessions, describe what member actions were helpful and unhelpful and help make decisions about what member actions should be continued or changed. Such processing enables teams to focus on group maintenance, facilitates the learning of social skills, ensures members receive feedback on their participation, and reminds members to practice social skills consistently. Allow sufficient time for processing to take place and make it specific rather than general.

EXERCISE 3.3　　**Plane Wreck***

PURPOSE

Most cooperative efforts require a division of labor. The purpose of this exercise is to give you a chance to be part of a division of labor in doing a task.

PROCEDURE

1. Divide your group into two groups of three. Select one person to be an observer, one person to be "A," and one person to be "B."
2. Each group of three needs the following materials:
   a. A blindfold.

*Adapted from an exercise in Napier and Gershenfeld (1973).

    b. Five or six odd-sized pieces of cardboard.

    c. A roll of cellophane tape or masking tape.

    d. A piece of rope at least three feet long.

3. *The Situation:* A and B were flying in a plane across some islands. Their plane suddenly developed engine trouble and crashed on a desert island with no water. They will be rescued in a few days, but they must have water if they are to survive. They have some materials for making a container to hold rainwater. The only problem is that Person B received a heavy blow on the head and is now both blind and mute. Person A burned both hands badly and is not able to use them at all. But they must build the container if they are to survive. A rain cloud is quickly approaching, and they must have the container finished before it reaches the island. A few drops are already beginning to fall.

4. Tie the hands of Person A behind her back. Blindfold Person B and tell him not to say a word during the entire building process.

5. The observer takes notes on how well the two persons work together. How good are the directions? How well are they carried out? How cooperative are they? What communication problems exist? What could they have done differently?

6. If the container is not finished in twenty minutes, the two people are stopped. Then, in your group of six, discuss what happened in each trio. Use the following questions as a guide:

    a. How did Person A feel?

    b. How did Person B feel?

    c. What does the container look like? If it were made of wood and nails instead of cardboard and tape, would it hold water? (If there is a hole in the bottom, the answer is no.)

    d. What would have improved the cooperation?

    e. What did you learn about a dvision of labor on a cooperative task?

DALE'S DINER IS LIKE A TREE

Dale's Diner is like a tree. Both have a cooperative divsion of labor to ensure life, growth, and productivity. A tree divides its labor into the following parts: The roots anchor the tree and transport water and nutrients up to the sapwood. The sapwood carries the water and nutrients from the roots up to the leaves. The leaves make food for the tree by combining carbon dioxide from the air and water from the soil, in the presence of sunlight, to form sugar. The inner bark then carries the sugar made in the leaves down to the branches, trunk, and roots where it is converted to other substances vital for the tree's growth. The outer bark protects the tree from insect and disease attack, excessive heat and cold, and other injuries. The heartwood gives the tree strength and stiffness. This division of labor ensures that the tree lives, grows, and produces.

    Dale's Diner divides its labor into the following parts: Roger and Francis, the roots, buy all the ingredients and supplies needed for the meals. Dale, the sapwood, carries the ingredients and supplies from the trucks to the kitchen. Edythe, the leaf, with the aid of heat from the stove converts the ingredients and supplies into meals. Frank, the inner bark, distributes the delicious meals to the customers, collects money, and handles all financial matters vital for the growth of Dale's Diner. Helen, the outer bark, repairs the building so that the people inside are protected from insect attack, excessive heat and cold, and other injuries. David, the heartwood, provided the original capital to give Dale's Diner financial strength. This division of labor ensures that Dale's Diner lives, grows, and produces.

Coordinating the Work

○   ○   ○

The fundamental facts that brought about cooperation, society, and civilization and transformed the animal man into a human being are the facts that work performed under the division of labor is more productive than isolated work and that man's reason is capable of recognizing this truth. But for these facts men would have forever remained deadly foes of one another, irreconcilable rivals in their endeavors to secure a portion of the scarce supply of means of sustenance provided by Nature. Each man would have been forced to view all other men as his enemies; his craving for the satisfaction of his own appetites would have brought him into an implacable conflict with all his neighbors. No sympathy could possibly develop under such a state of affairs. . . . We may call consciousness of kind, sense of commu-

nity, or sense of belonging together the acknowledgment of fact that all other human beings are potential collaborators in the struggle for survival because they are capable of recognizing the mutual benefits of cooperation.

Ludwig Von Mises (1949)

○   ○   ○

A ship is being piloted into and out of San Diego harbor and involves six people with three different job descriptions. On the deck two people take visual sightings of predetermined landmarks, using special telescopic devices mounted on gyrocompasses that yield exact readings of direction. They call out their readings to two other individuals, who relay them by telephone to a specialist on the bridge. This individual records the bearings in a book and repeats them aloud for confirmation. Next to the recorder, another individual uses specialized tools to plot the ship's position on a navigational chart and to project where the ship will be at the next fix and beyond. These projections of position are used to decide what landmarks should be sighted next by those on deck and when a course correction will be required. The entire cycle is repeated every one to three minutes. No individual in the system can pilot the ship alone. The knowledge necessary for successful piloting is distributed throughout the whole team.

A division of labor is like a jigsaw puzzle. Only when the pieces are placed in the right order can the puzzle be completed. Your work is part of a division of labor. When you work, your efforts have to be coordinated with the efforts of other employees if the overall task is to be completed. Work is coordinated when the efforts of several employees are put in the right order. One person may buy a product from a wholesaler, another person may put the product on the shelves of a store, and another person may sell the product. Everything has to be done in the right order for the organization to be successful.

There are two major ways for coordinating the work of several employees. The first is through job roles. The work you contract to perform is your **job role**. For example, you may contract to program computers, to write reports, or to type. For coordinating work, every organization has a master plan that describes every employee's job role. It tells how the roles are coordinated so that the overall task can be completed. Within a restaurant, for example, such roles as cooks, waiters, busboys, bookkeepers, janitors, and manager are coordinated so that the restaurant can make a profit. Being good at your work and being reliable are important for the overall master plan. What you do affects the success of other employees and the entire organization.

The second way to coordinate a division of labor is through the organization's norms. **Norms** define the ways in which you are expected to behave. Your supervisor and your coworkers may expect you to be friendly. That is an example of an organizational norm. You may be expected to arrive at work on time, to dress neatly, to be skilled in handling customers. All such expectations are organizational norms. Norms may even include how you should address your boss or how long your coffee breaks should be. If most employees conform to the organization's norms, their work is coordinated more easily.

Through defining your job responsibilities and prescribing appropriate behavior on the job, an organizaton can successfully coordinate the efforts of many different employees.

In the Plane Wreck exercise, one person had to plan and direct how the container was to be built. Another person had to carry out the directions and actually build the container. Most organizations have some people who plan how a job is to be done and some people who carry out the directions of supervisors. Such a situation is a clear division of labor. Sometimes the planners get frustrated when the doers do not understand what they are supposed to do, and sometimes the doers get angry when the directions from the planners are not clear. Sometimes planners forget that the doers are real people, not machines. Communication between planners and doers can be a problem, and conflicts can occur. **A division of labor often creates problems that only persons with good interpersonal skills can solve.**

Civic Virtue

Historians claim that the decline and fall of Rome was set in motion by corruption from within rather than by conquest from without. Rome fell, it can be argued, because Romans lost their civic virtue. You have **civic virtue** when you meet the letter and spirit of your public obligations based on your society's common objectives and your membership in the community of shared values. You respect other people's rights and property. You pick up litter to keep your community clean. You live a life aimed at improving the quality of life for all members of your family, community, society, and world. When a society is inhabited by those who believe in nothing but individualistic values, people stop obeying the law. The individualist, for example, may go through a red light beause he thinks it is rational for him to do so. He will arrive at his destination sooner. A pedestrian, then, might meet his demise. But each of us is at some time a pedestrian. Voluntary cooperation is central to economic success and it does not occur amongst people who are narrowly interested in him- or herself only.

How to Make Friends on the Job

1. Be cooperative. Help others whenever you can. Be concerned about their goals and needs. Share your assets to help them reach their goals. Do your work in ways that help other employees do their work better and easier.

2. Do your work well. Take your responsibilities seriously and do a good job. Be dependable. Keep seeking out new training programs to increase your expertise. Your fellow employees will respect you for this.

Acts Of Caring Move The Team Forward And Onward

○   ○   ○

A faithful friend is a strong defense, and he that hath found him, hath found a treasure.

Ecclesiastics 6:14

○   ○   ○

Long-term, hard, persistent efforts to achieve come not from the head, but from the heart. Cooperative teams are powered by the caring developed among team members. Vince Lombardi, the famous coach of the Green Bay Packers, once said, "Love is loyalty. Love is teamwork. Love respects the dignity of the individual. Heartpower is the strength of your corporation." Major General John H. Stanford, Commander of the United States Army once said, "Love 'em and lead 'em." Many business executives have noted the importance of developing caring relationships among team members. Consider Dave Joyner's description of the Penn State football team and its coach, Joe Paterno:

○   ○   ○

"The reason we were so good, and continued to be so good, was because he (Joe Paterno) forces you to develop an inner love among the players. It is much harder to give up on your buddy, than it is to give up on your coach. I really believe that over the years the teams I played on were almost unbeatable in tight situations. When we needed to get that six inches we got it because of our love for each other. Our camaraderie existed because of the kind of coach and kind of person Joe was."

○   ○   ○

When Competition Is in Order

There will be times during your career when you will need to know how to compete. For example, only one person can receive a promotion; only one person can be hired for a job. Sometimes there is not enough money for everyone to get a raise. And only one person can end up president of the company. Your getting a raise or promotion may depend on how your work compares to the work of others. There are also times when competition can be fun.

There is an element of competition in every career. But usually the person who is promoted excels at organizing cooperative efforts. The person who is most skillful in organizing cooperative efforts will probably end up getting the promotion.

Acting independently often provides a chance for you to feel success on your own. It sometimes feels good to be by yourself, to do something entirely by yourself. Everyone needs to be alone part of the time. In an organization, you can work by yourself as part of a division of labor. You may do an individual job, but your work contributes to the work of others. It becomes part of an overall cooperative effort.

It is important for you to be able to compete. It is important for you to have the skills to work on your own. **But there is no place in an organization for extreme competition or extreme individualism.** You need to make sure your feelings of competition and your feelings of wanting to do things by yourself do not interfere with the cooperation necessary for the task to get done.

Using Your Assets

An effective group uses the assets of all members in order to do the best work possible. If you've got them, use them. Finding out what assets group members have and figuring out ways to use members' assets are important cooperative skills. Identifying assets of the group means knowing the skills, talents, abilities, experiences, and knowledge of fellow group members. Figuring out **how** to use members' assets involves deciding which ones are most helpful in a given situation. Every group has a large number of assets available. The better the group, the more clearly it will know the assets of its members and the more fully it will use them.

There are only two ways in which a group can get to know the assets of its members. The first is for each member to be open about her assets. Each member may honestly tell other group members about her assets when it is appropriate. The second way is for group members to ask each other about their assets. There is a dual responsibility in being a group member. One side of the coin ensures that your assets are known and used by the group. The other side asks your fellow group members what their resources are and makes sure the group uses them. You have a responsibility to make your assets known, and to use them. You have a responsibility to find out the assets of other group members and use them to help the group achieve its goals.

In Chapter 2 you did an exercise to find out the assets of your group members. In Section IV, there will be another exercise aimed at knowing the assets of the group members. Successful cooperation depends on knowing the assets available and using them effectively.

Some Major Points

1. Your work is part of a cooperative effort. Therefore, cooperate with superiors and coworkers.
2. The more skillful you are in cooperating, the more successful you will be within your organization.
3. To be a good cooperator, you need a high level of interpersonal skills.
4. Try to visualize the overall task to be done.
5. Plan how you will contribute to completing the task.
6. Plan how you will get others to contribute to completing the task.
7. Be helpful to others. Share any resources you have that will be helpful.

8. Understand the division of labor. Think about how your work fits in with the work of other employees.
9. Be reliable in your job performance.
10. Conform to organizational norms.
11. Be prepared to resolve misunderstandings and conflicts with other employees, especially with your supervisor.
12. Remember: Your work plus my work equals our product, and if we are to be successful we need to help each other.

4

FOLLOW ME

Taking Leadership

After completing the Questionnaire that follows, you should be able to define and give examples of:

- Leadership
- Subordinates
- Authority
- Authority hierarchy
- The authority law of organizations
- The two basic objectives of cooperative groups
- Leadership actions
- Task leadership
- Maintenance leadership

The answers are given on the right side of the page. Work with a partner and keep the answers covered until you have agreed on your response. Remember to check each answer before going on to the next item, as explained on page 1.

QUESTIONNAIRE: Main Concepts in Chapter 4

1. *Leadership* is influencing other group members or fellow employees. When you influence your co-workers, you are engaging in _____.

leadership

2. John convinces Sue and Sam to change their coffee breaks from twenty minutes to fifteen minutes. John has influenced Sue and Sam. He has, therefore, demonstrated _____.

leadership

3. Some persons are assigned leadership positions within an organization. They have the power to influence their subordinates. A *subordinate* is a person who works under a superior. A superior may have a number of _____ working under him.

subordinates

4. Your boss is your organizational superior. You are one of your boss' _____.

subordinates

5. When the organization gives a person the power to influence her subordinates, the person has authority. *Authority* is power placed in a job role. The job role of supervisor includes authority over subordinates. The purpose of authority is to ensure that subordinates meet the requirements of their job role. When the organization creates a job role that has power over their job roles, they are assigning _____.

authority

6. Your boss has the _____ to make sure you are doing your job.

authority

7. An *authority hierarchy* defines who has authority over whom in an organization. A supervisor has authority over a worker. A manager has authority over a supervisor. A vice-president has authority over a manager. A president has authority over a vice-president. When an organization decides who has authority over whom, it is deciding on an _____ _____ .

authority hierarchy

8. Your boss has a boss, who has a boss, who has a boss, who has a boss. This is an example of an _____ _____.

authority hierarchy

9. A basic law of organizations is that subordinates *obey* their superiors on matters relating to job performance. When a person is assigned authority over you, you are supposed to _____ her suggestions about how you do your job.

obey/follow

10. Every cooperative group has two basic objectives. One is to complete its *task*. The other is to *maintain* the relationships among group members in good working order. The two objectives of a cooperative group deal with the group's _____ and _____.

task
maintenance

11. Purifying water is an example of a group _____. To get Mary and Sam to stop arguing about the best way of purifying water is an example of group _____.

task

maintenance

12. Authority is not the only type of leadership in an organization. Whenever an employee acts in a way that helps his group complete its task, he is providing leadership. All employee actions that help the group complete its tasks and maintain itself in good working order are _____ _____ .

leadership
actions

13. An example of task leadership is summarizing what the group knows about a problem it is trying to solve. When Joan summarizes what the group knows about purifying water, she is providing _____ _____.

task
leadership

14. An example of maintenance leadership is encouraging silent members to participate. When Jonathan asks Herman what his opinion about purifying water is, Jonathan is providing _____ _____.

maintenance
leadership

15. There are two ways of being a leader in an organization. The first is to be given _____. The second is to engage in actions which help the group complete its _____ and _____ itself in good working order.

authority

task
maintain

What Is Leadership?

Have you ever looked around at a state of chaos and wondered who was in charge? Have you ever looked around for someone to tell you what to do? Have you been part of a group that just could not get started, or been at a party that just could not get off the ground?

All cooperative efforts take leadership. To work together to achieve a goal and to solve problems and make decisions in a group take leadership. Leadership is needed to coordinate a division of labor and to ensure that every employee is carrying out his job responsibilities. All during your career you will lead others and be led by others. Providing leadership and following someone else's leadership are part of every job.

What is leadership? How do you tell when you are being a leader? Anytime one person influences another person, that is leading. Leadership is influencing other group members or fellow employees. Good leadership is influencing fellow group members in ways that help achieve the group's goals. Poor leadership is influencing fellow group members in ways that interfere with the achieving of the group's goals.

Leadership is a relationship between two or more people. There has to be an influencer and an influencee, a superior and a subordinate. One person leads and another person is led; one exerts influence, and another accepts it.

○   ○   ○

Who built the seven towers of Thebes?
The books are filled with the names of kings.
Was it kings who hauled the craggy blocks of stone? . . .
In the evening when the Chinese wall was finished,
Where did the masons go?

BERTOLT BRECHT

○   ○   ○

Within a cooperative group, every member must accept influence when it helps the group achieve its goals. What helps the group helps you. If someone has a good idea about how to improve the group's work, everyone is grateful and will do it that way. Having good leadership helps everyone in the group. Providing leadership helps every other group member. Influencing others in a cooperative group is usually easy because everyone trusts the other members to do what is best for the group.

Are Some Born to Lead and Others Born to Follow?

One of the oldest views of leadership is that some people are born to lead and others are born to follow. Aristotle believed this was true. Some people do seem to dominate others through the force of their personalities or through what they stand for. There are great women, such as Helen Keller, and great men, such as Abraham Lincoln, in the world. People who believe in the "great person" view of leadership think that leaders are discovered, not trained.

In an attempt to prove the "great person" theory, many researchers have compared presidents of companies with low-level workers. They have not been able to tell the difference between a president and a worker. Sometimes they find that leaders are more intelligent and better adjusted emotionally than are non-leaders. At other times they find that the most intelligent people never become leaders. And many leaders, such as Adolf Hitler, show signs of being emotionally

maladjusted. In short, there is no evidence that leaders are born. Anyone who has the determination to succeed can become a leader. Anyone who has the energy to work hard at learning how to become a leader can become a leader.

The Chosen Few, or Why You Marry the Boss

Within an organization, some are passed by, and some are chosen to lead. The chosen few are given the authority to influence their **subordinates.** They are put in charge of other employees and given the responsibility to make sure their subordinates work hard and correctly. Rodney, for example, was made a supervisor over four keypunch operators. But no one in their right mind would trust Rodney to do a good job at that. So Rodney is placed under a manager. The manager supervises Rodney and Rodney supervises the keypunch operators. But sometimes managers are careless, so there are vice-presidents to supervise the managers. There is also a president to make sure the vice-presidents do not let all that power go to their heads and do something dumb (such as promoting Rodney to be a manager). The president is then supervised by the Board of Directors. The Board of Directors is supervised by the stockholders, who own the company. Everyone in the company (except for the stockholders) is supervised by someone else who has greater power. That is what is known as an **authority hierarchy.**

Authority is power placed in a job role. The purpose of authority is to make sure that persons in lower job roles do the activities they contracted for. Rodney, for example, was given the authority to make sure that the four keypunch operators were doing their job.

One of Max Weber's most famous statements was that an employee must always obey a person with more authority on matters relating to job performance. The four keypunchers have to obey Rodney about how to do their work. They can tell Rodney to go jump when he tries to tell them how to eat their lunch. But when he tells them what to keypunch next, they are supposed to obey. Everything does go more smoothly in an organization when the directions of a superior in the authority hierarchy are obeyed.

Because your supervisor has more authority than you do, you are supposed to follow his directions and suggestions. The supervisor can influence how you do your job. But your supervisor is not the only person who influences how you do your job. Your coworkers also influence you. Sometimes you influence how your coworkers do their jobs, and occasionally you even influence the way your supervisor does her job. Even if you are the worker with the least authority in the organization, you can be a leader. You can develop leadership skills without having any authority at all. After the following exercises, we will explain how.

**EXERCISE
4.1**   **Leadership Behavior**

PURPOSE

Any action that helps a group complete its task is a leadership action. Any action that helps a group maintain good working relationships among members is a leadership action. When you are a member of a group, what leadership actions do you engage in? How do you influence other group members to complete the task and maintain good working relationships? This exercise has two purposes. The first is to make you more aware of your typical leadership actions. The second is to help your group look at its patterns of leadership.

PROCEDURE

1. Working by yourself, complete the "Questionnaire on Your Leadership Actions," which starts below.
2. Instructions on how to score your answers are in Appendix B. Determine your score.
3. Using the Key to Task-Maintenance Styles (page 97), place yourself on the Task-Maintenance Grid (page 98).
4. In your group, take a Task-Maintenance Grid and place all six members on it. Write a description of the leadership pattern of your group. Then write a description of how the leadership pattern of your group could be improved.

Questionnaire on Your Leadership Actions

Each of the items listed below describes a leadership action. On a sheet of paper write down the numbers 1 through 12. For each item, put 5 if you *ways* behave that way; 4 if you *frequently* behave that way; 3 if you *occasionally* behave that way; 2 if you *seldom* behave that way; and 1 if you *never* behave that way.

When I Am a Member of a Group,

_____ 1. I offer facts, give my opinions, ideas, feelings, and information to help the group discussion.

_____ 2. In a friendly way, I help the other members take part in the discussion. I am open to their ideas. I let them know I value their contribution to the group's discussion.

_____ 3. I ask for facts, information, opinions, ideas, and feelings from the other group members to help the group discussion.

_____ 4. I tell jokes and suggest fun ways of doing the work in order to reduce tension in the group and increase the fun we have working together.

_____ 5. I give direction to the group by planning how to go on with the group work and by calling attention to the tasks to be done.

_____ 6. I help communication among group members by using good communication skills. I make sure that all group members understand what other members say.

_____ 7. I pull together related ideas or suggestions made by group members and restate and summarize the major points discussed by the group.

_____ 8. I ask members how they are feeling about the way the group is working. I share my own feelings about the group work and the way members are interacting.

_____ 9. I pull together group work by putting different ideas and suggestions in the proper order. I also make sure the actions of different members are coordinated.

_____ 10. I observe the way the group is working. I use my observations to help discuss how the group can work together better.

_____ 11. I give the group energy. I encourage group members to work hard to achieve our goals.

_____ 12. I listen to and serve as an interested audience for other group members. I restate their ideas to make sure I understand them.

Key to Task-Maintenance Styles

(1,1): Only a minimum effort is given in order to get the required work done. There is general noninvolvement with other group members. Such a person may well be saying "To hell with it all." Or he may be so inactive in the group as to have no influence whatsoever on other group members.

(6,1): Getting the job done is emphasized in a way that shows very little concern

(1,6): High value is placed on keeping good relationships within the group. Thoughtful attention is given to the needs of other members. He helps to create a comfortable, friendly atmosphere, and work tempo. Such a person may be great running a social club or a country club but may never help the group get any work accomplished.

(6,1): Getting the job done is emphasized in a way that shows very little concern with group maintenance. Work is seen as important, while relationships among group members are ignored. Such a person would make a great army drillmaster. But the productivity of the group would soon suffer.

(3,3): The task and maintenance needs of the group are balanced. Such a person will be making compromises between task needs and maintenance needs continually. While being a great compromiser, this person does not look for or find ways to creatively put together the task and maintenance needs for best productivity.

(6,6): When everyone plans and makes decisions together, all the members become committed to getting the job done. At the same time, they build relationships of trust and respect. A high value is placed on sound, creative decisions that result in understanding and agreement. Ideas are sought out and listened to, even when the ideas, opinions, and attitudes differ from one's own. The group as a whole defines the task and works to get it done. Such a person encourages the creative combining of both task and maintenance needs. Such a person is the ideal leader for a group.

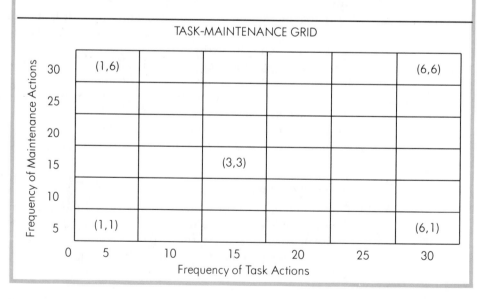

TASK-MAINTENANCE GRID

EXERCISE 4.2   **Murder on the Amtrak Express***

PURPOSE

In this exercise, your group is asked to solve a murder mystery. An observer will focus on the leadership actions of group members. The purpose of the exercise is to provide a chance to practice leadership actions.

PROCEDURE

1. Your group is to work cooperatively to solve a murder mystery. You are to decide who the victim is, who the murderer is, the weapon used, the time and place of death, and the motive.

2. Divide the group into four participants and two observers. The observers should study the observation sheets on page 101. One observer will take note of members who perform task actions; the other is to observe and note members' maintenance actions. The actions to be observed are defined in the Questionnaire on Your Leadership Actions (pp. 96–97). The number by the action to be observed corresponds to the question of the same number in the questionnaire. Discuss the observation sheets with the instructor to make sure you understand what you are to do.

3. The instructor will give each group a deck of 3 × 5 cards. On each card is written a clue to solving the murder mystery. Keep the cards face down so you cannot read the clues. Deal out all the cards so that each participant has several.

4. Each participant silently reads the clues on his cards. These cards are not to be shown to anyone else. All clues are to be communicated verbally.

5. The group has solved the mystery when they know: the victim, the murderer, the weapon (or means), the time and place of death, and the motive. The group should also decide: What is the moral of the story? Write out your group's answers and hand them in to the instructor.

6. Discuss the following questions in your group. Use your observers as your major resource.
   a. What leadership actions were most frequent in the group?
   b. What leadership actions were least frequent in the group?
   c. What leadership actions did each member engage in?
   d. What leadership actions were needed that no one engaged in?

*Adapted from a mystery developed by Gene and Barbara Stanford (1969). Materials and instructions for the teacher are given in Appendix B.

7. The instructor will announce the correct answer to the mystery.
8. Discuss the following questions in your group:
    a. Did the group get the correct answers?
    b. What could the group do to improve its performance in the future?
    c. What good leadership actions were taken that the group should repeat in the future?

**EXERCISE
4.3**   **Selecting a City***

PURPOSE

Many people act the same way in every group they belong to. They always make suggestions, or sit silently, or want to joke around. If a group is going to be effective, however, the members may have to act quite differently, depending on what leadership actions are needed. The purpose of this lesson is to give you some practice in providing the leadership actions needed by the group.

PROCEDURE

1. Join with another group so that there are twelve people sitting together. Then ask two people to volunteer to be observers. The observers will use the following observation sheets for Task and Maintenance Actions. They should look for (1) what actions are present and absent in the group, (2) how participation is distributed in the group, and (3) what specific behaviors are being provided by each group member.
2. The instructor will place in the center of your group a large envelope containing the role-playing instructions for the lesson. Read the instructions written on the large envelope and follow them.

*Teacher's instructions for preparing the materials for this exercise are given in Appendix B.

OBSERVATION SHEET FOR TASK ACTIONS

Actions

Members

1. Information and Opinion Giver						
3. Information and Opinion Seeker						
5. Direction Giver						
7. Summarizer						
9. Coordinator						
11. Energizer						
Other (describe):						
Other (describe):						

OBSERVATION SHEET FOR MAINTENANCE ACTIONS

Actions

Members

2. Encourager of Participation						
4. Tension Reliever						
6. Communication Helper						
8. Evaluator of Emotional Climate						
10. Process Observer						
12. Active Listener						
Other (describe):						
Other (describe):						

Where Do Leadership Skills Come From?

By now you know that you are not born a leader. No one else is either. By now you realize that your fairy godmother will not magically make you president of the

United States. She will not make anyone else president either. Leadership skills are not inborn, do not magically appear, and do not come with a promotion. *You have to learn to be a leader.* You have to master the basic skills and practice, practice, practice. Only by hard work and persistence can you master leadership skills.

You can be elected to a leadership position, chosen for a promotion, put in charge of other employees, be a member of an important committee, or be part of a decision-making group that deals with important problems. But being in a leadership position does not mean that you will be a skillful leader. Being on an important committee does not mean that you will be skillful in providing leadership. *Leadership skills have to be learned.* If you do not learn them, you will not have them. There will be times when you will be in charge of a mess. Hopefully you will have the skills to straighten it out, to turn the mess into a cooperative working group.

A cooperative group has two basic objectives. One is to complete its tasks. The other is to maintain relationships among members in good working order. The most important view of leadership deals with the actions group members have to take to help the group complete its task and maintain itself. You have already participated in several exercises where your group had to make decisions and solve problems. For the group to be successful, the group members have to get the information needed to make a decision. Then they have to put the information together in such a way that a correct decision can be made. To do this, certain task leadership actions are needed. Members have to contribute, ask for, summarize, and coordinate the information. They have to give direction to the group's efforts and provide energy to work hard in making the decision. For any group to be successful, such task leadership actions have to be provided.

But it does no good to complete a task if it is done in a way that makes several group members angry. If part of the group refuses to come to the next meeting, the group has not been successful. Thus, members must pay attention to maintaining good working relationships. The task must be completed in a way that increases the ability of group members to work together in the future. To do this, certain maintenance leadership actions are needed. Members have to encourage each other to participate. They have to relieve tension when it gets too high, facil-

itate communication among members, and evaluate the emotional climate of the group. They have to discuss how the group work can be improved, and they have to listen carefully and respectfully to each other. These leadership actions are necessary to maintain friendly relationships among members. For any group to be successful, such maintenance leadership actions have to be provided.

Any member can provide leadership actions. You do not have to be the appointed or elected leader to provide leadership. In fact, in good groups, every member will provide leadership. In poor groups, members leave all the leadership actions up to the appointed or elected leader.

There are two steps in providing task and maintenance leadership actions. The first is to figure out what actions the group needs in order to complete its task and maintain itself in good working order. The second is to provide these actions or get another group member to do so. Anyone can learn to do this skillfully. First, information about how the group is doing must be collected through observation. Second, leadership actions must be provided.

Any leadership action may affect both task completion and group maintenance. A member can give information in a way that makes the other members laugh and enjoy themselves. Most leadership actions, however, help either complete the task or keep relationships friendly. Sometimes a group member will push hard to finish a task. This may help the group complete its task, but it also may hurt the relationships among group members. Some group members always tell jokes. This may help the group enjoy itself, but it also may hurt the group's ability to complete its task. It does little good to complete a task if the group falls apart afterward. Likewise, it does little good to keep the group together if it never completes a task. Both completing tasks and maintaining good relationships are important.

A skilled leader has to be flexible. People who behave the same way in every group will not provide good leadership. In one group, it may be helpful to provide more information. In another group, it may be helpful to summarize the information the group already has. In one group, it may be helpful to get more members to participate. In another, it may be helpful to improve the listening and reduce the talking. A person with good leadership skills will not do the same thing in every group or every meeting. She will keep her behavior flexible in order to provide the actions the group needs at any given time.

Finding and Organizing Information

For a group to complete its tasks successfully, it has to find and organize information. The more the group knows about a problem, the more likely the group will solve it. Much of the activity of decision-making groups is focused on obtaining and organizing information. This means that in order to find all relevant information, all members have to participate. When a group meeting begins, some information is known to all members. Other information is known to only two or three members. Sometimes important information is known only to one member. By

the end of the meeting, all relevant information needs to be known to all members. Only when all members know all relevant information does the group have a good chance to make correct decisions. An important part of task leadership is to ensure that all relevant information known to group members is shared.

Keeping Old Betsy Running

Cooperative groups have to be maintained in good working order. You would not think of driving a car without putting oil in the engine. If the engine did not have oil, it would fall apart. If relationships among group members are not maintained, the group will fall apart. Whenever you are working cooperatively with others, you should try to keep the relationships friendly and pleasant. Most of us know that machines have to be maintained properly if they are going to continue to work. Many people do not realize, however, that cooperative relationships have to be maintained properly if they are going to continue to exist. Do not overlook the need to maintain relationships among group members in good working order.

One of the most important leadership actions you can take in maintaining relationships in good working order is to encourage all members to participate. Participation by all members is important if the group is going to work effectively. There are at least three reasons why this is so. The first is that if members do not participate, their ideas, skills, and information cannot be used by the group to solve the problem. This hurts the group's effectiveness.

There is a second reason why the participation by all members is important. Members are committed to what they help build. Members who participate become more committed to the group and what the group has done. Members who remain silent will not care about the group and what it has done. It is the silent members who are most likely to drop out of the group. The more a person feels he has influenced the group and contributed to the group's work, the more committed he will be to the group.

○   ○   ○

The type of person I want to work for me is a person who can show a little leadership when it's needed. So many people won't lift a finger unless they're ordered to do something. I can leave the place for two hours and come back and find a complete mess. No one seems to have the initiative to do things on their own anymore. I want people working for me who can take hold of a situation and make sure what is needed gets done.

Ralph Understreet, Hotel Manager in
STUDS TERKEL, *Working*

○   ○   ○

The third reason why everyone needs to participate is that active members often get angry at or worried about the silent members. When people are working hard to complete a task, they begin to wonder why others are sitting quietly and not contributing. They may be irritated about the silent member's lack of concern about task completion. Or they may be worried about what the silent member is thinking. They may think the silent member is being critical of their actions. The greater the risks a member is taking in participating, the more concerned he or she will be about the silent members.

Often there are two reasons why a member does not participate. Some people are shy and naturally silent. They belive they have nothing to contribute. They are happy to sit quietly during the group meetings. Other people want to be more active, but they believe that no one will listen to them if they speak. Often they disagree with what the group is doing, but they think that no one values their opinion. They feel a lot of frustration while being silent. Both types of silence hurt the group's work. Both types of silence indicate problems in maintaining the group in good working order.

There are members in almost every group that need to be encouraged to participate more. They will have to feel supported and accepted when they do talk. Encouraging all members to speak their piece is one of the most important ways of maintaining the group in good working order.

HOW TO MAKE FRIENDS ON THE JOB

Pay attention to the actions that help maintain good relationships amongst your fellow employees. *Be a maintenance leader!* Include everyone. Respect everyone. Relieve tension among coworkers. Help others communicate.

Organizational Leadership

○   ○   ○

"Whenever anyone asks me (how to be a leader) I tell them I have the secret to success in life. The secret to success is to stay in love. Staying in love gives you the fire to really ignite other people, to see inside other people, to have a greater desire to get things done than other people. A person who is not in love doesn't really feel the kind of excitement that helps them to get ahead and lead others and to achieve. I don't know any other fire, any other thing in life that is more exhilarating and is more positive a feeling than love is."

Army Major General John H. Stanford (Kouzes and Posner, 1987)

○   ○   ○

On July 15, 1982, Don Bennett, a Seattle businessman, was the first amputee ever to climb Mount Rainier (reported by Kouzes and Posner, 1987). He climbed 14,410 feet on one leg and two crutches. It took him five days. When asked to state the most important lesson he learned from doing so, without hesitation he said, **"You can't do it alone."**

What did he mean? There were many ways in which others helped him achieve his goal, including his daughter. During one very difficult trek across an ice field in Don Bennett's hop to the top of Mount Rainier, his daughter stayed by his side for four hours and with each new hop told him, "You can do it, Dad. You're the best dad in the world. You can do it, Dad." There was no way Bennett would quit hopping to the top with his daughter yelling words of love and encouragement in his ear. The encouragment of his daughter kept him going, strengthening his commitment to make it to the top. The team and the organization are similar. With members of their cooperative group cheering them on, members amaze themselves and their superiors with what they can achieve. With members of their team cheering them on, members amaze themselves and their colleagues with what they can accomplish.

There is growth and decline. Staying the same is not an option. Growth takes leadership, not management. There is a difference. Some individuals manage, some individuals lead. The difference may be found in the root meanings of "lead" and "manage" (Kouzes and Posner, 1987). The root origin of **lead** is a word meaning "to go," denoting travel from one place to another. Leaders are those who "go first," pioneering unexplored territory and showing others the direction they should take. By comparison, the root origin of **manage** is a word meaning "hand." Managing seems to connote "handling" things by controlling and maintaining the status quo. Managers tend to handle things, leaders tend to get us going somewhere. **The unique role of the leader is to take us on journeys to places we have never been before.**

The metaphor of the journey may be the most appropriate metaphor for discussing the tasks of leaders. Individuals can manage what now exists, the status

quo, or take staff members on a journey to increase their expertise in order to create a new and better organization.

Perhaps more than anything else, leadership is about the creation of a new way of life within organizations. Leadership is inextricably connected with the process of innovation, of bringing new ideas, methods, or solutions into use. Leaders are agents of change. Change requires leadership, a "prime mover" to push for implementation of strategic decisions. The leader highlights the challenges the organization faces and makes them shared challenges for the staff. **Leaders create a "family" within which staff members care deeply about each other and the mutual vision they are trying to actualize.** Managers get other people to do, but leaders get other people to want to do.

There are a series of leadership issues that must be faced in order to maximize the productivity of the organization (Kouzes and Posner, 1987; Johnson and Johnson, 1989):

1. How to **challenge the status quo** of the traditional competitive and individualistic models of management.

2. How to **inspire a clear mutual vision** of what the team and/or organization should and could be, a clear mission that all members are committed to achieving, and a set of goals that guides members' efforts.

3. How to **empower members through cooperative team work.** Doing so enables each individual member to take action to increase his or her expertise and effectiveness, both technically and interpersonally.

4. How to **lead by example** by (a) using cooperative team procedures and (b) taking risks to increase expertise.

5. How to **encourage the heart** of members to persist and keep striving to improve their technical and interpersonal expertise.

Challenging The Status Quo

Organizations (and groups) are sites for an inevitable and external conflict. On one side are the forces of maintenance and continuity (i.e., the status quo), that strive to create and sustain the use of orderly, predictable procedures. Opposing them are the forces of innovation and discontinuity, that seek to alter established practices. Both seek the same goal of team and organizational productivity. Both are needed. The creative tension between the two is what powers considered and thoughtful development and change.

These same two forces operate within the individual member. Group members will experience the conflict between the security of the past and the satisfactions of growth in expertise and accomplishment. The status quo side wants to continue what has been done in the past. The enhanced expertise side strives for growth, change, and increased competence. Leaving the status quo and risking current success against the potential of a better future requires courage.

Leaders challenge the status quo and inspire team and organization members to recognize that **if they are not working to increase their expertise, they are losing their expertise.** Expertise is a process, not an end product. Any person or organization is constantly changing. If expertise is not growing, then it is declining. The minute a person believes he or she is an expert and stops trying to learn more, then he or she is losing their expertise. **Leaders must lead members toward enhanced expertise, not manage for bureaucratic control. And the clearest and most direct challenge to traditional competitive and individualistic actions is the adoption of cooperative teams within the organization.** The organization needs to be transformed into an interlocking network of cooperative teams in order to increase productivity, promote more supportive and committed relationships, and increase members' psychological adjustment and self-esteem.

Creating A Shared Vision

O   O   O

If a man does not know to which port he is sailing, no wind is favorable.

Seneca

O   O   O

The second leadership responsibility is to create a joint vision of what the team or organization should and could be, a clear mission that all members are committed to achieving, and a set of goals that guide members' efforts. **To do so a leader must:**

1. Have a vision/dream of what the team and/or organization could be.
2. Communicate that vision with commitment and enthusiasm.
3. Make it a **shared** vision that members adopt as their own.
4. Make it a rational vision based on theory and research and sound implementation procedures.

Leaders enthusiastically and frequently communicate the dream of the team and organization being places where individuals share, help, encourage, and support each other's efforts to achieve and succeed. Places where **we** dominates **me.** Where working together to get the job done creates caring and committed relationships that propel people forward in their mutual search for excellence.

Leaders inspire a **shared** vision. It is the common vision that creates a basic sense of "sink or swim together" (i.e., positive interdependence) among members. Leaders breathe life into the hopes and dreams of others and enable them to see the exciting possibilities the future holds by striving for a common purpose. **The vision and its advocacy have to be rational.** The new practices have to be backed up with a knowledge of the relevant research and theory. A person with no followers is **not** a leader, and people will not become followers until they accept a vision

as their own. It is the long-term promise of achieving something worthwhile and meaningful that powers an individual's drive toward greater expertise. **You cannot command commitment, you can only inspire it!**

Empowering Members Through Cooperative Teams

○   ○   ○

I never got very far until I stopped imagining I had to do everything myself.

Frank W. Woolworth

○   ○   ○

The most important of all the five leadership practices is empowering individuals by organizing them into cooperative teams. To be effective, a cooperative team must be carefully structured to include positive interdependence, face-to-face promotive interaction, individual accountability, social skills, and group processing (Johnson, Johnson, and Holubec, 1986, 1988).

The one-word test to detect whether someone is on the road to becoming a leader is *we*. Leaders do not achieve success by themselves. It is not *my* personal best leaders inspire, it is *our* personal best. The most important thing a leader can do is to organize members so that they work cooperatively with each other, for at least two reasons.

The first is to promote committed and caring relationships among organization members. This is achieved through a "team" approach. Having members work as part of cooperative teams fosters committed and caring relationships. Cooperative efforts result in trust, open communication, and interpersonal support, all of which are crucial ingredients for productivity. When trust is broken by competition, harsh feelings, criticism, negative comments, and disrespect, productivity suffers.

The second is to empower staff members through teamwork. The "real world" involves working with and through many different people to get the job done. By organizing members into cooperative teams, leaders increase members' confidence that if they exert effort, they will be successful. Teams empower their members to act by making them feel strong, capable, and committed. Being part of a team enables members to innovate, experiment, take risks, and grow professionally.

Leading By Example

○   ○   ○

One does not improve through argument but through examples . . . Be what you wish to make others become. Make yourself, not your words, a sermon.

Henri Frederic Amiel

○   ○   ○

A Chinese proverb states, "Not the cry, but the flight of the wild duck, leads the flock to fly and follow." To provide leadership, you will need to model by (a) using cooperative procedures and (b) taking risks to increase your technical and interpersonal expertise. To model, you must practice what you preach. **You lead by example.** To do so, you must be clear about your belief in cooperative efforts, you must be able to speak coherently about your vision and values, and your actions must be congruent with your words. **You begin leadership by becoming a role model that exemplifies the organizational and leadership values you believe are important.** You show your priorities through living your values.

One thing you can count on for certain. **Every exceptional leader is a learner.** The self-confidence required to lead comes from trying, failing, learning from mistakes, and trying again. We are all involved in a continuous process of increasing our technical and interpersonal expertise. From making your own journey to actualize your vision, you model the way for others. Remember, it is not the cry, but the flight of the wild duck that leads the flock to fly and follow .

Encouraging The Heart Of Members

○   ○   ○

"Love 'em and lead 'em."

Major General John H. Stanford, Commander, United States Army

○   ○   ○

Leaders are vigilant about the little things that make a big difference. Each spring at Verstec, annual bonuses are given to about 2,000 nonmanagerial personnel (Kouzes and Posner, 1987). In a recent year, the president arrived at the celebration dressed in a satin costume, riding atop an elephant, accompanied by the Stanford Marching Band. The president frequently says, "If you are going to give someone a check, don't just mail it. Have a celebration."

This example may seem extreme. It usually does not take a marching band and an elephant to make organizational members feel appreciated. **What makes a difference to each individual staff member is to know that his or her successes are perceived, recognized, and celebrated.** Leaders search out "good news" opportunities and orchestrate celebrations. Striving for increased technical and interpersonal expertise is an arduous and long-term enterprise. Members become exhausted, frustrated, and disenchanted. They often are tempted to give up. **Leaders must inspire members to continue the journey by encouraging the heart** (Kouzes and Posner, 1987). Leaders inspire staff members by giving them the courage and hope to continue the quest. This does not require elephants and marching bands (although they are not a bad idea). What it does require is:

1. The recognition of individual contributions to the common vision.
2. Frequent group celebrations of individual and joint accomplishments.

Members do not start the day with a desire to fail. It is the leader's job to show them that they can succeed. **The primary tools for doing so are individual recognition and group celebration.** A leader becomes a master of celebration. Leaders should give out stickers, t-shirts, buttons, and every other conceivable award when members achieve a milestone. One leader sends out cards that have "I heard something good about you" printed at the top. **Leaders find ways to celebrate accomplishments.** If you do not show your appreciation to your members, they are going to stop caring, and then, in essence, you are going to find yourself out of business.

To give individual recognition and have a group celebration requires a cooperative organizational structure. In competitions, to declare one person a winner is to declare all others losers. Group celebrations do not take place in competitive/individualistic organizations. In such environments, praise may be perceived to be phony or satirical and recognition may be the source of embarrassment and anxiety about future retaliation by colleagues. **Within cooperative enterprises, however, genuine acts of caring draw people together and forward. Love of their**

work and each other is what inspires many members to commit more and more of their energy to their jobs. Establishing a cooperative structure and encouraging the development of caring and committed relationships among members may just be the best-kept secret of exemplary leadership.

Leaping The Abyss Of Failure

○　　○　　○

"When you look into the abyss, the abyss is looking into you."

Nietzsche

○　　○　　○

Leaders give members the courage they need to take the risks necessary to increase technical and interpersonal expertise. Members can choose to play it safe in the short-run by traveling on the path of the status quo, thereby facing guaranteed long-term failure through obsolescence, atrophy, and burnout. Adherents to the status quo slowly and gradually descend into the abyss of failure. They are descending even though they may not always realize it. Managers organize the easy walk downward into the abyss of failure along the path of the status quo. Leaders encourage and inspire members to take the difficult leaps toward increased technical and interpersonal competence. They take a leap over the abyss of failure to reach enhanced expertise. Sometimes their leap falls short and they fail. Sometimes they soar high above the abyss to land safely on the other side. Leaders encourage the risks of short-term failure in order to enhance long-term productivity.

What If You Do Not Want To Be A Leader?

If you follow the rules given below carefully, you can be guaranteed to never be a leader:

1. Be absent from group meetings as frequently as possible.
2. When you do attend, contribute nothing.
3. If you do participate, come on strong early in the discussion. Demonstrate your knowledge of everything, including your extensive vocabulary of big words and technical jargon.
4. Indicate that you will do only what you have to and nothing more.
5. Read the paper or knit during meetings.

EXERCISE 4.4   **How Do You Explain This Leader**

PROCEDURE

Form a group of three. Read the following case study. Review the theories of leadership presented in this chapter and develop an explanation of the leadership demonstrated within the following situation. Then join with another group and compare your explanations.

Jim Jones was ordained as a minister in the Disciples of Christ Christian Church. In the early 1960's, he built his California-based church into a massive organization of dedicated followers. Preaching a mixture of Christianity and Marxism, he emphasized interracial harmony. He was a dynamic, entrancing speaker who could hold an audience in rapt attention. In 1963 he formed his own church, the People's Temple Full Gospel Church and soon had 8,000 members. While the People's Temple was considered to be civic-minded and altruistic for some time, rumors began to surface concerning Jones' demands for absolute dedication from his followers and the punishment he would inflict on members. Exmembers reported that he demanded to be called father, frequently made sexual demands on both male and female members, and required large financial contributions of even the poorest members.

Jones was reported to be obsessed with suicide. Occasionally, he would announce that the sacramental wine the congregation had drunk had been poison and all would be dead in a half hour. Jones even had confederates in the congregation simulate collapse, complete with stage blood flowing from their mouths. After convincing everyone that they were dying he would announce that he was merely testing their faith in him. Through repetition of this ceremony the thought of mass suicide became commonplace to his church members.

Feeling persecuted, Jones moved his church and congregation to the South American country of Guyana, and established Jonestown in the jungle. His press releases described the settlement as a utopian community. Rumors, however, kept surfacing that the community was a prison in which members were brutalized. Armed guards to prevent desertion were reported and the suicide rituals were practiced repeatedly. In response to the rumors, congressional representative Leo Ryan visited Jonestown and was murdered. Realizing that a full investigation would be made of his church, he ordered a suicide ritual. Over the loudspeaker system Jones explained the need for the "revolutionary suicide of the faithful" and ordered his followers to take their own lives and the lives of their children.

The next day, when authorities reached the settlement, they viewed a scene of unbelievable ghastliness. More than 900 people from infants to adults, as well as Jones himself, had committed suicide. Whole families had taken the poison on Jones' orders and died side by side.

(See Krause (1978) for a detailed description of development and demise of Jones' cult.)

Leadership Quotes

"Something is happening to our country. We aren't producing leaders like we used to. A new chief executive officer today, exhausted by the climb to the peak, falls down on the mountaintop and goes to sleep."

Robert Townsend, Former president of Avis

"He who never learned to obey cannot be a good commander."

Aristotle

"A business short on capital can borrow money, and one with a poor location can move. But a business short on leadership has little chance for survival."

Warren Bennis and Burt Nanus

"Never tell people 'how' to do things. Tell them 'what' to do and they will surprise you with their ingenuity."

George Smith Patton

"Anyone can hold the helm while the sea is calm."

Publius

"The final test of a leader is that he leaves behind him in other men the conviction and will to carry on."

Walter Lippmann

"Leadership is the courage to admit mistakes, the vision to welcome change, the enthusiasm to motivate others, and the confidence to stay out of step when everyone else is marching to the wrong tune."

E. M. Estes, President, General Motors Corporation

Making Decisions by Yourself or in a Group

During your career, you will have to make many decisions. You usually can ask other people to help make an important decision. Or you can make it by yourself. There is a great deal of research comparing individual decisions with group decisions. In general, it indicates that decisions made by groups are better than are decisions made by individuals. Why is this so? What makes groups better than individuals in making decisions? Some of the reasons are as follows.

1. To make a good decision, you need to have the information about the situation and the problem you are considering. Usually there are other people who have information you do not have. You will make a better decision if they discuss their information with you.
2. Most people work more seriously when other people are also involved.
3. In a group, the different information everyone has can be pooled, analyzed, and put together in a productive way.
4. Another person can often see an error in your thinking before you do. Thus your errors can be corrected before the decision becomes final.
5. Most people have blind spots that other people may not have. Thus, a group will bring up ways of looking at a problem that you may not think of.
6. Other people's ideas stimulate new ideas in you.

Major Points

1. To get a cooperative effort from the group, you will have to help provide leadership.
2. You provide leadership by taking actions that help the group complete its task.
3. You provide leadership by taking actions that help the group maintain relationships among members in good working order.
4. Generally, follow the instructions of your supervisor and do what you are

told cheerfully. The organization requires him to direct your work. The supervisor is just doing his job by telling you what to do.

5. Do not be a silent member. Participate and contribute.

6. Be supportive of other people's participation. You may not agree with what they are saying, but you can be thankful that they feel free to say something.

SUMMARY AND REVIEW: Chapters 3 and 4

Setting Learning Contracts

You are to make a learning contract with your group summarizing the most important things you have learned from Section II. Chapters 3 and 4 focused on cooperation and leadership. Your contract should include a specific plan for applying what you have learned.

Procedure

1. Working alone, make a list of the most important things you have learned about cooperating and leading. List at least five things you have learned.

2. Select the five most important things you have learned. For each one, plan an action you can take in the next two weeks to apply that learning. For example, if you learned the importance of maintenance leadership, you might plan where you can be a maintenance leader. In making your action plans, be specific and practical. Do not try to do either too much or too little.

3. Copy the Learning Contract form on page 61. Fill it out, but do not sign it.

4. In your group, draw numbers to see who is going to go first. The member selected reviews his learnings and action plans with the group. The group helps the member clarify any vague items, add to his list, and improve his plans with concrete suggestions for implementing goals. Some members may plan to do more than is possible; other members may not plan to do enough. You may be able to think of a better way to put the learning into action.

5. The member's learning contract is modified until both he and the rest of the group are satisfied with it. He then signs the contract, and then the rest of the group signs as witnesses. The member is now committed to the group to carry out his action plans.

6. The whole process is repeated until every member of the group has a learning contract with the group.

7. The instructor will set a date for the group—about two weeks hence—to review each member's progress in completing his action plans.

8. Working alone, keep a record of your progress in implementing your action

plans. Copy and fill out the Learning Contract Progress Report on page 60. Use it when you give a progress report to your group.

9. In the progress review session, you will report to your group the day and date of the actions taken, describe what you did, what success you had, and what problems you encountered.

Reviewing Learning Contracts

At the end of Section I, you made a contract with your group. Your contract dealt with what you learned from the exercises in Section I and how you were going to apply those learnings. At that time, you were told that in a progress review session you would be asked to give the day and date of the actions taken, describe what you did, and state what success you had and what problems you encountered. The purpose of this session is to review your contract dealing with Section I.

Procedure

1. Draw numbers to see who will go first. Then go around the group clockwise. Each person is to review the tasks and activities she was to engage in to apply learnings from Section I. She then is to give the day and date on which the tasks and activities were completed, tell what success she experienced, and state what problems she encountered. Group members are to praise a person's successes and are to provide helpful suggestions to overcome any problems a person is having in completing a learning contract.

2. When a learning contract has been completed, it is considered fulfilled. If a member has not fulfilled her learning contract, she is expected to do so in the near future. An unfinished contract will be discussed again at the next session set aside for that purpose.

5

Sending and Receiving

After completing the Questionnaire that follows, you should be able to define and give examples of

- Communication
- Sender
- Receiver
- Message
- Effective communication
- Owning
- Evaluating
- Paraphrasing

The answers are given on the right side of the page. Work with a partner and keep the answers covered until you have agreed on your response. Remember to check each answer before going on to the next item, as explained on page 1.

QUESTIONNAIRE: Main Concepts in Chapter 5

1. *Communication* is one person sending a message to another person. The message is aimed at getting a response. When one person tries to get a response from another person by sending him a message, _____ is taking place.

   communication

2. When one person yells, "Stop that nonsense and pay attention!" he is trying to _____ with someone.

   communicate

3. The person sending the message is the *sender*. In communication, the message is sent by the _____.

   sender

4. I am sending you a message by writing this sentence. I am an example of a _____.

   sender

5. A *receiver* is the person receiving the message. The person receiving the message is a _____.

   receiver

6. You are receiving a message by reading this sentence. You are an example of a _____.

   receiver

7. A *message* is a group of words or actions that has meaning to the sender and the receiver. When the one person wants to share a thought, feeling, or need with another person, he sends a _____.

   message

8. This sentence is a _____ from me to you.

   message

9. In _____, a _____ sends a _____ to a _____.

   communication
   sender, message, receiver

10. *Effective communication* occurs when the receiver understands a message to be what the sender intended it to be. When the receiver understands a message in the same way that the sender meant it, _____ _____ has taken place.

    effective communication

11. Taking *ownership* of your thoughts, feelings, and needs is using the personal pronouns, *I, me, my,* and *mine*. When you use personal pronouns in a message, you are _____the message.

    owning

12. In the statement, "I want to stop working and eat lunch," the sender is _____ her need to eat lunch.

    owning

13. *Evaluating* a message is judging whether the sender is right or wrong. When the receiver makes judgments about the sender's message, he is _____.

    evaluating

14. If you think I am crazy, you are _____ the messages in this book.   evaluating

15. *Paraphrasing* is restating what the sender says, feels, and means. When you restate the thoughts and feelings in a message, you are _____.   paraphrasing

16. If I say, "I want to teach better communication skills," and you say, "You want readers to improve their communication skills by reading your book," you are engaging in _____.   paraphrasing

What Is Communication?

Heather Lamb is a long-distance operator. She works for a communications company, but she is not allowed to communicate with customers on a personal basis. She works in close physical contact with other employees, yet she does not know their first names. Her work is organized so she can communicate very little with her coworkers. She likes her job, yet she longs for more personal communication with customers and coworkers. She spends all her time communicating with other people, but her communication is limited by the mechanics of her job.

Many jobs are similar to Heather's. Because of the nature of the job, there is very little possibility for personal communication. Other jobs have a great deal of face-to-face communication. On these jobs, it is possible to be personally involved with customers and coworkers. But no matter what your job is, you will have to communicate with other people. Whether you are a maintenance engineer or president of the United States, you will have to communicate with other people as part of your work. If you cannot communicate effectively you will not be successful. You cannot survive on the job without being able to communicate to supervisors, coworkers, suppliers, and customers. If other people do not understand what you are saying or if you cannot understand what your supervisor and coworkers are saying, your work will suffer. A major part of any job is communicating with other people. Regardless of whether you are planning to be a cook, computer technician, secretary, mechanic, social worker, or mechanical artist, you will have to communicate daily with other people.

Some people are shy; some people do not care if they communicate with anyone else at work or not; and some try very hard *not* to communicate with anyone else. I once worked with an engineer named Steve. Steve was afraid to speak to anyone at work unless it had to do with a specific engineering problem. When people said hello in the hallways, he would look away and pretend he did not see them. When someone in the cafeteria would say, "Hi, Steve!" he would look at his food and again pretend he did not hear them. He was trying not to communicate. Steve was terrified by the thought of saying something that would make others dislike him. Yet his behavior communicated a great deal about what kind of person he was and how he felt about other people.

○　　○　　○

It's a strange atmosphere. You're in a room about the size of a gymnasium, talking to people thousands of miles away. You come in contact with at least thirty-five an hour. You can't exchange any ideas with them. They don't know you, they never will. You feel like you might be missing people. You feel like they put a coin in the machine and they've got you. You're there to perform your service and go. You're kind of detached.

There are about seven or eight phrases you use and that's it. . . . A big thing is not to talk with a customer. If he's upset, you can't say more than "I'm sorry you've been having trouble." If you get caught talking with a customer, that's one mark against you. You can't help but want to talk to them if they're in trouble or if they're just feeling bad or something. For me it's a great temptation to say, "Gee, what's the matter?" You don't feel like you're really helping people that much.

One man said, "I'm lonesome, will you talk to me?" I said, "Gee, I'm sorry, I just can't." . . . I'm a communications person but I can't communicate.

Heather Lamb, Long-Distance Operator
in STUDS TERKEL, *Working*

○　　○　　○

Whenever two people can see or hear each other, they are communicating. Two people cannot work together, cooperate, or even pass by each other in the restroom without some communication taking place. If a person sees you, she gets an impression of what you intend to communicate by your clothes, posture, hair style, facial expression, and way of walking. *What you see is what you get!* It is impossible *not* to communicate if someone sees or hears you. Whenever you are noticed by another person, you are communicating.

Our daily work lives are filled with one communication experience after another. Without communication, no work could take place. Having a job means you will be communicating with other people, because work is coordinated through communication. Through communication, you get to know, trust, and understand your coworkers. A major part of any job is being able to communicate effectively with your supervisor, coworkers, suppliers, and customers.

Whenever someone says, "Let me make one thing perfectly clear," you can usually be sure that you will end up confused. Definitions of what communication is usually leave people confused. So let me make one thing perfectly clear about communication: ***Communication*** is one person sending a message to get a response from another person. One person says, "How are you today?" to get a response, such as "Fine," from another person. A teacher shakes his head to get two students to stop throwing erasers. Any message that is intended to influence another person in any way is communication.

It takes three things for communication to take place. First, there must be a *sender,* a person who communicates the message. Second, there is a *receiver,* a person who responds to the message. Third, there is a *message,* a group of words or actions that has meaning. The way you dress, the expression on your face when you talk with your boss, and the words you say are all messages. When you tell your boss how much you love your job, you are the sender, your boss is the receiver, and the words indicating how much you love your job are the message.

Effective Communication

Sometimes communication is effective. At other times, communication breaks down and there is a misunderstanding. When the receiver interprets a message in the same way the sender intended it, communication has been effective. If the receiver interprets a message differently than the sender intended it, there has been a misunderstanding. For example, let us say that John wants to communicate to Jane that it is a wonderful day and he is feeling great. He looks at Jane, smiles warmly, and says, "Hi!" If Jane thinks John is really feeling good because it is a beautiful day, communication has been effective. If Jane thinks John wants to ask her for a date, communication has not been effective. Let's take another example. You walk into this class, feel a surge of joy, and say, "Teacher, I'm glad I'm here!" If the teacher believes you, your communication has been effective. If the teacher thinks you are being sarcastic, then a misunderstanding has taken place.

Effective communication is not just a matter of opening your mouth. It is not just a matter of luck. It takes skills. These skills do not magically appear on your eighteenth birthday. You are not born with these skills—they have to be learned. This section deals with skills in sending and receiving messages so that both you and the sender understand them.

POWER AND EFFECTIVE COMMUNICATION

When I was six years old, I learned a lesson in effective communication from my older brother's horse. In Jay's absence, I had decided to saddle Maud and go for a ride. Maud, it seems, had other plans.

As I was trying to put the saddle on her back, Maud positioned herself firmly on my foot. I tried different ways of communicating that she should get off. First I asked her politely to please release my foot. She didn't move a muscle. Next I tried to push her off. She didn't budge. Then I shouted in her ear that if she didn't get off my foot I would beat her over the head. At that she blinked, but stood her ground. By now my foot was hurting.

Making good my threat, I took a board lying within reach and hit her on the head as hard as I could. She shifted her weight but did not release my foot. Even when I poked her in the side with the board, she refused to acknowledge and respond appropriately to the message I was sending her so loud and clear.

Finally, Jay arrived on the scene. He was twelve and much bigger than I. "Maud," he said calmly and quietly, "you get off Dave's foot." Instantly, Maud did as she was told.

To this day, Jay insists that all I had to do was ask Maud nicely to move. My belief is that she had gotten the message all right, but would not accept it from a six-year-old kid. My brother had an advantage over me—he was the master, the authority figure. The moral of this story is: For effective communication, a little bit of power can be a big help!

Saying What You Mean and Meaning What You Say

Saying what you mean is not always easy. And the more personal the ideas and feelings you want to communicate, the harder it is. Sometimes people are not really sure what they want to say. At other times, people know what they want to say but are not sure how best to say it. In either case, people want to say what they mean in a way that is understood.

The first step of communication is figuring out what you want to say. Activate brain before engaging mouth! Often this means being aware of your feelings and reactions. The second step of communication is phrasing your message so it can be

easily understood by the receiver. The third step in communicating is being able to understand what other people mean when they send messages to you.

The four basic sending skills that we will focus on in the next part of this chapter are:

1. Speaking for yourself or taking ownership of your statements.
2. Describing other people's behavior without implying judgment.
3. Focusing statements on a relationship between yourself and another.
4. Taking the viewpoint or perspective of the other person into account in phrasing your message.

The basic receiving skill discussed in this chapter is paraphrasing or reflecting the sender's message.

I'll Speak for Me, You Speak for You: Taking Ownership

The most basic sending skill is speaking for yourself. You are an expert on your ideas, feelings, and needs. Other people are not as good at stating what you are thinking, feeling, and needing. And you are not an expert on what other people think, feel, and need. You speak for yourself when you use the pronouns *I, me, my,* and *mine.* You take **ownership** of your ideas, feelings, and needs when you say, "I think . . . ," "I feel . . . ," and "I want. . . ." The more you speak for yourself, the clearer your messages will be. The less you speak for yourself, the more confused your messages will be. For example, there is a difference between saying, "I like my job," and saying, "Some people like this job, some don't."

There are two ways you can confuse the ownership of your messages. The first is *to speak for no one.* To speak for no one you substitute words such as *it, some people, everyone, they,* or *one* for *I.* Or you can use no pronoun at all. As a result, it is not clear who the owner of the ideas or feelings is. Examples of speaking for no one are "Most people believe that students from Southeast Central are chickens!" or "It is commonly believed that students from Southeast Central have a big yellow streak down their backs!"

You can also speak for others. When you speak for another person, you state you know more about what he thinks, feels, and needs, than he does. You speak for others when you substitute *you, we,* or the person's name for *I.* Speaking for another person also makes it confusing as to who is the owner of the ideas and feelings. Examples of speaking for another person are "You have always liked your mother's cooking best," "Bill doesn't like you—he thinks you are a lousy boss," and "We are bored to tears!" Speaking for another person may make him angry. At the very least, he may feel "boxed in" by your statements. And he will be confused as to what your thoughts, feelings, and needs are.

Not speaking for yourself confuses the people you are talking to. Speaking for no one and for other people confuses the people you are talking to. Speaking for yourself is a sign of trust and openness. It implies that you are willing to let your fellow workers know where you stand and how you are reacting. Whenever you want to communicate clearly, be sure to speak for yourself. You can trust other people to speak for themselves without your help.

EXERCISE 5.1   **Who Owns This?**

PURPOSE

A basic communication skill is to speak for yourself by taking ownership for your thoughts, feelings, and needs. You should avoid speaking for no one or for other people, unless you want to confuse the receiver. The purpose of this exercise is to give you some practice in recognizing who owns the thoughts, feelings, or needs in a message. A message can be owned by the sender, no one, or someone other than the sender. The sender can be speaking for himself, for no one, or for someone else. This exercise will give you a chance to identify who is speaking for whom.

PROCEDURE

1. Working alone, read each of the statements listed below. On a separate sheet of paper, write your answers. Put an "S" for each statement in which the sender is speaking for himself. Put an "N" for each statement in which the sender is speaking for no one. Put an "O" for each statement in which the sender is speaking for someone else.

2. Working as a group, decide whether each statement is an "S," "O," or "N." Discuss any disagreements among members until all members agree on the answers. Then rephrase the "O" and "N" statements to make them "S" statements. Finally, check your group's answers against the correct answers given in Appendix B, and discuss any statements the group missed.

3. Review the material on ownership of statements in the book.

Statements

____ 1. Everyone here hates the boss.
____ 2. I love you.
____ 3. Rumor has it that you are a beautiful person.
____ 4. We think work is groovy.
____ 5. I feel nervous when you look at me that way.
____ 6. You make people feel good just by smiling at them.
____ 7. I can tell by looking at your face that you feel terrible.
____ 8. No one would quit this job.
____ 9. You think I have big feet and it isn't true!

_____ 10. Bill thinks you're strange.

_____ 11. I'm really excited about my raise.

_____ 12. Most people would be mad if you did that to them.

_____ 13. My boss thinks I'm great!

_____ 14. I believe in the United States of America.

_____ 15. I need more time to think about it.

_____ 16. It would be good for the people in this office to be more trust-
ing.

_____ 17. I want to find a better job.

_____ 18. It is commonly felt that I am a terrific athlete.

Describe but Don't Judge

Priscilla wasn't the nicest boss I ever worked for. I was working as a typist and had just finished typing a report for her. She took one look at it and commented, "You stupid fool, it's all wrong. Type it over and do it right!" She then marched off before I could find out what was wrong with the way I had done it. Judgments and generalities do not help communication. They just confuse and anger the receiver.

Describe, don't judge! When you are discussing another person, describe behavior, don't make judgments. Say, "She was five minutes late for work today," not "That shiftless, lazy, no-good woman can't get to work on time to save her life!" Communication is always clearer when you describe rather than judge. When you describe, you let the receiver make his own judgments. When you evaluate, you make judgments and ask the receiver to agree with you. Your judgments tell more about you and your feelings than they do about the person you are discussing. There will be many times when you are expected to discuss the behavior of fellow employees, suppliers, and customers. Be sure to de-scribe, not judge.

Being skillful at describing without judging is important for effective com-munication. The following exercise will give you some practice in doing so.

**EXERCISE
5.2**   **Describing**

PURPOSE

The purpose of this lesson is to give you some practice in describing another person's behavior without passing judgment.

PROCEDURE

1. Working alone, read each of the statements listed below. On a sepa-rate sheet of paper, write your answers. Put a "D" for each statement

that *describes* a person's behavior. Put a "J" for each statement that *judges* a person's behavior.

2. In your group, review the answers of each member for each statement. Discuss any disagreements until all members agree on each answer. Check your group's answers against the answers in Appendix B. Discuss any statements your group missed.

3. Working alone, write the name of each group member at the top of a sheet of paper. You should have five sheets of paper, each having the name of one group member written at the top. On the sheet of paper, write down a few of the typical behaviors of the group member. Take two minutes for each group member. Use the following rules for doing so:
   a. Report specific behaviors that you observed;
   b. Do not judge or evaluate the behaviors;
   c. Do not make any inferences about the person's motives, personality, or attitudes.

4. In your group of six, hand each member of the group the sheet of paper on which you described her behavior. Each group member should end up with five sheets of paper with her name written at the top. On each sheet will be a description of her behavior.

5. Draw numbers to see who will begin. Then go around the group in a clockwise direction. Each group member will read the descriptions of his behavior. The group member can make any comments about the descriptions he wants to.

Statements

1. Sam interrupted Sally when she tried to talk about the Minnesota Vikings.
2. Mark is very sincere.
3. Sue never understands what Jack is saying.
4. Sally is rude and ungrateful.
5. Sam changed the subject.
6. Jane's trying to make me mad.
7. It's a great day out today.
8. That's the fourth time in the past half-hour that you finished one of my sentences.
9. Sam and Mark have made the most statements during this exercise.
10. Jane is very shy.
11. I don't like Sally.
12. Sam has not made a statement for the past three sessions.
13. During the group session yesterday, you sat staring into space for the first half-hour.
14. Today on my way to school, I saw three butterflies.

Relationship Statements

Happiness is having good relationships. How well two people work together depends on how good their relationship is. With some coworkers, you automatically become friends. With other coworkers, you automatically become enemies. But most relationships on the job do not "just happen." They have to be built and maintained. At times your relationships at work will be smooth and enjoyable. At other times, conflicts and problems will arise that have to be solved. At such times, you and a fellow employee will have to sit down and discuss the current problems in your relationship. Such a talk will focus on how the relationship can be changed so the two of you can work together better. During such conversations, you will need to make relationship statements.

The term *relationship statements* refers to descriptions of how you see the relationship. A relationship statement describes some aspect about the way the two of you are relating to each other. It focuses on the relationship, not on you or the other person, and it speaks only for yourself. An example of a relationship statement is, "I appreciate your listening to me carefully." A good relationship statement indicates clear ownership and is descriptive. A poor relationship statement speaks for the other person and makes judgments about the relationship.

EXERCISE 5.3   **"You and Me" Relationship Statements**

PURPOSE

The purpose of this exercise is to give you some practice in differentiating between good and poor relationship statements.

PROCEDURE

1. Divide into groups of three.
2. Working as a group, read each of the Relationship Statements listed below. Write one answer that all members of the triad agree is correct. Put an "R" for each good relationship statement that describes how the speaker sees the relationship. Put "No" for all poor relationship statements.
3. Review your answers for the poor relationship statements. Decide as a triad on the reason the relationship statements are poor. Put a "J" for a poor relationship statement that judges. Put an "O" for a poor relationship statement that speaks for the other person. Put a "P" for a statement that is about a person, not a relationship.
4. As a triad, rewrite the poor relationship statements to make them good relationship statements.
5. Turn to Appendix B and check your triad's answers against the correct answers. Discuss any statements the group missed.

6. In your triad, decide who will be Person A, B, or C. Person A is the observer for the first round, Person B for the second round, and Person C for the third.

7. Persons B and C discuss their relationship, using good relationship statements to do so. They have three minutes to make several good relationship statements to each other.

8. Person A observes. He or she takes notes about whether the relationship statements are good or poor. He or she also times the conversation and stops it after three minutes.

9. At the end of three minutes, Person A reports his or her observations. Persons A, B, and C then discuss how they could have improved their relationship statements.

10. The same procedure is used for Rounds 2 and 3.

11. Combine two triads into a group of six. Discuss the following questions:
    a. How did I feel making relationship statements?
    b. What did I learn about making good relationship statements?
    c. When are skills in making relationship statements important?

Relationship Statements

1. We really enjoyed ourselves last night.

2. Our relationship is really lousy!

3. For the past two days, you have not spoken to me once. Is something wrong with our relationship?

4. You look sick today.

5. You really make me feel appreciated and liked.

6. You're angry again. You're always getting angry.

7. We are great at communicating.

8. I think we need to talk about our disagreement yesterday.

9. I think you can finish that job today.

10. I feel you're making nasty comments. Are you angry with me?

11. You really are mean and vicious!

12. My older brother is going to beat you up if you don't stop doing that.

13. I'm concerned that when we go to lunch together we are often late for work in the afternoon.

14. You really seem happy about your promotion.

15. This job stinks!

16. I'm confused by your behavior. Last week you were really friendly to me. This week you have not even said hello once.

Different Shoes, Different Perspectives

Betsy and Juanita work together as laboratory technicians in a large hospital. Betsy comes from a well-off, upper middle-class family. Juanita's parents had a hard struggle sending their daughter through college. Betsy and Juanita buy tickets for a state lottery in which they could win up to $50,000. When the drawing is held, they learn that they are both winners. Betsy says, "Hey, I won $50,000 in that lottery. Imagine that." Then she continues eating lunch and reading a magazine. Juanita starts jumping up and down shouting, "I won! I won! I won $50,000! She throws her arms around her friend, crying and laughing in her excitement.

Why did Betsy and Juanita react so differently to the news that they had each won $50,000 in a state lottery?

You see things from your shoes. I see things from my shoes. From your shoes, a person you work with is sexy, attractive, desirable; from my shoes, the person is only so-so. From your shoes the movie is fantastic; from my shoes, it certainly is! Sometimes we see things the same; sometimes we see things differently.

Different people have different perspectives. Misunderstandings often occur because we assume that everyone sees things from the same perspective we do. If we like Italian food, we assume that all our friends like Italian food. If we are interested in sports, we assume that everyone is interested in sports. If we get angry when someone laughs at our behavior, we assume that everyone will get angry when they are laughed at. If we think our boss is stupid, we are surprised

when a coworker thinks the boss is brilliant. As children, we can see things only from our perspective. As we become adults, we learn that different people have different perspectives, and we learn how to understand other people's perspectives.

You can have different perspectives at two different times. When you are a tired clerk who wants to go home to get ready for an important date, a customer's behavior may seem unreasonable. When you are a manager who is trying to increase sales, the same customer behavior may seem very understandable. On Monday, if a clerk overcharges you, you may laugh it off. But on Tuesday, when you have been overcharged at the last three stores you have visited, a careless clerk may make you angry. If you have been lifting 100-pound bags of cement and someone tosses you a 40-pound bag, it will seem very light. But if you have been lifting 20-pound bags, the 40-pound bag will seem very heavy. As your job role, experiences, assumptions, and values change, your perspective will change.

The same message can mean two entirely different things to two different people. If you provoke your coworker, she may laugh. But if you provoke your boss, she may get angry and fire you! *Different perspectives mean the message will be given different meanings.* From one perspective, a message may be interpreted as a joke. From another perspective, the same message may be interpreted as hostile insubordination.

To be skilled in communicating, you need to understand the perspective of the *receiver*. When you are deciding how to phrase a message, you need to take into account:

1. The receiver's perspective
2. What the receiver already knows about the issue
3. What further information the receiver needs and wants about the issue

By taking these factors into account, you can phrase the message so the receiver can easily understand it.

To be skilled in communicating, you need to understand the *sender's* perspective. When deciding what a message means, you need to take into account:

1. The sender's perspective
2. The meaning of the message from the sender's "shoes"

By taking these factors into account, you can decide accurately what the message really means.

There is nothing more helpful for effective communication than being skilled in seeing things from the other person's perspective. Try standing in someone else's shoes. It will really improve your communication with that person.

PURPOSE

When you send messages, you need to phrase them so that they are appropriate to the receiver's perspective. The purpose of this exercise is to give you some practice in doing so.

PROCEDURE

1. In your group, read the story below, entitled, "The Laboratory Technicians." Write out what Edythe might say to Buddy, to Helen, to Dr. Smith, and to Mrs. Jonathan.

2. Your teacher will have each group read some of their answers to the whole class.

3. In your group, discuss the following questions:
   a. How did your group's answers compare with the answers of the other groups?
   b. What did your group learn about making messages appropriate? Write out a list of what you learned.
   c. How do you find out what another person's perspective is? Write out a list of the ways you can.

4. Go around the group and have each member describe a recent situation in which he phrased messages differently to people with different perspectives.

The Laboratory Technicians

Buddy and Edythe are laboratory technicians in a large hospital. They have just worked with each other for a few days and do not know each other very well. One morning their supervisor, Helen, asks them to do a rush job on a blood sample for Dr. Smith. The patient's name is Mrs. Jonathan. Edythe has never met either Dr. Smith or Mrs. Jonathan.

Edythe quickly conducts a series of blood tests. The results indicate that Mrs. Jonathan has blood cancer. As she finishes writing up the results of the tests, Buddy comes over and asks, "What'd you find?" Then Helen rushes in and asks, "What were the results of the blood tests for Dr. Smith?" Dr. Smith then calls on the phone for a quick report from Edythe. Finally, later in the day, Mrs. Jonathan calls up Edythe and says, "Look! I'm the person paying the bills! I want to know the results of my blood tests! And don't tell me to ask Dr. Smith! I already did and he won't tell me!"

If you were Edythe, would you say the same thing to Buddy, Helen, Dr. Smith, and Mrs. Jonathan? If the answer is no, what would you take into account in replying to each person? You might want to take the following factors into consideration:

1. Who the person is.
2. What his or her position in the hospital is.
3. How much the person knows about blood tests and blood cancer.
4. What the nature of the relationship between Edythe and the person is.
5. How appropriate it is to be fully honest about the results of the blood tests.

Let Me Tell You What You Just Said

There is no skill more important in a relationship than being a good listener. A good listener is always liked and is always sought out for conversations. Listening skills are a major asset for your career. If you are a good listener, you have it made.

The keystone to good listening is **paraphrasing.** Restating, in your own words, what the person says, feels, and means improves communication in several ways. First, it helps you avoid judging and evaluating. When you are restating, you are not passing judgment. Second, restating gives the sender direct feedback as to how well you understand the messages. If you do not fully understand, the sender can add messages until you do. If you are interpreting the message differently from the way he intended it, the sender can clarify. Being able to clarify and elaborate are important for making sure communication is taking place.

Third, paraphrasing communicates to the sender that you *want* to understand what he is saying. It shows that you care about him enough to listen carefully, that you are interested, that you take what he is saying seriously, and that you want to understand. Finally, paraphrasing helps you get into the sender's shoes: It helps you see the message from the sender's perspective. By restating the message as accurately and fairly as possible, you begin to see things from the sender's point of view.

The simple act of paraphrasing is perhaps the most powerful thing you can do to reduce conflict and misunderstandings. It works by correcting inaccuracies

WHAT YOU SAID

"Did you see that! Did you see that! He's done it to me again! That *$)#@*boss did it to me again!

"He's always giving me the dirty jobs! Whenever there's some really low, scummy job to be done, he singles me out! This time I'm not going to do it!

"I am going to stop it! I'm going to stop it by not doing it and then telling him where to put his job when he asks me why it isn't done! Nobody is going to treat me this way!"

PARAPHRASED

"You're really upset and angry about what the boss just asked you to do."

"You feel he's picking on you by giving you all the dirtiest jobs. You don't know why, but you want to do something to stop it."

"By refusing to do the job and telling him so, you think he will stop giving you dirty jobs to do."

of communication. It also indicates empathy—trying to see things from the sender's shoes.

Paraphrasing is often a simple restatement of what has been said. At first, it may feel dumb to restate what another person has said. It may feel awkward and unnatural until you get used to doing it. But the speaker will be grateful for a chance to clarify or add to his original statement, and he will feel grateful for being understood.

Paraphrasing becomes harder when it includes feelings as well as ideas. And it is not limited to only the words the sender uses. Nonverbal cues are also important. Examples of paraphrasing are given in the following conversation.

Paraphrasing may sound simple. But it is often difficult to do. To be skilled in communicating, you must be skilled in paraphrasing. It has very powerful and constructive effects. It is one of the most essential skills of effective communication.

This does not mean that you will want to paraphrase every statement made by anyone who speaks to you. Some statements aren't important enough to bother with. When someone says hello, there is no need to paraphrase. When someone says "Nice day," there is no need to paraphrase. When someone says "Look at that!" there is no need to paraphrase. Paraphrasing is for important messages: When you are not sure what the sender means, when your boss is giving important instructions, or when someone is being very emotional, you paraphrase. In the middle of a conflict, when you want the sender to feel understood, or when you want to be absolutely sure what is being said before you reply, you paraphrase. Paraphrasing is essential in important conversations.

When you use paraphrasing, there is a rhythm to your statements. The rhythm is *You said . . . ; I say. . . .* First you say what the sender said ("You said"). Then you reply ("I say").

Remember the paraphrasing rule. *Before you can reply to a statement, restate what the sender says, feels, and means correctly and to the sender's satisfaction.*

EXERCISE 5.5   Sending and Paraphrasing

PURPOSE

When you communicate with fellow employees, you need skills in phrasing your messages appropriately. You also need skills in accurately understanding what the other person is saying. In this lesson, you will have the chance to do both. The purposes of the lesson are to give you a chance to practice (1) sending messages so they can be easily understood and (2) paraphrasing to understand another person's messages correctly.

PROCEDURE

1. Divide into groups of three. Decide who are Persons A, B, and C.
2. The schedule for the lesson is as follows:

	Round 1	Round 2	Round 3
Sender	A	B	C
Receiver	B	C	A
Observer	C	A	B

3. Item 7 gives several open-ended sentences. The *sender* will finish these sentences while speaking to the receiver, following the rules for sending messages. The rules for the *sender* are:
    a. Make your messages complete and specific.
    b. Include all the information necessary for the receiver to really understand your message.
    c. Repeat your message twice, using different words the second time.
    d. Be brief. Do not take more than sixty seconds for each statement.
4. The *receiver* paraphrases the sender's statement. Paraphrasing means that you restate what the sender says, feels, and means correctly and to the sender's satisfaction. The rules for paraphrasing are
    a. Restate the sender's ideas and feelings in your *own* words, rather than mimicking or parroting his or her exact words.
    b. Start out your remarks with, "You think . . . ," "Your position is . . . ," "It seems to you that . . . ," "You feel that . . . ," and so on.
    c. Do not show indication of approval or disapproval, agreement or disagreement. Your restatement must not be evaluative.
    d. Make your unspoken messages agree with your spoken paraphrasing. Look attentive, interested, and open to the sender's ideas and feelings. Show that you are concentrating on what the sender is trying to communicate.
    e. State as correctly as possible what you heard the sender say. Describe the feelings and attitudes involved.
    f. Do not add or subtract things from the sender's message.
    g. Put yourself in the sender's shoes and try to understand what the sender is feeling and what the message means to him or her.
5. The *observer* watches the communication exchange between the receiver and the sender and takes notes to give a report on how well each followed the rules for sending and paraphrasing. The observer may not speak until it is time to report. It is the observer's responsibility to tell the sender and receiver when the time is finished.
6. Each round lasts ten minutes (or less) followed by a three-minute observer report.
7. The statements for the sender to finish are as follows. In finishing the statement, do not give just a name or a word. Say at least two sentences about each topic:

a. Basically, the job I'm studying for is . . .
b. On this job I'm best at . . .
c. My greatest weakness on this job is . . .
d. I want to do this job because . . .
e. I prefer to work with people who . . . .
f. The best boss I ever had . . .
g. The best coworker I ever had . . .

8. After all three rounds have been completed, discuss the following questions:
   a. How did it feel to make a statement and have the receiver paraphrase it? Was he or she receiving the message accurately?
   b. How did it feel to paraphrase a statement made by the sender?
   c. Did you find you had any difficulty in listening to the sender? Why?
   d. How did the way the sender phrased his or her message affect the receiver's ability to understand it?

9. As a group of six, discuss the material in the book on sending and paraphrasing.

Communication Failure

You have just been through a lesson in which you practiced both sending and receiving skills. Such skills may seem easy. But to be really good at them takes a lot of practice. Many people have a hard time communicating because they make some simple mistakes in sending and receiving messages. Were you guilty of any of the following common mistakes?

_____ Not organizing your thoughts before speaking

_____ Including too many (and sometimes unrelated) ideas in your messages

_____ Not including enough information and repetition to be understood

_____ Ignoring the information the receiver already has about the subject

_____ Not making the message appropriate to the receiver's perspective

_____ Not speaking for yourself

_____ Speaking for other people

_____ Making judgments rather than describing thoughts or ideas

_____ Not giving your undivided attention to the sender

_____ Thinking about your reply before listening to everything the sender has to say

_____ Listening for details rather than for the entire message

_____ Evaluating whether the sender is right or wrong before you fully understand her message

HOW TO ACCEPT CRITICISM

1. Listen carefully. Paraphrase the criticism. Be sure you understand the actions other employees are critical of.
2. Try to see your actions from the other person's shoes. If you can assume his perspective, you may understand the criticism of your actions much better.
3. Do not make the assumption that criticism is hostile and a put-down. You can learn a great deal from constructive criticism. It takes time and effort to give criticism in a helpful way. The other person may be showing that he really wants to help you do better.

HOW TO GIVE CRITICISM

1. Try to see the situation from the receiver's shoes. You will be able to phrase your criticism more effectively when you understand his or her perspective.
2. Speak for yourself.
3. Describe the person's actions that you are critical of. Do not pass judgment on or belittle the actions. Merely describe them.
4. Describe what makes the actions ineffective or undesirable. This may include a description of your reactions and their effects on your relationship with the person.
5. Check out how the receiver is feeling both during and after the discussion.
6. Remember that recognizing positive actions is much more powerful than criticizing negative actions. Be sure to give a balanced report on what the person is doing right and what he is doing wrong. Follow the discussion by praising positive changes in the person's actions.

These are not the only mistakes you can make in communicating on the job. But they are some of the most common mistakes. They *all* need to be avoided if you are to be effective in communicating with your fellow employees. This is especially true of judging—let's take this case of Steve as an example:

Steve once had a job. And he could communicate fairly well at times. But he had a bad habit of making judgments about everything his boss said. For a time, when she gave him directions, he would interrupt. Then he would tell her how she was wrong. She kept getting angry and telling him to keep his mouth shut, so he began to let her finish before he told her how she was wrong. This helped some, but not much. He did not know that the biggest mistake you can make in communicating is to evaluate and judge. He did not realize that the surest way to cause misunderstandings is to be judgmental when sending and receiving messages. And he did not care that being judgmental can be received as a put-down. So he was fired.

EXERCISE 5.6 **Communication Networks**

PURPOSE

The communication pattern structured by the organization you work for will have definite effects on the relationships you form and the way you feel about your job. In this lesson, you will have the opportunity to experience the effects of three different communication patterns. The purpose of the lesson is to highlight the effectiveness and morale of different organizational and group communication patterns.

PROCEDURE

1. Each group needs five participants and one observer. The five participants are seated in a straight line with everyone facing the same way. Each member is dealt five cards from a regular deck of playing cards. No verbal communication is allowed, but participants may write notes to the person in front of or behind them and pass cards to the person in front of or behind them. The *task of the group* is to select one card from each member's hand in order to make the highest-ranking poker hand possible. The *observer's task* is to time how long it takes the group to complete its task and to make notes about the behavior and feelings of the participants. After the group has decided on a poker hand, each participant should write an answer to the following questions:
   a. How satisfied are you with the group and its work?
   b. How did you feel?
   c. What did you observe?

2. The same task with the same rules is repeated, but this time the participants are arranged in a cross pattern, where one participant is in the middle and one person on her right, one person on her left, one person in front of her, and one person in back of her. Participants can only pass notes and cards to the person in the middle. The person in the middle can pass notes and cards to anyone. No verbal communication is allowed.

3. The same task is repeated. This time the participants sit in a circle and may communicate to anyone else in the group. Participants can pass notes and cards, and *may* speak to whomever they wish in the group.

4. Using the reactions of the participants and the observer's impressions the group should discuss the advantages and disadvantages of each communication pattern. Some of the questions the group may wish to answer are:
   a. What were the feelings of the persons in the middle of a communication pattern and on the fringe?
   b. Which communication pattern was most efficient in terms of the time it took to arrive at a group poker hand?
   c. If you were in charge of a company, which communication pattern would you try to use?

5. The instructor will ask each group to share its conclusions with the whole class.

The Communication Network

The way in which communication is structured on the job does make a difference in how well work gets done and how employees feel about their jobs. Some of the conclusions reached about the effects of communication networks are as follows:

1. When a task is simple and requires only the collection of information, a centralized network is most efficient. But when the task is more complex and requires analyzing information, decentralized networks are more efficient in terms of time and lack of errors.

2. The morale of a group is higher in decentralized communication networks compared to centralized ones. Persons who occupy a central position in a communication network are usually more satisfied with the group's work than are persons who occupy fringe positions.

3. The person who occupies a central position in a communication network usually emerges as the leader of the group. Because the central person has more information, she can coordinate group activities.

A Final Thought

All work requires effective communication. Effective communication depends on good sending and receiving skills. To survive on the job, you will have to master the basic skills of sending and receiving messages effectively. The following suggestions for effective sending and receiving of messages will help you master these basic communication skills.

Suggestions for Good Sending

1. Talk. It is hard to send messages if you are not talking.
2. Speak for yourself, not for others. Describe your own thoughts, feelings, and needs. Use personal pronouns such as *I, me, my,* and *mine*. Do not present yourself as an expert on how others are thinking, feeling, and needing.
3. Describe other people's behavior without making value judgments. Do not make interpretations about their personality and motives.
4. Make your messages appropriate to the receiver's perspective. Be sure the words you use have the same meaning for both you and the receiver.
5. Ask for feedback about the receiver's understanding of your messages.
6. Repeat your messages more than once. Use more than one way to communicate them. Besides saying them, write them down in memos.

7. Seek eye contact when you want to be listened to.

8. Make sure your nonverbal cues agree with your spoken message. Confusion will result if your facial expression, posture, tone of voice, and gestures indicate one thing, and your words indicate just the opposite. For example, do not smile when you say, "I'm angry at you."

9. Make your messages complete and specific. Concretely identify the subject (for example, do *not* say, "*This* is important" or "*They* say so"). You may need to include information about your perspective, your assumptions, your leaps in logic, and so forth.

10. Speak clearly. Do not mumble.

Suggestions for Good Receiving

1. Stop talking. You cannot listen if you are talking!

2. Paraphrase accurately without making value judgments about the ideas and feelings of the sender.

3. Keep clarifying until both you and the speaker are satisfied that you understand his message.

4. Look attentive. Act interested. For example, do not read your mail while the sender is talking.

5. Remove distractions. Do not doodle, tap, or shuffle papers, for example.

Communicating thoughts and facts is important for your job survival. There is a great deal of information that has to be exchanged on the job. But far more difficult is the communication of feelings. Your job survival depends as much on effectively communicating feelings as it does on communicating information, and most of us find feelings much harder to express. The next two chapters, therefore, focus on the communication of feelings.

Telling People How You Feel

After completing the Questionnaire that follows, you should be able to define and give examples of

- Feelings
- Perception check
- Senses
- Interpretations
- Intentions

The answers are given on the right side of the page. Work with a partner and keep the answers covered until you have agreed on your response. Remember to check each answer before going on to the next item, as explained on page 1.

QUESTIONNAIRE: Maine Concepts in Chapter 6

1. *Feelings* are your inside reactions to your experiences. When you have an internal reaction to an experience, you are having a _____.

   feeling

2. Your little sister hits you. You react with joy, because you can now hit her back. Joy is an internal reaction to your experience. It is a _____.

   feeling

3. When you are not sure of how a person is feeling, you need to check to see if your impression is correct. A *perception check* is a question which asks if your impression of how a person is feeling is correct. When you share your impressions of how a person is feeling, without making any value judgments about the feeling, and ask if you are or are not correct, you are engaging in a _____ _____.

   perception check

4. "You appear really worried today. Are you?" is an example of a _____ _____.

   perception check

5. Your feelings begin with gathering information about your experiences. Such information is gathered through your *senses* (sight, sound, touch, taste, smell). When you gather information about your experiences by seeing, hearing, touching, tasting, and smelling, you are using your _____.

   senses

6. You see your little sister throwing a raw egg at your face. You hear the splat as it hits you right between the eyes. You feel the egg dripping down your face. You smell it as it drips past your nose. And you taste it as it drips into your mouth. You have been gathering information about one of your experiences through your _____.

   senses

7. Your feelings are based on your *interpretations* of the information your senses provide. The meaning you attach to the information gathered through your senses is your _____.

   interpretation

8. "My little sister is a mean, vicious, brat" is an _____ based on your experience of her throwing an egg on your face.

   interpretation

9. After becoming aware of your feelings, you decide how you intend to express them. Your *intentions* are what you want to do to express your feelings. They are your guides for action. When you decide what

you want to do to express your feelings, you have
decided on your _____.   intentions

10. When you have decided to take your little sister
over your knee and spank her for spattering egg on
your face, you have formed your _____.   intentions

Saying What You Feel

Everyone experiences many different feelings while on the job. Here is a partial list of words describing ways you may feel.

happy	upset	pressured	discontented
pleased	surprised	cautious	sad
daring	tense	confident	proud
bored	lonely	glad	anxious
satisfied	elated	hopeful	frustrated
ecstatic	apathetic	excited	confused
uncomfortable	content	delighted	overjoyed
angry	weary	fearful	frightened
shy	jealous	embarrassed	humiliated
worried	appreciated	supported	accepted

It is natural to have feelings. You are human, so you feel. Your *feelings* are internal reactions based on your experiences: Things happen and you interpret what they mean. The meaning you place on your experiences creates your feelings. The way in which feelings are caused is discussed in more detail in the next section.

Your feelings are expressed in physiological reactions inside your body. For example, you may begin to tremble, sweat, or have a surge of energy. Your heart may begin to beat faster, and tears may form. These internal reactions have outward signs. For example, sadness is inside you, but you cry or frown on the outside. Anger is inside you, but you may stare and shout at the person you are angry at. Happiness is inside you, but you may smile and laugh on the outside. Feelings are always on the inside. You use outward signs to communicate to other people how you feel inside.

Feelings are the best part of being alive. They are especially wonderful when they are shared with other people. One of the things that makes relationships so rewarding is sharing personal feelings. The more feelings you can have and can share, the better your life will be.

That does not mean that expressing feelings is easy. Sometimes it is very hard. Consider the following two situations. Jane and John are working as dental assistants in the same office. John consistently borrows Jane's dental tools and for-

gets to return them. Jane gets really angry about this, but she does not know how to express her anger to John without ruining their friendship.

Jack is a radio and television service technician. His boss recently asked him to start using a new set of forms for reporting his work. The new forms take much longer to fill out, than did the old forms, and they seem confusing to Jack. They interrupt his work, and he gets angry every time he fills one out. When Jack's boss asks him how he likes the new forms, Jack does not know what to say.

Whenever there is a risk of being rejected or laughed at, expressing feelings becomes very difficult. The closer the feelings are to yourself, the person you are talking with, and your relationship, the greater the risk may feel. This holds true whether you are expressing positive or negative feelings. It's difficult to say, "I love you," if you think you may be laughed at. It's hard to say, "Stop borrowing my tools! You take them but never return them!" if you think the person will hate you forever after. There is nothing easy about communicating feelings, but you have to do it.

It is also difficult to control your feelings. You must often think before you express feelings. Sometimes you may express your feelings too quickly, or you may not think of how to best express the feelings, or you may not think about how to make your feelings appropriate for your situation. For example, you may throw this book out the window before considering how your teacher may feel about your action. You may hit someone before thinking about what appropriate ways of expressing anger in the situation might be. You may cry before considering what the result of such an expression may be.

The constructive expression of your feelings includes both being aware of your feelings and deciding how best to express them. Not expressing your feelings is a bad idea. But expressing your feelings without some thought is also a bad idea.

The purpose of this chapter is to help you gain the skills needed to communicate your feelings constructively. Communicating feelings clearly takes skills, that you *can* develop. By learning the material in this chapter and by practicing, you can become quite skillful in communicating your feelings.

Becoming Aware of Your Feelings*

You cannot enjoy your feelings if you are not aware of them. You cannot express feelings that you refuse to acknowledge. And you cannot communicate feelings that you refuse to accept as your own. To express your feelings, you have to be aware of them, to accept them, and to truly "own" them and know how to communicate them effectively.

Feelings are internal reactions to your experiences. To be aware of your feelings, you have to be aware of how you are reacting to what is currently happening. There are five stages involved in internal reactions:

*This section is based on the excellent treatment of self-awareness in Miller, Nunnally, and Wackman (1975).

1. You gather information about what is going on through your five senses (seeing, hearing, touching, tasting, smelling).
2. You decide what the information means; this is an *interpretation.*
3. You have a feeling based on your interpretation of what the information you sense means.
4. You decide how you want to express your feeling; this is an *intention.*
5. You express your feeling.

An example may help you understand the five aspects of experiencing and expressing a feeling: I see you reading and looking around (*sensing*). I think you must be looking for an excuse to stop for lunch (*interpreting*). I feel sorry that you can't take a break from reading (*feeling*). I want to give you a chance to enjoy yourself for a few minutes (*intending*). So I ask you if you'd like to each lunch with me (*expressing*).

When we are relating to other people, we sense, interpret, feel, intend, and express all at the same time. It all happens faster than you can read a word. *Everything happens so fast that it seems like it is only one step instead of five!* To become aware of each of the five steps, you have to slow the process down. Here is another example that may help: "I hear my boss telling me to sweep the floor (*sensing*). I think he's picking on me again by giving me the dirtiest job he can find (*interpreting*). I get angry (*feeling*) and want to get even with him (*intending*). So I decide to show my displeasure by doing a bad job (*expressing my anger*)."

To express your feelings skillfully and appropriately, you must understand

the five parts of your inside reactions. This is especially true for feelings such as anger, sadness, depression, hopelessness, frustration, and fear. Happiness can just be enjoyed, but anger needs to be understood, so you can get back to a more pleasant state. And expresing anger constructively is much more difficult than expressing happiness. Very few people will be offended if you tell them you are happy, but many people will get offended if you tell them you are angry.

To communicate skillfully, you need to be aware of all five aspects of reacting. This awareness will help you build good relationships. To be able to change your negative feelings to positive ones, you need to be aware of all five aspects of reacting. We now turn, therefore, to discussing each aspect in more detail.

Sensing

The only way you can gather information is through your five senses: seeing, hearing, touching, tasting, and smelling. All information about the world and what is taking place in your life comes to you through one of the five senses. You look, listen, touch, taste, and smell to know what is going on in your life. These senses give you *descriptive* information only. You hear a person's voice get louder. You see a person's frown. You feel his fist hit your nose. You smell and taste the blood dripping from your nose. *Such sensory information only describes what is taking place. It does not give any meaning to what is happening.*

Deciding What It Means: Interpreting

After your senses make you aware of what is going on, you have to decide what the information means. *The information is neutral—you decide what it means.* Interpretations are yours; they take place inside you. They are not in another person's behavior. Different people, for example, interpret the same sensory information quite differently. One coworker may interpret the fact that your voice is loud as meaning that you are angry. Another coworker may decide that your loud voice means that you are nervous. The sensory information (your voice is loud) that they have is the same, but they give it two different meanings.

Your interpretations of what is going on depend on three things:

1. The information you get through your senses
2. What you think is causing the other person's actions
3. The assumptions you make about what is good or bad, what you do or do not need, and what causes what in the world

The information you receive through your senses has already been discussed. So we will now look at deciding what is causing another person's actions. When someone's voice gets louder, you look around to see what's causing it. If you see a huge dog with its teeth sunk in the person's leg, you decide that pain and fear are causing that person's voice to get louder. If, instead, you see someone else tickling him, you interpret the loud voice as indicating happiness. If you notice that the person has just paid $1,000 for a new stereo and it has fallen apart when he picked it up to take it home, you decide his loud voice means he is angry.

What you decide is causing the person's actions will influence your interpretation of the meaning of the information you sense. Let's take another example. You feel pain in your nose. You see that a fist of another person has just landed on your nose. You then decide whether the person intended to hit you, or whether it was an accident. If it was an accident, you will be less angry than if you decide the person did it on purpose. If you decide the person intended to hit you, you then must decide whether he had just cause (perhaps you kicked him) or whether he did not have just cause. All of this happens so fast that for the most part you are not aware that it is going on. Your interpretations follow your gathering of information much faster than a speeding bullet!

Finally, your perspective influences your interpretations. If you *assume* that people are mean and nasty, your interpretation of someone's fist landing on your nose may be biased. You may immediately jump to the conclusion that this is another example of how mean and nasty people are. Or if you *assume* that people are basically gentle and harmless creatures, you may jump to the conclusion that the person hit you accidentally. Your assumptions and your overall perspective have a powerful effect on your interpretations.

It is through your interpretations that you change and control your feelings such as anger, depression, sadness, resentment, fear, and frustration.

Feeling

First you sense. Then you interpret. Then you feel. You decide what the information gathered by your senses means. Your interpretations determine your feelings. Your feelings are a spontaneous reaction to your interpretations. This may be clearer with an example. You hear and see a coworker say, "Hope you're feeling well this morning!" Your feeling about the statement is based on what you decide it means. If you think the coworker is being sarcastic and making fun of you, you will feel angry. If you think he is expressing liking and concern for you, you will feel warmth and appreciation. All this happens immediately and automatically. The important thing to remember is that the coworker's words did not cause your feeling. Your feeling was caused by your interpretation of the meaning of the coworker's statement.

Every feeling you have is based on an interpretation about the meaning of the things you sense. Your feelings are based on your interpretations, not the actions or words of other people. You can, therefore, control what you feel. By changing your interpretations, you can change your feelings. This does not mean that changing your feelings is easy. Most people make interpretations so automatically that it is very difficult to change them. But it can be done if they want to work at it.

Feelings promote an urge to take action. They prepare your body for action. If you feel angry, for example, your muscles get tense and adrenalin is pumped into your bloodstream. Your heart starts to beat faster. All this prepares you for either running away or physically fighting. Feelings activate the systems within your body so they are ready for action.

It is very unhealthy to avoid expressing your feelings, both physically and

psychologically. Yet many people do try to avoid or ignore their feelings. Some people deny that they have feelings. They believe that if they refuse to allow the feeling to come out, the feeling will be controlled. They may think, "What I'm not aware of doesn't exist!" or "What I don't know won't hurt me!" However, when you have a feeling, your body gets ready to express it. If you develop the habit of keeping feelings inside by ignoring or denying them, your body will become very confused. The adrenalin and muscle tension to express anger, for example, will confuse your body if you are smiling and speaking in a friendly way to the person at whom you are angry.

It takes energy to hide your feelings from yourself and others. The more you are aware of your feelings, accept them as yours, and express them to others, the more energy you will have for enjoying yourself and your friendships. It will also help to make communication much easier and clearer.

Feelings will keep trying to be expressed until you express them in a way that ends them. Sadness, for example, can be expressed by crying and talking to an understanding friend. Walking around with a smile on your face will not end the sadness inside you. When you refuse to express your feelings, they start to control you. If you are holding sadness inside, for example, you will begin to avoid anything that makes you sad. When your friends become sad, you will get angry at them. Pretty soon your whole life will be organized around avoiding sadness because you will be afraid your own sadness will come out if you do not.

You *do not* control feelings by holding them inside, by pretending they really don't exist. You *do* control feelings by accepting them as being yours and expressing them. Let them happen—do not fight them or hold them back. Be aware of them and take responsibility for them, because they are yours. Usually things will be OK if you let your feelings take their natural course. It is even helpful to try to feel them more. If you are happy, take it higher. If you are sad, feel it deeply. The important thing is to allow them to exist and to be expressed appropriately. Feelings do not have to be justified, explained, or apologized for. As you become more and more aware of your feelings, you will recognize what they are telling you about yourself and the situation you are in. *You "control" feelings by being aware of them, accepting them, giving them direction, and expressing them appropriately.* And if you are constantly depressed, anxious, or unhappy, you can change your feelings by changing the interpretations you are making.

Feelings activate your body physically so it is ready for action. They urge you to take action to express them. What is lacking is a sense of direction. Should you run? Fight? Hug? Move toward another person? Move away? Feelings get the body ready for action, but they do not provide you with a sense of direction. That is the purpose of your intentions.

Intending

Your senses provide you with information about what is going on. Your interpretations give the information meaning. Your feelings are your reactions to your interpretations. Your *intentions* are your guides to action: They point out how the feelings can be expressed. Your *intentions* are what you want to do to express your feelings. They are your immediate goals, what you *want* to have happen.

Intentions give direction to your feelings. When you decide what you are going to do about your feelings, you are forming an intention. For example, you may intend to

reject	love	play	be caring
cooperate	clarify	help	share
avoid	hurt	demand	understand
praise	persuade	accept	defend yourself
protest	support	resign	try harder

If you are angry, your intentions may be to hurt someone or something. If you are appreciative, your intentions may be to do something kind and caring for someone. If you are sad, your intentions may be to talk with a friend. Your intentions give your feelings a direction in order for them to be expressed.

Intentions are powerful because they have such a big impact on your actions. They organize your actions and identify what you want to do to express your feelings. They guide your actions so your feelings are expressed.

Once you decide how to express your feelings, the next step is to take action and actually express them.

Expressing

To express something, you can say it, act it out, smile, frown, laugh, cry, jump up and down, or run screaming out of the building. Your words and nonverbal actions express your sensations, interpretations, feelings, and intentions. This section of the book is about how to express yourself so you are clearly understood and how to make your expressions appropriate to the situation. Your sensations, interpretations, feelings, and intentions need to be expressed, correctly and appropriately. There are basic skills needed to do so. For the purposes of this chapter, it is the expression of feelings that you need to work on. (You can use the skills covered in the previous chapter to express your sensations, interpretations, and intentions.)

EXERCISE 6.1   **Saying What You Feel***

> ### PURPOSE
>
> Some of the most difficult things to communicate are your feelings. After you recognize a feeling, the next step is usually to express it. There are two purposes of this lesson. The first is to explain how to express your feelings constructively. The second is to give you a chance to practice doing so.
>
> ### PROCEDURE
>
> 1. Divide into groups of three.
> 2. Look at the questionnaire entitled, "Expressing Your Feelings." Working as a group, for Item 1 put a "D" before the sentence that describes the sender's feelings. Put a "No" before the sentence that conveys feelings but does not describe them. You must have full agreement among all three members in order to complete the item.

*Based on an exercise developed by John L. Wallen.

3. Turn to the answers (following the questionnaire). Compare your answer to Item 1 with the answer given. Discuss the correct answer until all three members understand the point being made.

4. Go on to Item 2. Decide as a group on your answers. Then check your answers with the answer given. Discuss the correct answers until all three members understand them. Then go on to Item 3.

5. When you have finished, discuss the material on verbally expressing feelings included in this chapter.

Expressing Your Feelings

1. ____ a. Shut your mouth! Don't say another word!
   ____ b. What you just said really annoys me.

2. ____ a. What's wrong with your eyes? Can't you see I'm trying to work?
   ____ b. I really resent your interrupting me so often while I'm working.
   ____ c. You don't care about anybody else's feelings! You're completely self-centered!

3. ____ a. I feel depressed about some things that happened at work today.
   ____ b. This has been a terrible day at work.

4. ____ a. You're such a wonderful person to work with.
   ____ b. I really respect your ideas. You're so well informed.

5. ____ a. When I work with you, I feel at ease and free to be myself.
   ____ b. We all feel you're really great to work with.
   ____ c. Everyone here at work likes you.

6. ____ a. If things don't get better around here, I'm going to find a new job.
   ____ b. Did you ever see such a rotten place to work?
   ____ c. I'm afraid you will think less of me for asking for help with my job.

7. ____ a. This is a very interesting place to work.
   ____ b. I feel this is a very good place to work.
   ____ c. I get very excited when I'm doing my work.

8. ____ a. I don't feel adequate to contribute to this group.
   ____ b. I am not adequate to contribute anything to this group.

9. ____ a. I'm a born loser. I'll never be able to do anything right.
   ____ b. That training program was terrible. It didn't teach me anything.
   ____ c. I'm depressed because I made some mistakes at work today.

10. ____ a. I feel warm and comfortable working here.
    ____ b. Someone working here always seems to be near when I want company.
    ____ c. I feel most people care that I'm a part of this organization.

Answers to "Expressing Your Feelings"

1. a. No   Commands like these show strong emotion but they do not name the feeling that brought them on.
   b. D   Speaker says she feels annoyed.
2. a. No   Questions like that express strong feelings without naming them.
   b. D   Speaker states he feels resentment.
   c. No   This statement is an accusation that expresses strong negative feelings. Because the feelings are not named, we do not know whether the accusations are based on anger, disappointment, hurt, or some other feeling.
3. a. D   Speaker says he feels depressed.
   b. No   The statement appears to describe what kind of day it was. In fact, it expresses the speaker's negative feelings without saying whether he feels depressed, annoyed, lonely, humiliated, rejected, or whatever.
4. a. No   This value judgment shows positive feelings about the other person. But it does not describe what they are. Does the speaker like, respect, enjoy, admire, love the other person, or what?
   b. D   The speaker describes his positive feelings as respect.
5. a. D   A clear description of how the speaker feels when working with the other person.
   b. No   First, the speaker does not speak for herself. She hides behind the phrase, "We feel." Second, "You're really great" is a value judgment and does not name a feeling.
   c. No   The statement does name a feeling ("likes"), but the speaker is talking for everyone and does not make clear that the feeling is within him. A description of a feeling must contain the words *I, me, my,* or *mine* to make clear that the feelings are within the speaker. Does it seem more friendly for a person to say, "I like you" or "Everybody likes you"?
6. a. No   This statement shows negative feelings by talking about the conditions of the job. It does not describe the speaker's inner feelings.
   b. No   This is a question that expresses a negative value judgment about the place where she works. It does not describe what the speaker is feeling.
   c. D   This is a clear description of how the speaker feels about his job—afraid. Expressions a and b are criticisms that could come from the type of fear described in c.

Negative criticisms and value judgments often seem like expressions of anger. Actually, they often stem from the speaker's fear, hurt feelings, loneliness, or disappointments.

7. a. No   This statement is a positive value judgment that shows positive feelings. But it does not state what type of feelings they are.

    b. No   Although the person begins by saying, "I feel . . . ," he does not then name what he is feeling. Instead, he makes a positive value judgment on the place where he works. Note that merely placing the words *I feel* in front of a statement does not make the statement a description of feeling. People often say "I feel" when they mean "I think" or "I believe." There is no difference between "I feel you don't like me" and "I believe (think) you don't like me."

    c. D   The speaker describes his feelings of excitement when he is working. Many times people who are unaware of or deny what they feel state value judgments. They do not recognize that this is the way their positive or negative feelings get expressed. Many arguments can be avoided if we are careful to describe our feelings instead of expressing them through value judgments. For example, if Joe says his job is interesting and Fred says it is boring, they may argue about which it "really" is. If Joe, however, says he is excited by the job and Fred says he is frustrated by it, no argument should follow. Each person's feelings are what they are. Of course, discussing why each person feels as he does may provide helpful information about him and about the job itself.

8. a. D   Speaker says he feels inadequate.

    b. No   Careful! This sounds much the same as the first statement. It says, however, that the speaker actually *is* inadequate—not just that he feels inadequate. The speaker has evaluated and labeled himself as inadequate.

    This small difference was introduced because many people confuse feeling and being. A person may feel too inadequate to contribute in a group, yet may make helpful contributions. Similarly, he may feel adequate, yet may perform very inadequately. A person may feel hopeless about a situation that turns out to be solved by his behavior.

    A sign of emotional maturity may be that a person does not confuse what he feels with the real situation around him. Such people know they can perform adequately, even though they feel inadequate to complete the task. Such people do not let their feelings keep them from doing their best. They know the difference between feelings and performance—that the two do not always match.

9. a. No   The speaker has evaluated himself. He passed a negative self-judgment by labeling himself a born loser.

    b. No   Instead of labeling himself a failure, the speaker blames the training program. This is another value judgment and not a description of feeling.

    c. D   The speaker says he feels depressed. Statements a and c show the important difference betwen passing judgment on yourself and describing your feelings.

Feelings can and do change. To say that you are now depressed does not mean that you will or must always feel that way. If you label yourself a born loser, however, or if you truly think of yourself as a born loser, you are likely to act like a born loser. One girl stated this important insight for herself this way, "I have always thought I was a shy person. Many new things I really would have liked to do I avoided. I would tell myself that I was too shy. Now I have discovered that I am not a shy person, although at times I *feel* shy." Many of us try to avoid new things, and thus avoid growing, by labeling ourselves. For example, someone may say, "I'm not artistic," "I'm not creative," "I'm not a good public speaker," or "I can't speak in groups." If we could recognize what our feelings are beneath such statements, maybe we would be more willing to risk doing things we are somewhat fearful of.

10. a. D   The speaker says he feels warm and comfortable.
    b. No   This statement expresses positive feelings, but it does not say whether he feels happy, warm, useful, supported, or what.
    c. No   Instead of "I feel," the speaker should have said, "I believe." The last part of the statement really tells what the speaker believes the others feel about him. It does not tell what the speaker feels. Expressions c and a relate to each other as follows: "Because I believe that most people care whether I am a part of this organization, I feel warm and comfortable."

Telling It the Way It Is

Feelings demand to be expressed. To express your feelings, you have to be aware of them and accept them as yours. And you have to know how to communicate them in a useful way. There are both direct, skillful, and indirect, harmful ways of expressing your feelings. Consider the following examples:

1. *Labels:* "You are rude, hostile, and self-centered!" versus "When you interrupt me, I get angry."
2. *Commands:* "Drive slower!" versus "When you drive like this, I get scared."
3. *Questions:* "Are you always this crazy?" versus "You are acting strangely and I feel worried."
4. *Accusations:* "You don't care about me!" versus "When you don't pay attention to me, I feel left out."
5. *Sarcasm:* "I'm glad you're early!" versus "You're late, and now I will feel embarrassed about arriving at my meeting late."
6. *Approval:* "You're wonderful!" versus "I like you."
7. *Disapproval:* "You're terrible!" versus "I don't like you."

Indirect ways of expressing feelings are common. But they are destructive. Indirect ways of expressing feelings do not give a clear message: The receiver is uncertain as to how you really feel, and the receiver usually feels "put down" by the remarks. We are taught how to describe our *ideas* clearly and correctly, but we are rarely taught how to describe our *feelings* clearly and correctly! We express our feelings, but we usually do not try to name and verbally describe our feelings. Here are four ways you can describe a feeling:

1. *Identify or name it:* "I feel angry;" "I feel embarrassed;" "I feel liking for you."
2. *Use comparisons:* Because we do not have enough names or labels to describe all our feelings, we make up comparisons to describe them: "I feel stepped on;" "I feel like I'm on Cloud Nine;" "I feel like I've just been run over by a truck."
3. *Report what kind of action the feeling urges you to do:* "I feel like hugging you;" "I feel like slapping your face;" "I feel like walking all over you."
4. *Use sayings to tell how you feel:* "I feel like God is smiling on me;" "I feel like a pebble on the beach."

You describe your feelings by identifying them. A description of a feeling must include:

1. A personal statement—that is, refer to *I, me, my,* or *mine*
2. A feeling name, comparison, action, urge, or saying

Any statement you make can show feelings. Even the comment, "It's a warm day," can be said so that it expresses resentment, anger, or joy. Expressing your feelings in ways that confuse people will make it hard to build and keep good relationships. Showing feelings by using commands, "put-downs," accusations, or judgments will tend to confuse your fellow workers. Describing your feelings will not. Describing your feelings skillfully is a must for useful communication.

When you describe your feelings, two things will usually happen. First, you will become more aware of what it is you really feel. Often your feelings may not be very clear to you. By trying to describe them to a fellow employee, you make your feelings clear to both yourself and others. Second, describing your feelings often starts a conversation that will improve your relationship with the other person. If a fellow employee is to react to your feelings, he must know what your feelings are. Even if your feelings are not pleasant, it is often helpful to express them. Negative feelings are signs that something may be going wrong in the working relationship. By describing your feelings, you give information necessary for understanding and improving your relationship.

Kicking the Wall

There will be times when you are furious or when you are deeply depressed, sad, or upset. And there will be times when you cannot express your feelings directly to the people who are helping cause them. If your boss is very insecure, for example, you may not be able to express anger toward him directly. In fact, there are

very few bosses in this world who will accept direct expressions of anger with true understanding.

When you have feelings you cannot express directly, you do need to find indirect ways of expressing them. This does not mean expressing them through commands, accusations, and "put-downs." It means going home and kicking the wall.

Feelings do need to be expressed. The stronger the feeling, the stronger the need for expression. In the privacy of your home, you can swear at your boss, hit a punching bag, or swim hard while imagining what you would like to say to a certain coworker.

The important thing is to express negative feelings in a way that ends them. You do not want to stay angry or depressed forever. The sooner you get rid of the negative feelings, the happier your life will be. Getting rid of them *indirectly* usually involves one or more of the following:

1. Engaging in physical activity, such as hitting a pillow, jogging, swimming, tennis, basketball, volleyball, handball, or even ping pong.

2. Strongly expressing the feeling by yelling, swearing, crying, or moaning.

3. Resolving the situation in your mind or resigning yourself to it. Give up thoughts of revenge and getting back at other people. You want to resolve

the problems. You can put up with an unfair boss. An obnoxious coworker is not really that bad. Let the negative feelings go. Do not hang on to them. They will only make your life unpleasant.

Do not forget to get rid of little frustrations and irritants as well as big ones. Small feelings, if they are kept inside and allowed to build up, become big feelings. You may explode in an overreaction someday if you store up all your little frustrations and annoyances. It is easier to express your feelings openly when they are small. That is the time to get rid of them. Do not let them build up.

EXERCISE 6.2   **Actions Speak Louder than Words**

PURPOSE

It takes more than words to communicate feelings clearly. It also takes nonverbal or unspoken messages. You need to be skillful in both verbal and nonverbal communication to express feelings clearly. Often nonverbal messages are more important than spoken messages in communicating feelings. *Nonverbal messages* include facial expressions, tone of voice, eye contact, gestures, manner of dress, posture, touch, and the rate, duration, and pauses in our speech. Especially important for expressing feelings are facial expressions and tone of voice. The purpose of this lesson is to give you a chance to practice nonverbal communication of feelings.

PROCEDURE

1. In your group, sit on the floor in a circle. Do not use a table. Deal out a deck of ordinary playing cards until everyone has the same number of cards and there are at least three cards left in the draw deck. The draw deck is placed face down in the center of the circle.

2. The winner of the game is the person who gets rid of all his cards first. You get rid of your cards by correctly identifying the feelings expressed by other group members and by accurately communicating feelings to the other group members.

3. Group members take turns expressing one feeling. To begin, the person on the dealer's left selects a card from his own hand and lays it face down in front of him. This person is now the expresser. The remaining group members are to identify the feeling he expresses correctly. The expresser then nonverbally expresses the feeling on the card. The feelings each card represents are listed in Item 9. The other people check their hands to see if they have a card that matches the feeling that was expressed. If so, they place the card(s) face down in front of them. If not, they pass.

4. When all the cards are down for the first round, they are all turned

face up at the same time. If one or more of the receivers have matched the expresser's card, the expresser puts his card and all the matching cards face down on the bottom of the draw deck.

5. Any group member who put down a wrong card must return it to his hand and draw an additional penalty card from the top of the draw deck. You draw the same number of penalty cards from the draw deck as the number of cards you put down in front of you.

6. If no other group member matched the expresser's card, then the expresser failed to communicate and he returns the card to his hand and draws a penalty card from the draw deck. In this case, the other people return their cards to their hands but *do not* draw penalty cards.

7. When you have two or three cards representing the same feeling, you must play all the cards if you play one of them. If you have several Queens, for example, you must play all of them if you play Queens at all. So, as expresser or receiver, you may get rid of two or three cards. Or you may have to draw two or three penalty cards.

8. The expresser may use any nonverbal or unspoken behavior he wishes to in order to communicate the feeling he is portraying accurately, except the use of words and sounds. No words may be spoken or sounds made. You may wish to use your hands, your head, your whole body, and you may involve other group members by touching them or engaging them in a nonverbal interchange.

9. Each card represents a different feeling:

2	=	contentment
3	=	shyness
4	=	indifference
5	=	fear
6	=	frustration
7	=	loneliness
8	=	sorrow
9	=	anger
10	=	hope
Jack	=	happiness
Queen	=	joy
King	=	warmth
Ace	=	love
Joker	=	admiration

10. Read the material on nonverbal communication and discuss it in your group.

Saying It Without Words: Nonverbal Messages

Linda and Sam have worked together in a hospital lab for two years. One day Sam asked Linda if she would like to have dinner with him on Friday. Linda smiled and walked away without answering. How would you feel if you were Sam? What did Linda mean? What was she feeling?

It is often difficult to know what another person really feels. People often say one thing but then do another. Someone may seem to like you but never say so. A person can say she has great affection for you, but somehow you do not feel she really means it.

There is a major problem in communicating feelings. Feelings are communicated less by the words a person uses than by nonverbal messages. Because nonverbal messages are open to several interpretations, feelings are often misunderstood. Nonverbal messages are harder to understand than are words. The same feeling can be expressed nonverbally several different ways. Anger can be expressed by jumping up and down or by a frozen stillness. Happiness can be expressed through laughter or tears. Any single nonverbal cue can express a variety of feelings. A blush may show embarrassment, pleasure, nervousness, or even anger. Crying can be caused by sadness, happiness, excitement, grief, pain, or confusion.

Another problem with nonverbal messages is that different people have been taught to interpret the same nonverbal message differently. Standing close to a person may be a sign of warmth to one person. It may be a sign of forwardness and boldness to another person. Anger may be seen as a sign of dislike by one person. It may be seen as a sign of caring to another person. In understanding nonverbal messages, you must decide what the messages mean. Because nonverbal messages are not always clear-cut, the chance for misunderstandings is always present.

Correctly understanding the feelings of your fellow employees is especially difficult when verbal and nonverbal messages do not agree. Sometimes different amounts of feeling are expressed at the same time through verbal and nonverbal messages. The person can say, "I really love you more than anyone else on earth," but his voice may be only luke-warm. Sometimes opposite feelings are expressed at the same time through verbal and nonverbal messages. The boss who screams, "I WANT IT QUIET AROUND THIS PLACE!" and the salesperson who says, "I've always got plenty of time to talk to a customer," while glancing at his watch and nervously beginning to close the store are examples. Sometimes a coworker says, "I like you," in a cold tone of voice while looking worried and backing away. His nonverbal messages are "Don't come close to me." *When receiving conflicting messages, we tend to believe the message that is hardest to fake. That is usually the nonverbal message.* People are more apt to believe your nonverbal messages than your verbal messages.

Your appearance is one of your most important nonverbal messages when you are applying for a job. You may say verbally, "You can trust me with responsibility." But if your appearance is sloppy and unkempt the nonverbal message may be, "I can't even be trusted to dress myself appropriately." The way you dress, the way your hair is cut, the neatness of your appearance, and your cleanliness are all nonverbal messages to the employer. These nonverbal messages are under your control. Before you interview for a job, you should think clearly about what you want to communicate nonverbally to your potential employer. Then your appearance should reflect the messages you want to send.

In summary, nonverbal messages are more powerful in expressing feelings than are words. But they are also more difficult to understand correctly. To communicate your feelings clearly to fellow employees, you need to be skilled in both verbal and nonverbal ways of expressing feelings. Above all, you need to make sure your words and your nonverbal messages agree with each other.

○   ○   ○

I had one gentleman the other day, and he wanted an outside call. I asked his name and room number, which we have to charge for his room. And he says, "What's it to you?" I said, "I'm sorry, sir this is our policy." And he gets a little hostile. But you just take it with a grain of salt, and you just keep on working. Inside you and in your head, you get mad. But you still have to be nice when the next call comes in. There's no way to let it out.

Frances Swenson, Hotel Switchboard Operator
In STUDS TERKEL, *Working*

○   ○   ○

EXERCISE 6.3   **Understanding Your Anger**

PURPOSE

Being aware of your feelings is an important and sometimes difficult task. Many of us were taught to hide our feelings. We learned to pretend we did not have them. This is especially true of feelings we consider negative, such as anger. We often keep our anger inside and act as if it were not there. We often deny to ourselves that we are angry. In order to be aware of your anger, so it is expressed appropriately, you must understand what makes you angry. Then, hopefully, you will be more aware of your angry feelings in the future.

PROCEDURE

1. Working alone, on a separate sheet of paper, write out your answers to the statements listed below.
2. In your group, discuss the answers of each member to the first statement. Then go on to the second statement.
3. After you have finished discussing all sixteen statements, write down:
   a. The five major things that make your group members angry on the job.
   b. The five major ways in which your group members express their anger.

c. Five major conclusions about what happens when anger is expressed on the job.

4. Your instrutor will have each group share their conclusions with the whole class.

5. In your group, discuss how your conclusions compared with the conclusions of the other groups. Does everyone feel anger for the same reasons? Does everyone express their anger in the same way? Does everyone feel the same way when someone is angry at them? Does everyone think that the same consequences will result from expressing anger at work?

Statements

Complete the following statements. Be specific. Try to think of times when you were angry or someone was angry at you. If you are not now working, you may wish to substitute "fellow students" for "coworkers" and "teacher or parent" for "boss."

1. I feel angry when my coworkers . . .
2. When I'm angry at my coworkers, I usually . . .
3. After expressing my anger, I feel . . .
4. The way I express anger usually makes my coworkers . . .
5. When my coworkers express anger toward me, I feel . . .
6. When I feel that way (Item 5), I usually . . .
7. After reacting to my coworkers' anger, I feel . . .
8. My reactions to my coworkers' anger usually result in their . . .
9. I feel angry when my boss . . .
10. When I'm angry at my boss, I usually . . .
11. The way I act when I'm angry at my boss makes me feel . . .
12. The way I act when I'm angry at my boss usually results in my boss . . .
13. When my boss expresses anger at me, I feel . . .
14. When I feel that way (Item 13), I usually . . .
15. After reacting to my boss's anger, I feel . . .
16. My reactions to my boss's anger usually result in my boss . . .

Sometimes you get mad. Why should this man be yelling at me? I do feel put down a lot.

Heather Lamb, Long-Distance Operator
in STUDS TERKEL, *Working*

Expressing Anger

John works as a mechanic. On Tuesday, he is sick and stays home. On Wednesday, he comes to work to find several of his tools missing. He is told that Sam borrowed them. John asks for his tools back and Sam cannot find them. Sam looks everywhere but cannot remember what he did with them. John is angry. What should he say? What should he do? Does he have a good reason to be angry?

Alice repairs television sets. On Tuesday, she repairs a set. On Friday, the customer brings it back and says it has not been repaired properly. Alice's boss tells Alice either she shapes up or he is shipping her out. Alice sits down to recover from her boss's statements when Ann walks by, trips, and spills coffee on Alice's

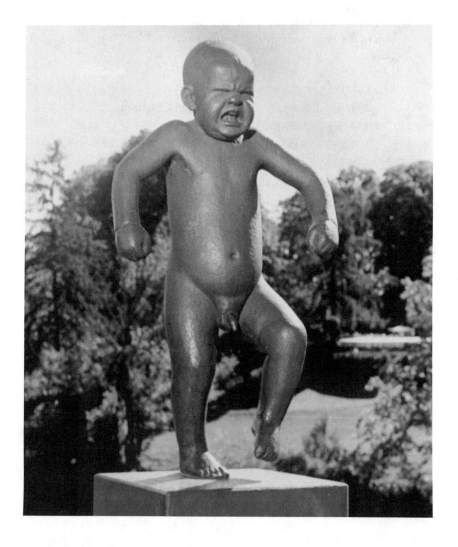

shoes. Alice is furious! What should she say? What should she do? Does she have a good reason to be angry? Who is she really angry at?

No matter how good-natured you are, there will be times when you get angry at your fellow employees or customers. Sometimes you will have to express your anger in order to be honest. At other times, you may wish to keep your anger to yourself. Sometimes you will have a good reason for being angry, and sometimes not.

○   ○   ○

I was angry with my friend:
I told my wrath, my wrath did end.
I was angry with my foe:
I told it not, my wrath did grow.

WILLIAM BLAKE

○   ○   ○

Being skillful in expressing anger is one of the hardest things for most people to do. In forming and maintaining relationships with fellow employees, it is important that you can express anger toward them and that they can express anger toward you. Anger is a sign that something is going on that needs to be changed. It is only through facing such problems that they can be solved. Being angry and having it help solve a problem builds the trust between you and your fellow employees. Knowing that the relationship is strong enough to handle future strains adds to the confidence you can have in your fellow employees. Many times, relationships are strengthened by an open discussion of why people are angry.

Don't Say It—Keep Me in the Dark!

So many people are uncomfortable with their feelings that they become afraid when another starts expressing his or her feelings. Many people have never learned that it is normal to have feelings, that feelings can be expressed constructively. And many people try so hard to keep their feelings inside that their feelings control them rather than they control their feelings.

There are difficulties in expressing feelings on the job. One is the mistaken belief that to be mature, you have to ignore your feelings. Nothing is further from the truth. You ability to solve problems improves as all the needed information (including feelings) is put on the table and discussed. Not being aware of your feelings makes for biased judgments. Not discussing them makes for biased actions. When feelings are not expressed and discussed, work relationships often fall apart.

Many people will ask you to ignore your feelings. They will tell you, "Don't feel that way." If you say, "I feel depressed," they will say, "Cheer up!" If you say, "I'm angry," they say, "Simmer down." If you say, "I feel great," they say, "The roof will cave in any moment now." All of these replies communicate, "Don't feel that way. Quick, change your feeling!"

In any relationship, it takes some time to develop the trust needed for easy communication of feelings. Some of your fellow employees will be very poor in expressing feelings. They may not want you to express yours. But with time, if you communicate your feelings, you will quiet their fears. Feelings are important information about relationships. And it is important that you express your feelings.

There are other difficulties with expressing feelings. There are difficulties in being aware of your feelings. There are difficulties with accepting some feelings as your own. Feelings of jealousy, envy, and greed are examples of this. Then there are beliefs that feelings should be private. "Men don't cry." "Women don't raise their voices, slam doors, or swear." Most of us have been taught to act in certain ways that limit the expression of our feelings. Many of us have been taught to keep our feelings to ourselves.

Expressing feelings is often risky. When you tell someone what your feelings are directly, they may put you down. They may laugh at or ridicule your feelings. Expressing feelings makes you vulnerable to rejection and to being seen as silly, weak, odd, unusual, or weird.

In spite of all these difficulties, life will be better if you describe your feelings directly when the time is right. You will learn to know yourself better if you do. And it will help your fellow employees get to know you as a unique person.

Feelings, Fun, and Health

Fully experiencing your feelings is the best part of being alive. Yet many people have been taught to ignore their feelings, to deny that they exist, and to try to keep them inside. Many people also express their feelings too quickly. They act before they think of the best way to express their feelings in the present situation.

One of the most important aspects of psychological and physical health is (1) being aware of your feelings, (2) accepting them as your own, (3) understanding how your interpretations are causing your feelings, and (4) being able to express your feelings clearly and appropriately. If you do not handle your feelings constructively, you will not be able to handle problems and conflicts with other people. Furthermore, migraine headaches, ulcers, colitis, and other physical problems can be caused by not being able to handle your feelings in healthy ways. In order to really enjoy yourself, keep yourself psychologically and physically healthy, and survive on the job, you need healthy ways of managing feelings.

Just for your own self-understanding, answer the following questions. Then write a description of how you usually handle your feelings.

EXERCISE 6.4   **Self-Awareness Check: How I Manage My Feelings**

Each of the following five questions has two parts. On a separate sheet of paper, select one of the two answers, "a" or "b," that best fits you. Think about each question carefully. Be honest. No one will see your answers. The results are simply for your own self-awareness.

1. ____ a. I am fully aware of what I am sensing in the present situation.
   ____ b. I ignore what I am sensing by thinking about the past or the future.

2. ____ a. I understand the interpretations I usually make about other people's actions. I work to be aware of the interpretations I am making.
   ____ b. I deny that I make any interpretations about what I sense. I insist that I do not interpret someone's behavior as being mean. The person *is* mean.

3. ____ a. I accept my feeling as being part of me. I turn my full awareness on it. I try to feel it fully. I keep asking myself, "What am I feeling now?"
   ____ b. I reject and ignore my feeling. I deny my feeling by telling myself and others, "But I'm not feeling anything at all." I avoid people and situations that might make me more aware of my feelings.

4. ____ a. I decide how I want to express my feeling. I think of what I want to result from the expression of my feelings. I think of what is an appropriate way to express the feeling in the present situation. I review the sending skills in my mind.
   ____ b. Since I've never admitted to having a feeling, I don't need to decide how to express it! When my feelings burst, I am too emotional to remember good sending skills.

5. ____ a. I express my feelings appropriately and clearly. Usually, this means describing my feeling directly. It also means using nonverbal messages to back up my words. My words and my nonverbal messages communicate the same feeling.
   ____ b. I express my feelings inappropriately and in confusing ways. Usually, this means indirectly through commands, accusations, "put downs," and evaluations. I may express feelings physically in destructive ways. I shout at people, push or hit them, avoid people, or refuse to look at them or speak to them. I may hug them, put my arm around them, give them gifts, or try to do favors for them. My words and my nonverbal messages often contradict each other. I sometimes smile and act friendly toward people I'm angry at. Or I may avoid people I care a great deal for.

Checking It Out

Feelings are inside. We can only tell what people are feeling from their outward actions and their words. Outward actions include smiles, frowns, shouting, tears, running away, and laughter. From outward actions and words, we get impressions of how people feel. When someone describes his feelings to us, we usually accept his feelings to be what that person says they are. But if someone expresses feelings indirectly (such as through sarcasm) or nonverbally (such as through a frown), we need to clarify how they actually feel. We may be unsure of how they feel. Or we may think we know how they feel. But we may be wrong. Before we respond to a person's feelings, we need to check to make sure we really know how he actually feels.

The best way to check out whether or not you understand how a person is feeling is through a perception check. A *perception check* has three parts:

1. You describe what you think the other person's feelings are.
2. You ask whether or not your perception is correct.
3. You do not express approval or disapproval of the feelings.

"You look sad. Are you?" is an example of a perception check. It describes how you think the person is feeling. Then it asks the person to agree with or correct your perception. And it does both without saying the feeling is either right or wrong. A perception check is asking, "I want to understand your feeling. Is this the way you feel?" It is an invitation for the person to describe his feelings more directly. It shows you care enough about the person to want to understand his feelings.

In conflicts, it is especially important to check out your impressions of the other person's feelings. There are often misperceptions about feelings in conflicts. Before you blast a coworker out of the saddle for being angry at you, be sure to clarify that he really is angry at *you*.

Checking out your impressions is an important communication skill. Our perceptions of how others are feeling are often affected by our own feelings. Our fears, present feelings, and expectations all influence our impressions of other people's feelings. If we are afraid of anger, and expect people to be angry, we may think they are angry when they are not. If we feel guilty, we may think other people are angry and about to punish us. How we perceive other people's feelings is often inaccurate. It is important to check out our impressions and make sure they are correct.

EXERCISE 6.5   **Perception Checks**

> *PURPOSE*
>
> It is important to make sure you correctly understand how other people are feeling. If they do not describe their feelings directly, you will have to figure out how they are feeling from their actions, facial expressions, posture, gestures, and so forth. When you have decided what they are feeling, you will

have to check it out. Checking out what we think other people are feeling is important as we often misperceive other people's feelings. We need to modify any incorrect impressions before we respond. The purpose of this lesson is to give you a chance to tell the difference between good perception checks and other types of statements.

PROCEDURE

1. Working alone, read each of the statements listed below. On a separate sheet of paper, write your answers. Put "PC" for each good perception check and put a "No" for all other statements.

2. Review your answers for the poor perception checks. Decide on a reason why the statement is a poor perception check. Put a "J" for each statement that makes a judgment. Put an "O" for a statement that speaks for the other person. Put a "Q" for each question that does not include a description of one's perceptions of the other's feelings.

3. In your group, review the answers of each member for each statement. Discuss any disagreements until all members agree on the answer. Compare your group's answers with the correct answers given in Appendix B. Discuss any statements the group missed.

Statements

_____ 1. Are you angry with me?

_____ 2. You look like you are upset about what Sally said. Are you?

_____ 3. Why are you mad at me?

_____ 4. You look like you feel put down by my statement. That's stupid!

_____ 5. What is it about your boss that makes you resent her so much?

_____ 6. Are your feelings hurt again?

_____ 7. You look unhappy. Are you?

_____ 8. Am I right that you feel disappointed that nobody commented on your suggestions?

_____ 9. Why on earth would you get upset about that? That's pretty crazy!

_____ 10. I get the impression you are fairly happy with my work. Are you?

_____ 11. Are your feelings hurt again?

_____ 12. If you are dumb enough to get angry about that, the hell with you!

_____ 13. You're always happy!

_____ 14. I'm not sure whether your expression means that I'm confusing you or hurting your feelings. Which one is it?

_____ 15. Half time you're laughing. The other half of the time you're staring off into space. What's going on?

Feelings and Friendships

We all want our fellow employees to like us. We all want to develop friends on the job. How you express your feelings will make a difference as to how well you are liked. People have negative reactions to feelings expressed indirectly. Feelings expressed through labels, commands, questions, accusations, sarcasm, and judgments will tend to turn fellow employees off. The more you avoid these indirect ways of expressing your feelings, the more you will be liked.

The direct expression of positive feelings will help build friendships. The more you directly communicate warmth, support, and liking for your fellow employees, the more you will be liked. They will tend to see you as being trustworthy, accepting, and understanding. They will think you have beliefs and values similar to theirs. The direct expression of warmth is one of the most powerful ways there is of building friendships.

Even the direct expression of negative feelings will build trust and respect. A coworker who will be honest with you is usually preferred to one who will cover up negative feelings. Being honest about your feelings helps build the trust needed for friendship and respect to develop.

Besides being skillful in describing your feelings, you need to like others. We tend to like people who like us, and people we dislike tend to dislike us. I once worked with a person named Dave. Dave disliked everyone. He would go around saying his fellow employees were "a bunch of creeps," "really stupid," "so ignorant I can't believe it," and "completely inferior to me." Yet Dave was deeply hurt when he was not liked! He expected his fellow employees to like and admire him!

Want to be liked by your fellow employees? Then like them. And directly communicate your warm feelings toward them.

Drugs and Feelings

Some people think that unpleasant feelings are an illness that can be cured by the use of drugs. How many times a day are you told in advertisements that if you have an unpleasant feeling you should take a drug to change it? If someone gives us a headache, what are we told to do about it? Take an aspirin! If we are tense about work and cannot sleep, what are we told to do about it? Take a sleeping pill! If we are angry and upset at one of our coworkers, what are we told to do about it? Take a tranquilizer to calm us down! Whether the drug is aspirin, alcohol, cigarettes, coffee, antidepressants, tranquilizers, sleep inducers, or even cold medicine, we are told over and over again to take drugs. The underlying message in all the advertisements for drugs is that the easiest way to change your unpleasant feelings is to take a drug.

Drugs can change your feelings for a short period of time. They can help you forget your problems. They *cannot* help you solve your problems. Conflicts with your boss will not be solved by taking sleeping pills. A disagreement with your coworkers will not be solved by getting drunk. A pain-killer will not increase your liking for your job. You can take a drug to cheer you up on Monday and find yourself still depressed on Tuesday. The cause of unpleasant feelings (with a few rare exceptions) is not the chemistry of your body. Usually, the causes are problems in your relationships. It is only through improving your relationships that you feelings will be changed permanently. *Popping a pill may be easy, but it is not an answer to changing unpleasant feelings!*

Some Major Points on Expressing Feelings

Suggestions for Good Sending

1. Describe your feelings by name, comparison, action, or figure of speech.
2. Describe what you think the other person is feeling. Then ask whether or not you are correct.
3. Make your nonverbal messages communicate what you want them to.
4. Make sure your nonverbal and verbal messages communicate the same thing.

General Suggestions

1. When two people avoid discussing an issue, the issue will reappear in a different form. You cannot avoid conflicts. Open discussion of conflicts is the best way.
2. Being angry and upset, refusing to listen, and being defensive, while often justifiable responses, do not help resolve conflicts. These do not help the relationship continue or get stronger.
3. Feelings that are ignored or denied will come out later in one way or another. Build healthy habits to manage your feelings.

7

Controlling Your Feelings

After completing the Questionnaire that follows, you should be able to define and give examples of

- Irrational assumption
- Rational assumption

The answers are given on the right side of the page. Work with a partner and keep the answers covered until you have agreed on your response. Remember to check each answer before going on to the next item, as explained on page 1.

1. An *irrational assumption* is a belief that makes you depressed or upset most of the time and that is accepted as true without any proof. A belief that you assume is true and that makes you unhappy and anxious most of the time is an _____ _____.

   irrational assumption

2. "I must be absolutely perfect all the time or else I will be destroyed," is an example of an _____ _____.

   irrational assumption

3. A *rational assumption* is a belief that leads to a valid and accurate interpretation of one's experiences and, thereby, to appropriate feelings. A belief that promotes a valid and accurate interpretation of one's experiences is a _____ _____.

   rational assumption

4. "It would be nice if I were perfect, but I can live with and recover from my mistakes," is an example of a _____ _____.

   rational assumption

How Does Your Work Make You Feel?

How does your work make you feel? Do you enjoy getting up in the morning? Do you spring out of bed ready for a great day at work? Do you look forward to getting back on the job? Or, are you like Todd? Todd is always depressed, worried, or angry about his job. Ask him how he is at 10:03 in the morning, and he will say, "Depressed about my job." Ask him how he is at 3:34 in the afternoon, and he will say, "Worried about my work." Ask him how he is at 9:47 in the evening, and he will say, "Angry about my job." Wake him at 2:23 in the morning and ask him how he is, and he will say, "Anxious about my career."

There are lots of things that can depress you about work. Being treated like an object by the organization you work for, rather than being treated like a person, can be depressing. Not doing your job as well as you want to and not being liked by your fellow employees can really be sources of anxiety. Being told to hurry up and work faster constantly can make you angry. Finding out that your organization is going bankrupt and that you will lose your job can be demoralizing. Being caught in a traffic jam on the way to work and missing an important meeting can be a source of worry, frustration, and anger. Not getting a raise or promotion can be depressing. There are lots of things that can happen on a job that can result in your feeling depressed, worried, anxious, angry, frustrated, helpless, powerless, and tense.

Everyone will be depressed about work or angry at the people they work with occasionally. If the feelings are dealt with constructively, they will not last very long. But if you have destructive patterns of interpreting what is happening in your life, you can be depressed and upset all the time. You can even turn small events into tragedies. You could, for example, react as if a coworker's not liking you was as serious as finding out you have incurable cancer. There are pepole who are talented at taking a small event that occasionally happens, and creating major feelings of depression or anger that stay with them for several days or weeks.

How you feel is important for your enjoyment of life and for your ability to work cooperatively and productively. If you are depressed, angry, worried, and anxious about your career, job, and relationships with fellow employees, then you need to take some sort of action. You need to get rid of negative feelings and to promote positive feelings, such as happiness, contentment, pride, and satisfaction.

To change negative or destructive feelings, you have two choices. You can try to change things outside of yourself. You can change jobs, friends, location, and careers. Your second choice is to change things within yourself. You can change your interpretations of what is happening in your life. As we discussed in the previous chapter, changing your interpretations will change your feelings. In choosing whether to try to change something outside of yourself or inside yourself, it is important to remember what psychologists say: *The easiest thing to change in your life is yourself.*

Let's take an example. Sam believes his boss is always picking on him. He thinks that his boss gives him the dirtiest jobs to do. Sam thinks that his coworkers are not required to work as hard as he is. The boss always seems to be criticizing Sam, but not criticizing Sam's coworkers. All this makes Sam angry, depressed, worried, and frustrated. Sam also feels that the situation is hopeless. "What can I do?" says Sam. "My boss has all the power. He can fire me, but I can't do anything to him."

Sam has two choices: He can try to change his boss, or he can try to change his feelings. Psychologists would tell Sam that it is easier to change his feelings than to change his boss. What do you think?

Disposable Feeling: Like It or Dump It

Do you remember the five stages of expressing a feeling that we discussed in Chapter 6? They are:

1. Gathering information through your fives senses
2. Interpreting what the information means
3. Experiencing the feelings appropriate to your interpretations
4. Deciding how you intend to express your feelings
5. Expressing your feelings

It is your interpretations that cause your feelings, not the things going on in your

life. Feelings are not caused by events and people around you; they are caused by the ways in which you interpret your experiences. Your boss cannot upset you—only the interpretations you make about your boss' behavior can upset you. Your coworkers cannot upset you; only the interpretations you make about your coworkers' behavior can upset you. This means that you can control your feelings. You can decide which feelings you would like to keep and expand. You can decide which feelings you would like to dump and get rid of. Your feelings are disposable!

TIPS ON SURVIVAL: HOW TO LIVE A LONG LIFE

Want to live a long time? Research studies on survival in concentration camps, prisoner of war camps, cancer and heart disease victims, and old age have found five factors that seem to be the most important for survival:

1. *Having deeply held goals and commitments.* These goals and commitments need to involve relationships with other people. People who lived the longest in concentration and prisoner of war camps, for example, were people who turned their concern outward and worked to help other people survive.
2. *Sharing your distress with other people.* Quiet, polite, passive, accepting, and well-behaved persons often die early. A person who openly shares her suffering with other people and is aggressive in getting her needs met will tend to live longer.
3. *High morale is important.* Depression kills. In concentration and in POW camps and among cancer patients, people who become depressed often die.
4. *Physical activity is an important survival factor.* Keeping yourself physically active will help you live longer.
5. *Friendships and love relationships are vital.* Lonely people often die early. Isolated people often die early. People with good friends and loving relationships survive longer. Many psychologists believe that loneliness is the biggest personal adjustment problem in the United States.

If you want to live a long and happy life, therefore, build goals and commitments that are important to you and that involve other people's welfare. Share your moments of distress and discomfort with other people. Learn how to talk with other people about how you feel. Avoid depression and keep your morale high. Keep physically active. And constantly build and renew friendships and love relationships. We will all die someday. Let us work to see that we do not die from lack of commitments, depression, inactivity, or loneliness rather than from disease or accident.

Depending on your interpretations, you can feel satisfaction, pride, enjoyment, fun, contentment, and challenge about your career. Or you can feel depressed, anxious, worried, angry, sad, hopeless, and helpless. When your interpretations result in feelings that contribute to a painful and troubled life, you are managing your feelings destructively. When you have feelings like depression and

anxiety, your work suffers, the people around you suffer, and you are just no fun to be around. Surviving work means that you are able to manage your interpretations so that you are not overly depressed, anxious, angry, or upset about your career.

Your interpretations are influenced heavily by the assumptions you make about what is good or bad, what you do or do not need, and what causes what in the world. Sometimes people have assumptions that cause them to be depressed or upset most of the time. You can assume, for example, that your boss has to like you more than any other employee. Since there may be somebody your boss will like better than you, such an assumption will keep you unhappy. You will be depressed because your boss does not like you best! Assumptions such as this one are irrational. An *irrational assumption* is a belief that makes you depressed or upset most of the time. Such beliefs (such as the boss has to like me best or else my life is ruined) are accepted as true without any proof. If you believe your boss has to love you or else life is unbearable, you are clinging to an irrational assumption. Believing that you have to be perfect or else you are absolutely worthless is an irrational assumption. So is believing that everyone in the world has to think you are absolutely marvelous or else you will be miserable, and believing you are unemployable because you cannot immediately find a job. *Irrational assumptions can only make you feel miserable because they lead to depressing interpretations.* All you have to do to ruin your life is to make a few irrational assumptions and refuse to change them no matter how much pain they cause!

It takes energy to have destructive feelings. It takes energy to hold on to irrational assumptions, to make interpretations that lead to miserable feelings, and to try to ignore, deny, and hide these miserable feelings. *The fewer irrational assump-*

tions you have, the more energy you will have for enjoying yourself and your relationships! The more quickly you get rid of your irrational assumptions and the destructive feelings they cause, the more energy you will have for enjoying yourself and your relationships!

To survive on the job, you need to:

1. Be aware of your assumptions
2. Know how they affect your interpretation of the information gathered by your senses
3. Be able to tell how rational or irrational your assumptions are
4. Dump your irrational assumptions
5. Replace your irrational assumptions with rational ones

You can change your irrational assumptions. The easiest way is to become highly aware of when you are making an irrational assumption. And then you think of a rational assumption that is much more constructive. Finally, you argue with yourself until you have replaced your irrational assumptions with rational ones.

Irrational assumptions are learned. Usually, they are learned in early childhood. They were taught to you by people in your past. Irrational assumptions are bad habits just like smoking or alcoholism. You can break your bad habits. What was learned as a child can be unlearned as an adult. You can replace your irrational assumptions with rational ones. If you keep arguing against your irrational assumptions, you will soon develop rational ones! *Do not let yourself feel bad just because you have bad thinking habits!*

EXERCISE 7.1   **What Are My Assumptions?**

What are common irrational assumptions? How do you know if your assumptions are rational or irrational? One way is to compare yourself to the following list of rational and irrational assumptions taken from the writings of Albert Ellis (Ellis and Harper, 1961). Do you make any of these assumptions? Can you tell the difference between the rational and the irrational?

On a sheet of paper, number lines from 1 through 20. Then read each of the following statements. Write "yes" for any assumption that describes how you think. Write "no" for any assumption that does not describe how you think. Do this for all twenty statements. Then begin again. Reread each statement. Write "R" for the rational assumptions. Write "I" for the irrational assumptions. Keep your answers to use in a later lesson.

Common Assumptions

_____ 1. I must be loved, liked, and approved of by everyone all the time or I will be absolutely miserable and will feel totally worthless.

_____ 2. It would be nice if I were liked by everyone, but I can survive very well without the approval of most people. It is only the liking and approval of close friends and people with actual power over me (such as my boss) that I have to be concerned with.

_____ 3. I have to be absolutely, 100 percent perfect and competent in all respects if I am to consider myself worthwhile.

_____ 4. My personal value does not rest on how perfect or competent I am. Although I'm trying to be as competent as I can, I am a valuable person regardless of how well I do things.

_____ 5. People who are bad, including myself, must be blamed and punished to prevent them from being wicked in the future.

_____ 6. What is important is not making the same mistakes in the future. I do not have to blame and punish myself or other people for what has happened in the past.

_____ 7. It is a total catastrophe and so terrible that I can't stand it if things are not the way I would like them to be.

_____ 8. There is no reason why the world should be like I want it to be. What is important is dealing with what is. I do not have to bemoan the fact that things are not fair or just or the way I think they should be.

_____ 9. If something terrible could happen, I will keep thinking about it *as if* it is actually going to take place.

_____ 10. I will try my best to avoid future unpleasantness. Then I will not worry about it. I refuse to go around keeping myself afraid by saying, "What if this happened?" "What if that happened?"

_____ 11. It is easier to avoid difficulties and responsibilities than to face them.

_____ 12. Facing difficulties and meeting responsibilities is easier in the long run than avoiding them.

_____ 13. I need someone stronger than myself to rely on.

_____ 14. I am strong enough to rely on myself.

_____ 15. Since I was this way when I was a child, I will be this way all my life.

_____ 16. I can change myself at any time in my life, whenever I decide it is helpful for me to do so.

_____ 17. I must become upset and depressed about other people's problems.

_____ 18. Having empathy with other people's problems and trying to help them does not mean getting upset and depressed about their problems. Overconcern does not lead to problem solving. How can I be of help if I am as depressed as they are?

_____ 19. It is terrible and unbearable to have to do things I don't want and don't like to do.

_____ 20. What I can't change I won't let upset me.

EXERCISE **Interpretations**
7.2

> *PURPOSE*
>
> The assumptions we make greatly influence interpretations of the meaning of events in our life. These interpretations determine our feelings. The same event can be depressing or amusing, depending on the assumptions and interpretations we make. The purpose of this exercise is to focus a group discussion on the ways in which assumptions affect our interpretations and how we feel.
>
> *PROCEDURE*
>
> In your group, discuss the following questions for each of the ten episodes described below.
>
> 1. What irrational assumptions is the person making? How do these assumptions cause him to feel this way?
> 2. What rational assumptions does the person need in order to change the way he feels into a more positive feeling?

Episodes

1. Sally likes to have her coworkers place their work neatly in a pile on her desk so that she can add her work, staple it all together, and give it to their supervisor. Her coworkers, however, throw their work into the supervisor's basket in a very disorderly and messy fashion. Sally then becomes very worried and upset. "I can't stand it," Sally says to herself. "It's terrible what they are doing. And it isn't fair to me or our supervisor!"

2. Jill has been given responsibility for planning next year's budget for her department. This amount of responsibility scares her. For several weeks, she has done nothing on the budget. "I'll do it next week," she keeps thinking.

3. John went to the office one morning and passed a person he had never met in the hallway. He said hello, but the person just looked at him and then walked on without saying a word. John became depressed. "I'm really not a very attractive person," he thought to himself. "No one seems to like me."

4. Dan is an intensive care paramedic technician and is depressed and worried constantly about whether he can do his job competently. For every decision that has to be made, he asks his supervisor what he should do. One day he came into work and found that his supervisor had quit. "What will I do now?" he thought. "I can't handle this job without her."

5. Jane went to her desk and found a note from her supervisor stating that she had made an error in the report she worked on the day before. The note told her to correct the error and to continue work on the report. Jane became depressed. "Why am I so dumb and stupid?" she thought to herself. "I can't seem to do anything right. That supervisor must think I'm terrible at my job."

6. Heidi has a knack for insulting people. She insults her coworkers, her boss, customers, and even passers-by who ask for directions. Her boss has told Heidi repeatedly that if she doesn't change she will be fired. This depresses Heidi and makes her very angry at her boss. "How can I change?" Heidi says. "I've been this way ever since I could talk. It's too late for me to change now."

7. Tim was checking the repairs another technician had made on a television set. He found a mistake and became very angry. "I have to punish him," he thought. "He made a mistake, and he has to suffer the consequences for it."

8. Bonnie detests filling out forms. Her job as legal secretary often requires her to fill out forms. "Every time I see a form my stomach ties itself into knots," she says. "I hate forms! I know they have to be done but I still hate them!"

9. Bob is very anxious about keeping his job. "What if the company goes out of business?" he thinks. "What if my boss gets angry at me?" "What if the secretary I yell at is the boss's daughter?" All day he worries about whether he will have a job tomorrow or not.

10. Jack is a very friendly person who listens quite well. All his coworkers tell their problems to Jack. He listens sympathetically. Then he goes home deeply depressed. "Life is so terrible for the people I work with," he thinks. "They have such severe problems and such sad lives."

EXERCISE 7.3   **Changing Your Feelings**

PURPOSE

Now that you have discussed how people can make their assumptions more constructive, you may want to apply your own advice to yourself. The purpose of this exercise is to give you a chance to discuss your own negative feelings and see what assumptions are causing them.

PROCEDURE

1. In your group, draw numbers to see who goes first. Then go around the group in a clockwise direction. Each member is to answer the following questions:
   a. What depresses me about school is . . .
   b. When I get depressed about school, I . . .
   c. The assumptions I am making that cause me to be depressed are . . .
   d. Constructive assumptions I can adopt to change my depression to more positive feelings are . . .

   Listen carefully to what each group member says. If he is not sure of the assumptions, help clarify them. Give support for making each member's assumptions more constructive.

2. Now go around the group again and discuss each member's answers to the following questions:
   a. The things I worry about are . . .
   b. What I do when I get worried is . . .
   c. The assumptions I am making that cause me to be worried are . . .
   d. Constructive assumptions I can adopt to change my worry to more positive feelings are . . .

3. Now try anger:
   a. The things I get angry about are . . .

b. What I do when I get angry is . . .
c. The assumptions I am making that cause me to be angry are . . .
d. Constructive assumptions I can adopt to change my anger to more positive feelings are . . .
4. Let's see how you feel about your career!
a. The negative feelings I have when I think about my career are . . .
b. The things I do when I feel those feelings are . . .
c. The assumptions I am making that cause the feelings are . . .
d. Constructive attitudes I can adopt to change these feelings to more positive ones are . . .

HOW TO MAKE FRIENDS ON THE JOB

1. Be a good communicator. Send and receive messages skillfully. Above all, be a good listener.
2. Be able to communicate feelings clearly.
3. Stay happy by avoiding destructive assumptions.

SUMMARY AND REVIEW: Chapter 7

Setting Learning Contracts

You are to make a learning contract with your group. The learning contract should summarize the most important things you have learned from Chapters 5, 6, and 7. It should include a plan as to how you will use what you have learned. Chapters 5, 6, and 7 focus on communication. It is time to reflect, with your group's help, on what you have learned about communicating and to plan how you can use what you have learned.

Be as specific as you can in stating what you have learned and how you will apply what you have learned. The following procedure is to be used in setting your learning contract with your group.

Procedure

1. Working alone, make a list of the more important things you have learned about communicating. List at least five things you have learned.

2. Select the five most important things you have learned. For each one, plan an action you can take in the next two weeks to apply that learning. For example, if you learned about the importance of paraphrasing, you might plan

where you can practice paraphrasing every day. In making your action plans, be specific and practical. Don't try to do either too much or too little.

3. Copy the Learning Contract form on page 59 and fill it out, but do not sign it.

4. In your group, draw numbers to see who is going to go first. The member selected reviews her learnings and action plans with the group. The group helps the member be more clear about learnings. Some members' learnings may be too vague. Or a member may have achieved an insight about her career plans that she has not listed. The group also helps the member make better action plans. Some members may plan to do more than is possible; other members may not plan to do enough. You may be able to think of a better way to put the learning into action.

5. The member's learning contract is modified until both she and the rest of the group are satisfied with it. She then signs the contract, and then the rest of the group signs the contract. The member is now committed to the group to carry out her action plans.

6. The whole process is repeated until every member of the group has a learning contract with the group.

7. The instructor will set a date for the group to review each member's progress in completing his action plans. Two weeks from signing would be a good time.

8. Working alone, keep a record of your progress in completing your action plans. Fill out a copy of the Learning Contract Progress Report form (see page 60), and use it to help you give a progress report to your group.

9. In the progress review session, give the day and date of the actions taken. You will be asked to describe what you did, what success you had, and what problems you encountered.

Reviewing Learning Contracts

At the end of Section II, you made a contract with your group. Your contract dealt with what you learned from the exercises in Section II and how you were going to apply those learnings. In this session you are to review your contract dealing with Section II.

Procedure

1. Draw numbers to see who will go first. Then go around the group clockwise. Each person is to review the tasks and activities she was to engage in to apply learnings from Section II. She then is to give the day and date on which the tasks and activities were completed, tell what success she experienced, and state what problems she encountered. Group members are to praise a person's successes and are to provide helpful suggestions to overcome any problems a person is having in completing a learning contract.

2. When a learning contract has been completed, it is considered fulfilled. If a member has not fulfilled her learning contract, she is expected to do so in the near future. An unfinished contract will be discussed again at the next session set aside for that purpose.

8

Making Decisions
In A Team

After completing this chapter, you should be able to define and give examples of

- Decision making
- Controversy
- Advocacy subgroup
- Differentiation
- Integration

The answers are given on the right side of the page. Work with a partner and keep the answers covered until you have agreed on your responses. Remember to check each answer before going on to the next item, as explained on page 1.

QUESTIONNAIRE: Main Concepts In Chapter 8

1. An important part of your job will be to contribute to team decision making as to how productivity and quality may be increased. **Decision making** involves considering possible alternatives and reaching agreement as to which of several courses of action is most desirable for achieving the group's goals. When a group tries to agree as to which of several alternative courses of action it should take, it is making a _____.

   decision

2. When people with different expertise and perspectives come together to make a decision, disagreement results. **Controversy** exists when one person's ideas, information, conclusions, theories, or opinions are incompatible with those of another, and the two seek to reach an agreement. When two members of a team have come to different conclusions based on different information, and they have to reach an agreement, a _____ exists.

   controversy

3. When a team wishes an alternative course of action to reach a fair and complete hearing, it may be assigned to an advocacy subgroup. An **advocacy subgroup** is two or more group members who are responsible for preparing and presenting the best case for an alternative course of action. When two team members are given responsibility for preparing and presenting the best case for an alternative course of action being considered by the team, they are an _____ _____ .

   advocacy subgroup

4. When making decisions, a team needs to differentiate the conclusions of members. **Differentiation** is seeking out and clarifying differences among members' ideas, information, conclusions, theories, and opinions. When team members highlight the differences among their reasoning and conclusions, they are _____.

   differentiating

5. After all the different conclusions are understood, the best ideas from all members must be integrated. **Integration** is the combining of diverse information, reasoning, and conclusions into a single position that satisfies everyone. When team members create a new position that combines the best thinking of all members, they are _____.

   integrating

Team Decision Making

An important aspect of all work is participating in decisions. Within most jobs, decisions will be made by self-managing teams continually. Certain members of each team will be members of linking groups such as quality circles and will be required to participate in making decisions that extend beyond the self-managing team. **Participation in group decision making becomes an important part of every employee's job.** In discussing your participation in group decision making it is necessary to understand what a decision is, what decisions self-managing teams are likely to be making, and what role ideas and conclusions play in making high-quality and creative decisions.

Decision making involves considering possible alternatives and reaching agreement as to which of several courses of action is most desirable for achieving the organization's goals (Johnson and F. Johnson, 1991). This means that when a problem or issue is considered, several alternative courses of action need to be identified, given a fair and complete hearing, and then ranked from best to worse.

Self-managing teams have a variety of decisions to make. Decisions about how to improve the quality of the team's product or service will be made continually. Decisions about how to improve the process by which the product is made or the service is provided will be made continually. As the team operates, maintains equipment, and carries out administrative functions, decisions have to be made. Frequently, teams carry out their own quality control inspections. Members participate in goal-setting and budgeting.

Individual Versus Group Decision Making

○   ○   ○

. . . instead of looking on discussion as a stumbling-block in the way of action, we think it an indispensable preliminary to any wise action at all.

Pericles

○   ○   ○

Making a decision is similar to the three blind men describing an elephant. One blind man, feeling the elephant's leg, stated that the elephant is like a tree trunk. Another, feeling the elephant's trunk, stated that the elephant is like a large snake. The third, feeling the elephant's side, stated that an elephant is big and broad like a house. Which blind man was right? The moral is that each person brings his or her own information, expertise, and perspective to a decision that describes only part of the problem or issue.

Typically, groups make better decisions than do individuals. There are a number of ways that individual decision making may go wrong. Since individuals are capable of all sorts of rationalizations enhancing the importance of their expertise, any decision made by a single group member is suspect. Individual deci-

sion makers have been found to be closed to considering information, especially information that is new and that opposes their perspectives. They use easy to recall, available information to form their opinions. They overestimate the importance of confirming information and dismiss opposing data. Individual decision makers often evaluate information inadequately and engage in faulty reasoning about the causes for a problem or the types of solutions that may be helpful. Decision makers are also anchored to their original positions; final estimates are biased toward their initial estimates. Individual decision makers often fall far short of a thorough, systematic exploration of the problem, development of alternatives, and selection of the optimal solution. They not only avoid digging into the problem and uncovering all relevant information, but they distort and dismiss new information. They have been found reluctant to develop alternative solutions. They become committed to their original solution early, fail to see the need to develop alternative plans, and easily dismiss emerging solutions that are not well defined and defended. Commitment to a course of action can intensify even when feedback suggests it is failing.

A team provides a variety of sources for differing information, expertise, and perspectives. **Rule 1 is to seek out differing information, expertise, and perspectives when making important decisions.** Within the complexities of current life, no one person has all the information needed to make high quality, creative decisions. No one person has all the types of expertise needed to make high quality, creative decisions. No one person can see the problem or issue from all relevant pespectives. A person's perspective determines how the problem is defined and what solutions seem reasonable. In today's complex world, most decisions require a number of sources of information and expertise as well as a variety of different perspectives. Most important decisions require more than one source of expertise. Organizations are filled with individuals who have expertise in their limited areas and must interact and make joint decisions with each other. Most decision makers are normally unaware of alternative perspectives and frames of reference and of their potential effects on the relative attractiveness of options. Thus two different group members, with different information and perspectives, can make directly opposing decisions without recognizing the limitations of their frames of reference.

Rule 2 is to not agree to the first reasonable solution proposed. It is not necessarily the best one. Many groups make the mistake of satisfying the minimal requirements for solving the problem. Instead, they should strive to find the solution that maximizes the quality of the solution.

Rule 3 is to challenge each other's conclusions and reasoning. When group members with different information and perspectives come together to make a joint decision, conflicts and disagreements result. Such controversy is an essential part of team and organizational decision making. Having the skills to manage the resulting conflicts, information exchange, exchange of expertise, and to see the problem from a variety of perspectives is essential for reaching a high quality decision.

Controversy exists when one person's ideas, information, conclusions, theories, and opinions are incompatible with those of another, and the two seek to reach an agreement. Decision making typically involves considering several possible alternatives and choosing one. By definition, all decision-making situations involve some controversy over which of several alternatives should be chosen. The management of disagreement among members' ideas, theories, conclusions, perspectives, and expertise is a critical and often ignored aspect of effective decision making. Within many decision-making groups controversy is avoided, suppressed, and ignored. Yet controversy is the source of creative, high-quality decisions based on a thorough examination of all alternatives.

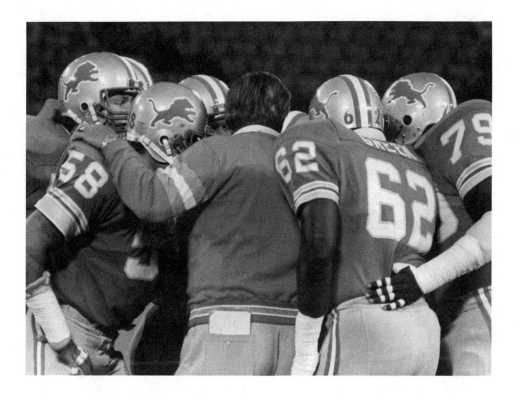

EXERCISE 8.1 **Who Should Get The Penicillin**

The purpose of this exercise is to examine the process of controversy and advocacy subgroups in a decision-making situation. Approximately one and a half hours are needed for this exercise. The procedure is as follows:

1. Introduce exercise.
2. Form groups of four members. Divide the group into two pairs. Give one pair a copy of the medical viewpoint and the other pair a copy of the military viewpoint.
3. Introduce the situation. Instruct the pairs to build as good a rationale for their assigned position as they can in fifteen or twenty minutes, using the information on the briefing sheet as a guide.
4. Instruct the pairs to meet together as a group of four. The group is to come to a decision that all four members can agree to. The decision should reflect the best reasoning of the entire group. The group discussion should follow these steps:
   a. Each pair presents its position as forcefully and persuasively as it can while the opposing pair takes notes and clarifies anything the two members do not fully understand.

b. Have an open discussion in which members of each pair: (1) argue forcefully and persuasively for their position, presenting as many facts as they can to support it; (2) listen critically to members of the opposing pair, asking them for the facts that support their point of view.

This is a complex issue and members need to know both sides in order to come to a thoughtful decision.

5. Instruct the pairs to reverse their perspectives by switching sides and arguing for the opposite point of view as forcefully and persuasively as possible. Members should see if they can think of any new facts that the opposing pair did not present in support of its position, and should elaborate on that position.

6. Instruct the groups to come to a joint decision by:
   a. summarizing the best arguments for both points of view.
   b. detailing the facts they know about World War II and the African campaign.
   c. achieving consensus among the members.
   d. organizing the rationale supporting the decision that they will present to the rest of the class. They should be ready to defend the validity of their decision to groups who may have come to the opposite decision.

7. Instruct participants to complete the postdecision questionnaire. Then have the observers determine the group mean for each question.

8. Summarize the decision of each group in front of the entire class. Then summarize the results of the postdecision questionnaire, using the summary table.

9. Instruct each group to discuss their experience, using:
   a. the decision and questionnaire results.
   b. the information collected by the observers.
   c. the impressions of the group members.
   d. the constructive-controversy checklist.

The following questions may help the groups discuss how they managed the controversy:
   a. How did the group manage disagreements among its members? (Use the checklist for constructive controversy as a guide.)
   b. From its experience, what conclusions can the group make about the constructive handling of controversies?
   c. Did the opinions of the group members change as a result of the group's discussion? Did members gain insight into the other point of view through the perspective-reversal procedure? Did members learn anything new about World War II?
   d. What did members learn about themselves and other group members? How did each member react to the controversy?

10. Have each group share its conclusions about the constructive management of controversy with the rest of the class.

Who Should Get the Penicillin Exercise Situation

In 1943, penicillin, which is used for the prevention of infection, was in short supply among the United States armed forces in North Africa. Decisions had to be made whether to use this meager supply for the thousands of hospitalized victims of venereal disease or for the thousands of victims of battle wounds at the front. If you were a member of a team of medical and military personnel, whom would you use the penicillin for?

_____ victims of venereal disease

_____ victims of battle wounds

Share your position and rationale with your group. Stick to your guns unless logically persuaded otherwise. At the same time, help your group achieve consensus on this issue.

Briefing Sheet: The Medical Viewpoint: Who Should Get the Penicillin Exercise

Your position is to give the penicillin to the battle-wounded. Whether or not you agree with this position, argue for it as strongly and as honestly as you can, using arguments that make sense and are rational. Be creative and invent new supporting arguments. Seek out information; ask members of other groups who may know the answers to your questions. Remember to learn the rationale for both your position and the military position. Challenge the military position; think of loopholes in its logic; demand facts and information that back up its arguments.

1. Our responsibility is to treat the wounded and save as many lives as possible. Without the penicillin many of the wounded will die needlessly. Minor wounds will get infected and become major, life-threatening wounds.

2. Our strategies must be based on the premise that human life is sacred. If one person dies needlessly, we have failed in our responsibility. The soldiers who have sacrificed so much to help us win the war must be treated with all the care, concern, and resources we can muster. Our soldiers must be able to fight harder than the German soldiers.

3. Troop morale is vital. Nothing raises troop morale as much as the men's knowledge that if they are wounded they will receive top-notch medical treatment.

4. Morale at home is vital. People must make sacrifices to produce the goods and materials we need to win the war. Nothing raises morale at home more than knowing that sons and brothers are receiving the most effective medical care that is humanly possible. It would be devastating for word to reach the United States that we were needlessly letting soldiers die for lack of medical care.

5. Even though we are at war, we must not lose our humanity. It will do no good to defeat Germany if we become Nazis in the process.

6. At this point the war is going badly in North Africa. Rommel and the German army are cutting through our lines like butter. We are on the verge of being pushed out of Africa, in which case we will lose the war. Rommel must be stopped.

7. Fresh troops and supplies are unavailable. The German submarines control the Atlantic, and we cannot get troop ships or supply ships into African ports. We have to make do with what we have.

8. Penicillin is a wonder drug that will save countless lives if it is used to treat the wounded.

Briefing Sheet: The Military Viewpoint: Who Should Get the Penicillin Exercise

Your position is to give the penicillin to the VD patients. Whether or not you agree with this position, argue for it as strongly and as honestly as you can, using arguments that make sense and are rational. Be creative and invent new supporting arguments. Seek out information that supports your position. If you do not have needed information, ask members of other groups who may. Remember to learn the rationale for both your position and the medical position. Challenge the medical position; think of loopholes in its logic; demand facts and information that back up its arguments.

1. Our responsibility is to win the war for our country at all costs. If we lose Africa, we will lose Europe to Hitler, and eventually we will be fighting in the United States.

2. Our strategies to win must be based on the premise of "the greatest good for the greatest number." We may have to sacrifice soldiers in order to win the war, save our democracy, and free Europe.

3. Troop morale is vital. Our soldiers must be able to fight harder than the German soldiers. Nothing raises troop morale like seeing fresh troops arrive at the front.

4. Morale at home is vital. People must make sacrifices to produce the goods and materials we need to fight the war. Nothing raises morale at home like hearing of battles won and progress being made in winning the war. Victories give our people at home more dedication.

5. At this point, the war is going badly in North Africa. Rommel and the German army are cutting through our lines like butter. We are on the verge of being pushed out of Africa, in which case we will lose the war. Rommel must be stopped at all costs!

6. Penicillin is a wonder drug that will send VD into remission, and within twenty-four hours the VD patients will be free from pain and able to function effectively on the battlefield.

Controversy And Decision Making

○　　○　　○

"Since the general or prevailing opinion on any subject is rarely or never the whole truth, it is only by the collision of adverse opinion that the remainder of the truth has any chance of being supplied."

John Stuart Mill

○　　○　　○

A large pharmaceutical company faced the decision of whether to buy or build a chemical plant (The Wall Street Journal, October 22, 1975). To maximize the likelihood that the best decision was made, the president established two advocacy teams to ensure that both the "buy" and the "build" alternatives received a fair and complete hearing. An **advocacy subgroup** is two or more group members who prepare and present the best case for a particular course of action to the decision-making group. The "buy" team was instructed to prepare and present the best case for purchasing a chemical plant, and the "build" team was told to prepare and present the best case for constructing a new chemical plant near the company's national headquarters. The "buy" team identified over 100 existing plants that would meet the company's needs, narrowed the field down to twenty, further narrowed the field down to three, and then selected one plant as the ideal plant to buy. The "build" team contacted dozens of engineering firms and, after four months of consideration, selected a design for the ideal plant to build. Nine months after they were established, the two teams, armed with all the details about cost, (a) presented their best case and (b) challenged each other's information, reasoning, and conclusions. From the spirited discussion, it became apparent that the two options would cost about the same amount of money. The group, therefore, chose the "build" option because it allowed the plant to be located conveniently near company headquarters. This procedure represents the structured use of controversy to ensure high quality decision making.

Controversies are common within decision-making situations. In the mining industry, for example, engineers are accustomed to address issues such as land use, air and water pollution, and health and safety. The complexity of the design of production processes, the balancing of environmental and manufacturing interests, and numerous other factors often create controversy. Most groups waste the benefits of such disputes, but every effective decision-making situation thrives on what controversy has to offer. Decisions are by their very nature controversial, as alternative solutions are suggested and considered before agreement is reached. When a decision is made, the controversy ends and participants commit themselves to a common course of action.

The Steps Of Using Advocacy Subgroups For Decision Making

○   ○   ○

"Conflict is the gadfly of thought. It stirs us to observation and memory. It insti-
gates invention. It shocks us out of sheep-like passivity, and sets us at noting and
contriving . . . conflict is a 'sine qua non' of reflection and ingenuity."

John Dewey

○   ○   ○

There are two reasons why controversy should be structured within any decision making situation. The first is that involved participation in groups will produce conflicts among ideas, opinions, conclusions, theories, and information of
members inevitably. Those conflicts can either divide a team and create negative
feelings, or the conflicts can increase the quality and creativity of team decision
making. The second is that the only way each alternative can receive a fair and
complete hearing is for a member to present the best case for that alternative. This
rarely occurs naturally. Teams cannot always count on controversies occurring
constructively or each alternative being given a fair and complete hearing. And
group members need a structure and a set of social skills in managing controversies when they do occur. For these and other reasons, controversies need to be
structured into team life carefully.

Using advocacy subgroups to ensure that controversy is utilized to make a
high-quality, creative decision begins with identifying a problem that both
needs to be solved, and warrants comprehensive consideration. Next, a number
of plausible, optional solutions are proposed. Once a number of alternative solutions to the problem have been identified, a decision has to be made as to which
one to adopt. The quality of this decision depends largely on whether team members will (a) challenge each other's conclusions and reasoning and (b) ensure that
all alternatives get fair and complete consideration. This requires that the team
use a controversy procedure with advocacy subgroups. A more detailed discussion of this process may be found in Johnson and R. Johnson (1987) and Johnson
and F. Johnson (1991).

Keeping Up With Change

A 3–M official stated recently that the products her company develops for other high-
tech companies are usually found to be obsolete within a year. To make a profit, 3–M
has to be very quick, then, in bringing a product to market and must be ready to drop
it for something else within a year. The company has 25,000 different products that
go into computers. The computers change continually and, therefore, many of the
25,000 products have to change. Product cycles are getting very short. Instead of a

two-year cycle for thinking of the product and getting it into the customer's hand, today companies need to bring a product from conception to the customer's hand in eight to ten weeks. It is estimated that 70 percent of 3–M's income in 1995 will come from products that are not yet invented. Instead of products, 3–M now has a **process** of bringing products to market quickly that makes it a profitable company. Such a process depends on high-quality, creative team decision making.

Step 1: Assigning Teams Positions

An example is as follows. You are a member of a team in a chemical company. As a result of making your chemicals sell, a number of hazardous wastes are produced by your company's manufacturing processes. A decision has to be made about how to best manage the disposal of the hazardous wastes. Your team leader conducts a meeting in which three options for disposing of the hazardous waste are identified: building a plant to burn the waste, buying a deep mine in which to bury it, or hiring a disposal company to ship it to a dump hundreds of miles away. The leader makes clear that the goal is to prepare a group report reflecting the best possible decision the group members are able to agree on. To do so requires that all alternatives get a fair and complete hearing. The leader, therefore, decides to use the controversy procedure to help the team decide. Members of the team are assigned to advocacy subgroups and given the responsibility to prepare the "best case" for the alternative assigned. You end up on the "bury" subgroup.

Step 2: Preparing Your Best Case

You and the other members of your advocacy subgroup gather and organize all available information in order to prepare the best case for advocacy as an alternative to the whole group. You try to find all the supporting facts, information, and evidence available for the bury position. You give any nonsupporting evidence to other members of the team who are representing the other positions. You organize what is known about the advantages of burying hazardous waste into a coherent and reasoned position. You plan how to present the best case possible so that all members of the team understand thoroughly the bury position and are convinced of its soundness. In doing so you should keep in mind that all conclusions involve a leap in faith and logic (see Figure 8.1). Making a conclusion involves (Johnson and Johnson, 1987):

1. Formulating your conclusion/claim.
2. Gathering, listing, and detailing the relevant facts, information, and experience and organizing them into a logical sequence so that your conclusion is supported.
3. Third, taking a "leap" over the "chasm of the unknown" to make a conclusion.

Figure 8.1 Making a Conclusion

Step 3: Presenting Your Best Case

○   ○   ○

The best way ever devised for seeking the truth in any given situation is advocacy: presenting the pros and cons from different informed points of view and digging down deep into the facts.

Harold W. Geneen, former CEO, ITT

○   ○   ○

You present your position and its supporting evidence as forcefully, persuasively, completely, accurately, and sincerely as possible. You also listen carefully to the other positions being presented. Taking notes is almost a must to remember the important points. You keep an open mind as to whether the company's hazardous waste should be burned, buried, or shipped away.

Step 4: General Discussion

○   ○   ○

To be persuasive we must be believable; to be believable we must be credible; to be credible, we must be truthful.

Edward R. Murrow, journalist

○   ○   ○

A general discussion is then held in which each advocacy subgroup (a) challenges the reasoning and conclusions of the other advocacy subgroups and (b) defends its position from others' challenges. You continue to advocate the bury position, defend it against others' attempts to challenge it. You challenge the burn and hire positions by pointing out the inadequacies in information, reasoning, and perspective. You remember that your goal is to reach the best decision possible about the need to regulate hazardous waste management and, therefore, point out the strengths of the two opposing positions as well as their weaknesses.

While evaluating and challenging the claims presented by the "burn" and "hire" groups, you use important skills, such as:

1. **Being critical of ideas, not of persons.** Arguments should concern ideas, not personality traits or motivation. There should be nothing personal in disagreement. Members should be highly critical of each other's ideas while affirming each other's competence. **Show personal regard for other team members.** They should look each other in the eye and say, "I can see why you think that from your perspective; I see it differently." Or, "I have great respect for your intelligence and, therefore, I am taking what you say very seriously; right now I have a different opinion." When disagreeing with another member, you should criticize his or her ideas and conclusions while communicating respect and appreciation for him or her as a person. Any inference of incompetence or weakness and any hint of rejecting another member should be avoided. Focus on the position and its rationale, not on the person. Do not provoke defensiveness by attacking the person. "I appreciate you, I am interested in your ideas; I disagree with your current position" should be communicated rather than, "You are stupid and ignorant and I do not respect you." In essence, you want to communicate, "We are teammates. I am interested in what you have to say. I do not agree with you. I have come to a different conclusion."

2. **Not taking personally other members' disagreements with and rejection of your ideas.** That other members disagree with your ideas and conclusions should be taken as an interesting opportunity to learn something new, not as a personal attack. Do not take disagreement with your ideas and opinions as personal rejection or a sign of disrespect. Always separate the quality of one's rationale from one's competence and worth as a person.

3. **Ensuring that there are several cycles of differentiation** (bringing out differences in positions) **and integration** (combining several positions into one new, creative position) before a final consensus is reached. Differentiation must come before integration is attempted. **Avoid premature evaluation.** More specifically:
   a. **Differentiation** involves seeking out and clarifying differences among members' ideas, information, conclusions, theories, and opinions. It involves highlighting the differences among members' reasoning and seeks to understand fully what the different positions and perspectives are. All

different points of view must be presented and explored thoroughly before new, creative solutions are sought.

    b. **Integration/synthesis** involves combining the information, reasoning, theories, and conclusions of the group members into a single position that satisfies them all. After it has differentiated positions, the group needs to seek a new, creative position that synthesizes the thinking of all members.

Never try to integrate different positions before adequate differentiation has taken place. The potential for integration is never greater than the adequacy of the differentiation already achieved. Most controversies go through a series of differentiations and integrations before a final consensus is reached.

4. **Asking questions to elicit information as to why the member's position is the correct or appropriate one.** Say, "Why do you think that way?" "What is the evidence that supports your position?" "Prove to me that what you are saying is correct." Clarify and seek another's rationale by questioning. Probe by asking questions that lead to deeper understanding or analysis, such as, "Would it work in this situation . . . ?" "What else makes you believe . . . ?".

5. **Refuting each other's evidence or reasoning.** To do so requires **analysis,** that is, **taking the opponent's position apart.** To charge the opposition with having faulty evidence is a standard basic approach to refutation.

6. **Emphasize the common decision to be made** by summarizing frequently and concisely, especially the points you have made to illuminate the strengths and weaknesses of all positions. Summarize what you can agree on and what you disagree on, what is "true" and what is "untrue."

During this discussion (as well as the initial presentation), when your position is challenged by others' conclusions and information (that are incompatible with and do not fit with your reasoning and conclusions), you are likely to feel uncertain as to the correctness of your position. Your uncertainty should motivate you to search for new information to support your position.

The general discussion of the issue may last for several team meetings. Between meetings you should (a) search for more information and experiences to support your position and discredit the other two positions and (b) seek to understand the burn and ship positions fully. **Consult relevant experts, reports, and research studies.** A variety of sources may provide information about the pros and cons of burying, burning, or shipping away hazardous waste. Visits to other companies with similar problems often help.

Step 5: Perspective Reversal

Put yourself in the others' shoes. The conflict is an opportunity to give all sides a complete and fair hearing. This involves seeing the issue from other perspectives besides your own. Demonstrate your understanding by summarizing the other positions accurately. Drop your advocacy and try to see the issue from all points of view. You summarize the other positions as forcefully, sincerely, accurately, and completely as you can. You correct the misperceptions and misunderstandings of your position as other team members summarize it. This results in freeing team members from their original position and helps them view the issue from more than one perspective. Understanding the statements of other members is not enough. The perspective from which the member is speaking must also be understood clearly.

Step 6: Making The Decision

Help your team reach a consensus and prepare a report on how the hazardous wastes should be disposed of. This requires a rethinking of the issue and a combining of the information and reasoning from all sides. The team's decision then reflects members' best reasoned judgment. Putting the best information and reasoning from all groups' members together into fewer words is **synthesis.** Avoid "either my way or your way" thinking and create a new solution. All the facts, information, and experiences gathered have to be synthesized into one or a set of conclusions. This involves recognizing relationships and patterns in the information, facts, and experiences gathered by different group members that at first may not be apparent, that is, **creative insight.** Rather than simply choosing an alternative decision, members' ideas should be integrated by combining the information, reasoning, and conclusions of the various team members so that a consensus can be achieved. If there is no new position that is acceptable from all perspectives, then probably not enough differentiation and critical thinking has taken place. You should:

1. **Emphasize your common ground in making the best possible decision.** Statements such as "We are all in this together" and "Let's make the best

possible decision" should dominate the group, not "I am right and you are wrong." The context within which the controversy takes place should be cooperative, not competitive. The issue is not to establish who has the best answer but to make the best group decision possible by exploring different perspectives and integrating different information.

2. **Follow the canons of rational argument.** Generate ideas, collect and organize relevant information, use deductive and inductive logical procedures, and make tentative conclusions. Avoid premature evaluations.

3. **Synthesize the best ideas from all viewpoints and perspectives.** The end result is a synthesis that is better than any single position advocated. Think creatively until it is discovered.

4. **Keep in mind that all conclusions are tentative** based on a person's understanding of currently known information. When more information is obtained, or current information better understood, conclusions must change. By definition, being rational can be thought of as keeping all conclusions flexible so that increased understandings and information can be considered and used to improve or modify what is currently believed accurate.

Summary And Conclusions

○   ○   ○

Difference of opinion leads to inquiry, and inquiry to truth.

Thomas Jefferson

○   ○   ○

Avoiding disagreement and argument becomes for many teams a matter of habit. They fail to express their own opinions and challenge each other's thinking because they assume that everyone agrees with the team's current reasoning. They make the false assumption that conflict is inevitably disruptive and antagonistic. They lack confidence in their own and others' competence in managing controversy constructively. They fear that disagreement will hurt their teammates' feelings.

Instead of avoiding controversies, seek them out. There are no cookbook rules for making controversies productive, but the following guidelines can help group members argue more constructively and transform disagreement among themselves into positive experience:

1. **Emphasize your common ground in making the best possible decision.** Statements such as "We are all in this together" and "Let's make the best possible decision" should dominate the group, not "I am right and you are wrong." The context within which the controversy takes place should be cooperative, not competitive. The issue is not to establish who has the best answer but to make the best group decision possible by exploring different perspectives and integrating different information.

2. **Look for opportunities to engage in controversy.** Highlight contrasting viewpoints, point out disagreements, and promote challenging tasks. Include diverse people in the group. People who differ in background, expertise, opinions, outlook, and organizational position are likely to disagree.

3. **Prepare the best case possible for your position.** Develop your thesis statement and research the best rationale possible to support it. It is up to you to ensure that your position is seen in its best light. Consult relevant articles, books, and experts to compile information and experiences to support your position. List relevant facts, information, and theories.

4. **Advocate your position forcefully but with an open mind.** Speak up. Make sure everyone listens. It is up to you to ensure that your position gets a fair and complete hearing.

5. **Encourage others to advocate their positions forcefully.** Express a warm, intense interest in all contributions. Every member should share his or her position and ideas in order to get comments and reactions from other members that will help improve the quality of group work. Value, respect, and take everyone's contributions seriously. Help all members, regardless of their status, to speak out confidently.

6. **Understand, then challenge, opposing ideas and positions.** Ask questions. Ask for the supporting facts, information, and theories in order to understand the opposing positions more thoroughly. Understanding the statements of another group member is not enough; the frame of reference from which the member is speaking must also be clearly understood. View the issue under discussion from a variety of perspectives. Then, point out fallacies in information and logic. Try to refute their thesis statements and claims. Group members should be critical of ideas, not of persons. Arguments should concern ideas, not personality traits. Group

members should be highly critical of each other's ideas, and at the same time affirm each other's competence by communicating respect and appreciation for the member as a person. Any implication of incompetence or weakness and any hint of rejecting another member should be avoided. **Criticize opposing ideas while confirming the competence of the other group members.** Combine personal regard with intellectual challenge. Say, "We are friends," "I am interested in what you have to say." Then say, "I do not agree with you on that point," "I have come to a different conclusion," "I appreciate you, I am interested in your ideas, but I disagree with your current position." Do not say, "You are stupid and ignorant and I do not like you!" Insults or imputations that challenge another member's integrity, intelligence, and motives are to be avoided.

7. **Do not take other members' disagreements and rejection of your ideas personally.** That other members disagree with your ideas and conclusions should be taken as an interesting situation from which something can be learned, not as a personal attack. Do not confuse rejection of your ideas and opinions with personal rejection. Separate the validity of your thinking from your competence and worth as a person.

8. **Ensure that there are several cycles of differentiation and integration. Differentiation** involves bringing out differences in positions and **integration** involves combining several positions into one new, creative position. Differentiation must come before integration is attempted.

9. **Put yourself in the other member's shoes.** Controversy is an opportunity to improve the quality of your own reasoning by seeing the issue from a variety of perspectives. Ensure that you understand the perspectives underlying positions as well as their content.

10. **Influence teammates through persuasion, not coercion.** Say, "Here is why I want you to consider this seriously," and "You may find this convincing." Ensure there is a give-and-take rather than dominance and passivity.

11. **Follow the canons of rational argument.** Generate ideas, collect and organize relevant information, use deductive and inductive logical procedures, and make tentative conclusions. Avoid premature evaluations.

12. **Synthesize the best ideas from all viewpoints and perspectives.** The end result is a synthesis that is better than any single position advocated. Think creatively until it is discovered.

Remember Nietzsche's observation: "When a fixed idea makes its appearance, a great ass also makes its appearance." Avoid the pitfalls of (a) assuming the position you are advocating is superior, (b) refusing to admit weaknesses in your position, (c) closed-mindedly attempting to prove your ideas are "right" and must be accepted, (d) interpreting opposition to your ideas as a personal attack, and (e) only pretending to consider ideas from other team members.

The New Career Pattern

The **new career pattern** is one in which you are oriented toward projects, the building up of your own professional expertise and reputation as a contributor who adds value to what they do, which you take to many places within the company. Technology is changing work so that companies can no longer employ narrowly skilled people who know only how to do one thing and do that their entire life. The new contract companies are offering their employees is that the company can not guarantee an employee's present job for life, but we can offer to keep training you to give you more and different skills so that you will continue to be employable. The company can only promise a career to those who take advantage of a perpetual learning environment.

Gaining Expertise

○   ○   ○

One learns by doing the thing; for though you think you know it, you have no certainty until you try.

Sophocles

○   ○   ○

Your job security and advancement rest on your ability to add value to your work by improving the quality of the product or service you help the company provide. This requires that you continually (a) increase your job-related expertise, knowledge, and experiences and (b) exchange your expertise, knowledge, and experience with those of others in decision-making situations. Important decisions are typically made by small groups of individuals with diverse expertise. To maximize the quality of the decision, expertise must be exchanged. Sales and manufacturing, for example, must exchange their knowledge and experience to ensure the profitability of a company.

Increasing your expertise requires procedural learning. Learning job skills is like learning how to play golf or fly an airplane. It involves more than simply reading material. **Procedural learning** exists when you:

1. Learn conceptually what the job procedures and skills are.
2. Translate your conceptual understanding into a set of procedures.
3. Take action and engage in the procedures and skills.
4. Eliminate errors in performing the procedures and skills.

Procedural learning differs from school learning due to a heavy reliance on feedback about performance and the modification of one's efforts until the errors of performance are eliminated. Through practice, practice, practice a progressive refinement of skills and knowledge is achieved. Jacob Bronowski noted the importance of actual practice when he said, "The hand is the cutting edge of the mind."

If you are not trying to increase your expertise, you are losing it. Expertise is not a state, it is a process. Either you are becoming better at your job or you are becoming worse. To become better, you must experiment with your behavior in order to (a) fine-tune and refine present competencies and (b) try out new strategies that hold some promise of being more effective than current ones. **Without risk there is no gain.** You must risk short-term, temporary failures in order to experiment with new practices that will eventually increase your long-term productivity. Remember, **you have to make deposits before you can collect any interest.**

There are three interrelated ways to increase your expertise. The first is through **training courses** and continuous formal education. The second is through the **continuous improvement** procedure where you (a) take action by trying something new, (b) assess how well it went and obtain feedback on your performance from other people, (c) reflect on how to do it better next time, and (d) take modified action by trying it again in a refined way. This procedure is characterized in Figure 8.2.

The third way to increase your job-related expertise is through informal apprenticeships. Apprentices increase their skills by working with "masters of the art" and other apprentices who are more experienced than they are. The **apprenticeship procedure** is as follows: **First,** as an apprentice you ask a more skillful person to explain how to do the job better. **Second,** you then watch them and copy what they do. It helps to watch a number of people do the same job in their own way to get a wide variety of ideas on how to improve your own productivity. **Third,** you perform the new skill or procedure with a more experienced person talking you through it step-by-step. In essence, the expert coaches you in how to do the new procedure by providing explanations, guidance, prompts, and hints. **Fourth,** you perform the new skill or procedure while explaining to your "coach" how to do it. You monitor and correct yourself under your coach's helpful eye. **Fifth,** you do it alone. This is sometimes called "soloing." **Sixth,** you find someone less experienced that you teach what you have just learned. This completes the apprenticeship procedure.

During your entire work life, you should be striving to increase your job-related expertise. Besides taking classes and attaining new knowledge that will help you do a better job, you must learn procedures that increase your productivity. This involves a combination of progressive refinement and apprenticeships. You never bcome too experienced or too old to get better at what you do. This is especially true of the interpersonal and small group skills you need to work as part of a team.

As you improve your job-related expertise continually, you are expected to function as part of teams that make decisions as to how productivity and quality may be improved. Within these teams diverse sources of expertise must be exchanged to maximize the quality and creativeness of the decisions made. The procedure for exchanging expertise is the controversy procedure involving the use of advocacy subgroups described in this chapter.

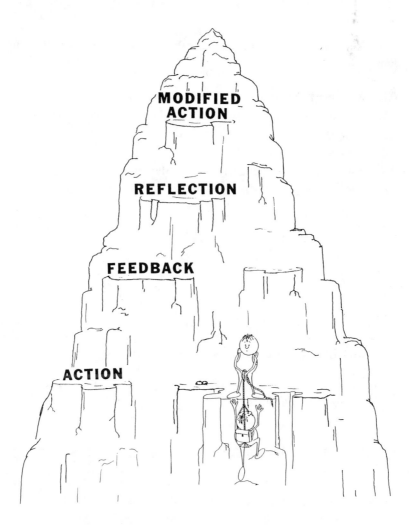

Surviving Working

The quality of your life at work and your work survival depends on your relationships with your coworkers and boss. Enjoying working, having solid support from fellow employees to rely on when things get rough, and feeling good about being at work all depend on how good your relationships are with your fellow employees. Your interpersonal skills will determine your ability to build and keep productive, cooperative, and good relationships with your fellow employees. Such relationships determine how well you survive the experience of working. When you have negative feelings about working, it is often a sign that there are problems in your relationships with coworkers that need to be dealt with. When such problems happen, you can ask yourself the following questions:

1. What are the problems I have at work?
2. How can I change the situation in which the problems occur?
3. How can I change my actions so that the problems are solved?
4. How can I change my feelings so that the problems are solved?
5. What personal assets can I use to solve the problems?
6. Who are the people at work who can help me solve the problems?

Using the skills discussed in this book can result in the solution of most problems you will have at work.

Mundane Work

People in jobs that used to be routine, such as janitors and food service workers must be retraining themselves continually, **because there is no such thing as a mundane job anymore anywhere.** No company can afford to have a single worker who is not "a sophisticated, project-oriented, value adder." There are no unsophisticated jobs anymore. Even being a janitor or a food service worker are now sophisticated "brain" jobs.

Getting Along with Your Boss

Surviving work means getting along with your boss. Your immediate supervisor may be the kindest, fairest, most understanding, and most consistent person in the world—but don't count on it. Not all people are easy to work under or easy to understand. It is difficult to develop an open, cooperative relationship with some bosses. Yet no other single working relationship is more important to your career survival. Here are some practical tips about keeping a good relationship with your boss.

1. Build good relationships with your coworkers. Being easy to work with begins with your coworkers and then spreads to your boss.
2. Keep your boss informed a little about your job performance:
   a. When you goof, let your boss know.
   b. When you do something well, let your boss know.
   c. Ask for a few minutes now and then to discuss how you are doing on the job.
   d. Do not expect your boss to build a relationship with you. You must build a cooperative, open relationship with her.
3. Do not let your coworkers dictate your opinion of your boss. Just because

your friend does not like your boss does not mean that you have to dislike your boss, too.

4. Be sensitive. Trust your own good judgment when it comes to communicating with your boss.

5. Do not be upset if your boss has a bad day. His job is probably more difficult than you think.

6. Do not go over your boss' head without his permission. Keep your boss informed whenever you want to talk to other management people.

No Two People are Exactly Alike

Each of us is unique. There is no one quite like you. You are different from everyone else, and every person we know is different from us.

Some differences seem more important than others. The color of your eyes is usually not seen as an important difference, but how much money your parents have often is. On the job, you may work with fellow employees and customers who come from entirely different backgrounds, communities, ethnic groups, and social groups. It may be important, in keeping your job, that you can relate to and cooperate with people very much different from yourself. America has been a melting pot for the world. There are many different kinds of people in our society. Your boss and your coworkers may be very different from you. Your skills in forming good relationships with people from different backgrounds may be very important for your job performance and for your enjoyment of your work.

I once worked as a pots-and-pans washer in a large restaurant while I was in high school. Working as an assistant cook was another high school student who was very witty and fun to work with. But the other employees kept giving me advice. "Stay away from Roy," they said, "he's not your kind."

In our society, many people believe that you should associate only with "your own kind" of people. We are taught to like only people we think are similar to ourselves—people who are "acceptable." People who are different are to be avoided. In the United States, however, we have all kinds of different people who have come from all kinds of different cultures. It is not possible only to associate with people who are similar to us. And we would not want to, even if we could. Despite the myth that being similar is good, differences among employees lead to increased productivity and more fun and enjoyment on the job.

If employees are skilled interpersonally, differences increase their ability to solve problems, be creative, and be effective in their work. There are two reasons for this. First, when a group is trying to solve a problem or make a good decision, the more different the group members are, the more different ways they have to look at the problem. People from different backgrounds may see a problem differently, may have different information and ideas about how to solve the problem. They may be experts in different areas. All of these differences help a group make better decisions and solve problems creatively and successfully. The second reason why differences among employees help increase productivity is that the differences promote conflict among ideas. Disagreements cause reevaluation of ideas and increased creativity. As will be discussed in the next three chapters, conflicts among ideas result in improved decisions and problem solving.

Differences among employees make work more interesting. People who have had different experiences, who have lived a different type of life, who have different ways of viewing the world, and who see work differently can be interesting and fun. Being around people who are different from you provides opportunities for learning.

Working with people from different backgrounds can also give you a much clearer understanding of your values, attitudes, abilities, background, motivations, and perspectives than will working with people who are similar to you. You learn who you are by comparing yourself with other people. Your ideas about who you are and what you are like are affected by who your fellow employees are. When you compare yourself with people from different backgrounds, you get a clearer picture of your own values and attitudes.

EXERCISE 8.2   **What Are Our Differences?**

PURPOSE

We are all different in many ways. We think some of our differences are important. Other differences we ignore. After we know each other for a while, we tend to forget how different we are. The purpose of this exercise is to review our differences.

PROCEDURE

1. In your group, list as many categories as you can of how people can be different from each other. Include such things as the following:
   a. Sex.
   b. Age.
   c. Place of birth: small town, farm, suburb, large city.
   d. Physical features: complexion, eye color, hair color, shape of nose, and so forth.
   e. Size and shape: height, weight, bone structure and other aspects of size.
   f. Dress and appearance: style of clothes, ornaments, etc.
   g. Speech manner: slang expressions, etc.
   h. Personal likes and dislikes
   i. Ethnic background; national origin of family.
2. Working as a group, make a list of the ways members of your group are different from each other. Make the list as long as possible. No difference is too small to list. You might, for example, even classify members by type of eyelashes.

3. Working as a group, classify each item on your list according to the importance society places on the difference. Use two categories: important and unimportant.

4. Working as a group, discuss each item and decide which is the positive way to be and which is the negative way to be for each item. Some items may be neutral. But in our society most differences have a "best" and a "worst" attached to them. It is usually considered, for example, better to be thin than to be fat, tall rather than short, small nosed rather than large nosed.

5. As a group, list how the differences among members have contributed in positive ways to the group.

6. As a group, discuss the following questions:
   a. Is it easy or hard to focus on the differences among members?
   b. Do you feel relaxed or tense while talking about differences?
   c. Do you feel accepted or rejected when someone points out a way in which you are different from him?
   d. Do you feel accepting or rejecting when you point out a way in which another member is different from you?

7. As a group, write your five conclusions about the way group members have been taught to react to differences among persons.

8. Your teacher will lead a discussion in which the conclusions of all groups will be shared with the entire class.

Skills for Working with Diverse People

I once worked with a woman named Renee. I was raised on a farm in Indiana. Renee was raised in New York City. I really liked Renee, and most of the time I thought Renee liked me. But when I made a mistake, Renee would become angry. To me, anger meant rejection, dislike, meanness, and nastiness. According to my upbringing, a person was not supposed to show anger unless it was an emergency! So one day I brought Renee a cup of coffee and asked her why she was so quick to become angry at me. "It's because I like you," Renee said. "Do you think I would waste my time being angry at someone I didn't really care for?" Renee had been raised to believe that anger was a sign of caring, concern, wanting to help the person do things better, and being interested in the well-being of the person. The differences in our background meant that we viewed anger completely differently.

The same feeling can mean different things to people from different backgrounds. What makes one person angry may make another person laugh. This is not the only communication problem people from different backgrounds have. A word that is quite innocent to one person may be a serious insult to another. Slang words may have different meanings, depending on where you are from. There are lots of possible communication problems when you work with people from different backgrounds. But when they have been talked through, whole new worlds of experience have been opened up!

All the interpersonal skills covered in this book are important for working with people from backgrounds other than yours. Of special importance is the skill of perspective taking. Being able to see a situation from another person's viewpoint is essential when working with diverse fellow employees. It helps you communicate, build good relationships, resolve conflicts, and be open-minded about other people's ideas and actions. It helps you appreciate and learn from other people. When working with diverse fellow employees, simply try to "walk in their shoes."

SUMMARY AND REVIEW: Chapter 8

Setting Learning Contracts

You are to make a learning contract with your group. The learning contract should summarize the most important things you have learned from Chapter 8 about forming good relationships. It should include a plan as to how you will use what you have learned. It is time to reflect, with your group's help, on what you have learned about forming relationships and on how you can use what you have learned.

Be as specific as you can in stating what you have learned and how you will apply what you have learned. The following procedure is to be used in setting your learning contract with your group.

Procedure

1. Working alone, make a list of the more important things you have learned about forming relationships. List at least five things you have learned.

2. Select the five most important things you have learned. For each one, plan an action you can take in the next two weeks to apply that learning. For example, if you learned about the importance of feedback, you might plan where you can obtain feedback on how other people see you. In making your action plans be specific and practical. Don't try to do either too much or too little.

3. Copy the Learning Contract form on page 61 and fill it out, but do not sign it.

4. In your group, draw numbers to see who is going to go first. The member selected reviews her learnings and action plans with the group. The group helps the member be more clear about learnings. Some members' learnings may be too vague. Or a member may have achieved an insight about her career plans that she has not listed. The group also helps the member make

better action plans. Some members may plan to do more than is possible; other members may not plan to do enough. You may be able to think of a better way to put the learning into action.

5. The member's learning contract is modified until both he and the rest of the group are satisfied with it. He then signs the contract, and then the rest of the group signs the contract. The member is now committed to the group to carry out his action plans.

6. The whole process is repeated until every member of the group has a learning contract with the group.

7. The instructor will set a date for the group to review each member's progress in completing her action plans. Two weeks from signing would be a good time.

8. Working alone, keep a record of your progress in completing your action plans. Fill out a copy of the Learning Contract Progress Report form (see page 60), and use it to help you give a progress report to your group.

9. In the progress review session, give the day and date of the actions taken. You will be asked to describe what you did, what success you had, and what problems you encountered.

Reviewing Learning Contracts

At the end of Section III, you made a contract with your group. Your contract dealt with what you learned from the exercises in Section III and how you were going to apply those learnings. In this session you are to review your contract dealing with Section III.

Procedure

1. Draw numbers to see who will go first. Then go around the group clockwise. Each person is to review the tasks and activities he was to engage in to apply learnings from Section III. Then he is to give the day and date on which the tasks and activities were completed, tell what success he experienced, and state what problems he enountered. Group members are to praise a person's successes and provide helpful suggestions to overcome any problems a person is having in completing a learning contract.

2. When a learning contract has been completed, it is considered fulfilled. If a member has not fulfilled her learning contract, she is expected to do so in the near future. An unfinished contract will be discussed again at the next session set aside for that purpose.

9

Conflict Styles and Their Uses

After completing the Questionnaire for this chapter, you should be able to define and give examples of:

- Conflict
- Beneficial conflict
- Conflict style

The answers are given on the right side of the page. Work with a partner and keep the answers covered until you have agreed on your response. Remember to check each answer before going on to the next item, as explained on page 1.

QUESTIONNAIRE: Main Concepts in Chapter 9

1. A *conflict* exists whenever the actions of one person prevent, block, interfere with, injure, or in some way make the achievement of another person's goals less likely. When one person acts in a way that prevents another person from achieving his goals, the two persons have a _____.

   conflict

2. John wishes to take a day off from work to visit a friend. His boss, Mrs. B., assigns John an extra task for that day. She tells John the task is urgent and has to be done. She refuses to allow him to take the day off. John and Mrs. B. have a _____.

   conflict

3. Conflicts are always occurring at work. You will never have a job that does not involve some conflict with superiors or with fellow employees. Because people act in ways that interfere with someone else's goals, you will not be able to avoid having _____ at work.

   conflicts

4. Conflicts are not always harmful. Often they have very important and helpful outcomes. What makes a conflict harmful or beneficial is the skill with which it is managed. When a conflict is skillfully managed, the conflict will likely be _____.

   beneficial

5. Everyone has a personal style of managing conflicts. Your *conflict style* is shown by your most frequent actions in conflict situations. How you usually act in conflicts reflects your conflict _____.

   style

6. The first step in improving your conflict skills is to be aware of your conflict style. The more aware you are of how you usually act in conflicts, the better able you are to improve your conflict skills. Improving your conflict skills begins with being aware of your present conflict _____.

   style

Starting A Conflict

It's really easy to start a conflict at work. You can begin a conflict any time: in the cafeteria, in the parking lot, during coffee break, or while you are working. All you have to do is tell your boss to stop bugging you, or tell your coworkers they are stupid, or be impolite to a customer. Conflicts are very easy to start. Resolving them is difficult.

I worked loading trucks for a while. One day my supervisor came over and grabbed my shoulder and shoved me. I punched him and knocked him down. I told him to keep his hands off me. I was doing my work. He didn't have to put his hands all over me. I got fired, but it was worth it. Working is bad enough without having some guy who thinks he's a big shot watching me and bugging me.

Art Wall, Factory Worker

SURE WAYS TO START CONFLICTS

1. Arrive late for work every day. Leave early every day. Take long coffee breaks and lunch hours.
2. Dress inappropriately.
3. Criticize and put down your boss and coworkers.
4. Make the assumption that your boss is trying to stick you with all the dirty jobs that no one else will do. Then refuse to do anything extra your boss asks you to do.
5. Make the assumption that your boss and the organization you work for are your enemies. Then rip them off whenever you get the chance.
6. Dislike your fellow employees. And let them know in no uncertain terms that you dislike them.

There will be conflicts wherever you work and no matter what you do for a living. Every work relationship contains elements of conflict, disagreement, and opposed wishes. The more involved with or committed you are to your work, and the better your work relationships, the more likely you are to have conflicts. It is easier to disagree with your friends than with people you do not know, and it is easier to disagree over things you care about than over things that really do not matter to you.

What are conflicts? A prominent psychologist who studies conflicts states that a *conflict* exists whenever the actions of one person prevent, block, interfere with, injure, or in some way make the achievement of another person's goals less likely (Deutsch, 1973). If you want to do a good job, and your coworker is always goofing off, you have a conflict. If you want to have a quiet place to work and the person next to you is singing at the top of her voice, you have a conflict. When you want to be promoted and the person next to you is also working for the same promotion, you have a conflict. Whenever your goals and another person's goals interfere with each other, you have a conflict.

Conflicts are a moment of truth in a relationship. They may contain the seeds of destruction or the seeds of a closer and more cooperative relationship. Conflicts may develop into lasting hostility or may increase mutual understanding and respect. Conflicts can be very harmful or very helpful. A conflict can be a crisis that either weakens or strengthens your relationships with fellow employees. Conflicts can push coworkers away from you or pull them closer to you.

Do Conflicts Lead to Chaos?

I once worked with a secretary named Ann. She was in constant conflict with her fellow employees. If the other secretaries did not ask her to eat lunch with them, she took it to be a declaration of war. Then she would try to do something nasty to them during the afternoon. If the secretaries did not ask her to have coffee with them, she would cry the rest of the day. She often became upset with her boss. The boss would give her some special typing to do right when she was trying to get the mail out. This would send her into a rage. One week she would be having a feud with Mary. The next week it was an all-out war with John. One week she would complain to the boss that the other secretaries were being mean to her. The next week she would complain to the boss that he was acting viciously toward her. Every other week she would quit. Then she would beg and plead to be rehired. Once a month she would be fired for not getting along with her coworkers. Then she would beg and plead to be rehired. She would argue. She would shout. She would cry. She would curse and sweat. She fought her way from one end of the office to the other. Ann did not enjoy her work very much, and her coworkers did not enjoy working with her.

Ann's style of managing conflicts was to take offense at everything. She expressed rage directly to her fellow employees. To Ann and her fellow employees, conflict appeared to lead to chaos. They longed for the day when no conflicts would arise.

Conflicts will always be present while you are working. But do they always lead to chaos? Many people in our society would say yes. They believe that conflicts are bad. They want to avoid conflicts, and they think a good relationship is one in which there are no conflicts. The same people will go to great lengths to avoid disagreements and feelings such as anger. They believe that conflict causes psychological distress, violence, social disorder, unhappiness, breakdown of authority, and the ending of relationships. What do you think? Do conflicts always turn out badly? Do they always lead to chaos?

It is not the presence of conflict that causes chaos and disaster, but the harmful and ineffective way it is managed. It is the lack of skills in managing conflicts that leads to problems. When conflicts are skillfully managed, they are of value.

The Value of Conflicts

Conflicts, when skillfully managed, can be of great value to you and your career. Let's take a few examples.

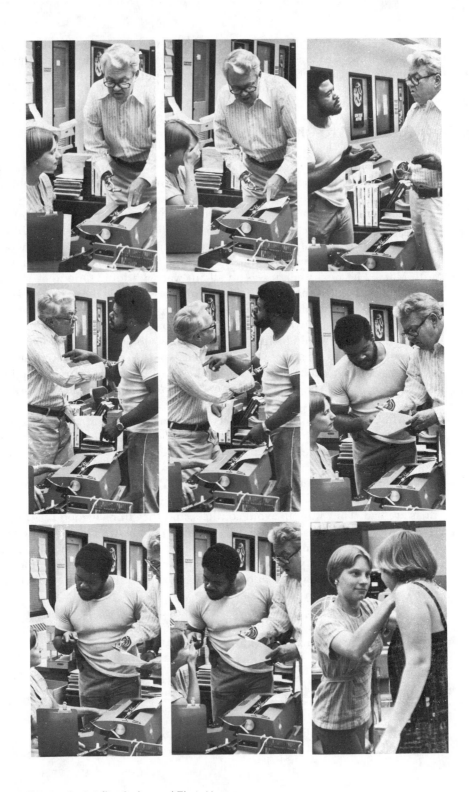

1. Being skillful in confronting your boss with the value of your work can lead to raises and promotions. Barbara Herrick (Terkel, 1972) said, "Men in my office doing similar work were being promoted, given raises and titles. Since I had done the bulk of the work, I made a stand and was promoted, too." Her willingness to confront her boss with the inequity of his policies led to her promotion.

2. Being aware of potential conflicts can increase your motivation to do your job well. John Fortune (Terkel, 1972) saw his meetings to sell advertising campaigns as being filled with conflict. He said, "Coming into a meeting is a little like swimming in a river full of piranha fish. If you start to bleed, they're gonna catch you." His awareness of the potential conflict increases his motivation to prepare fully for the meetings.

3. Conflicts make us more aware of job problems. They increase your awareness of what the problems are, who is involved, and how they can be solved. Art Wall's conflict with his superior (page 218) was a sign that there were problems with the way the company was selecting foremen. If all conflicts were ignored or covered up, then real and important problems about the way work is done would never be dealt with.

4. Conflicts encourage change. There are times when things need to change, when new methods are better than are the methods currently being used. Replacing current methods of work with better ones usually involves a conflict between the people who like the current methods and those who want to change.

5. Conflicts make work more interesting. Being in a conflict often sparks curiosity and stimulates interest. An argument about politics, company policy, or sports makes work less boring. When fellow employees disagree with your ideas, it may interest you in finding out more about the issue. Without some conflicts, you would get bored.

6. Better decisions are made when people disagree about what the decision should be. Disagreement causes the decision to be thought through more carefully.

7. Conflicts reduce the day-to-day irritations of working with other people. A good argument will do a lot to resolve the small tensions of working with other people.

8. Conflicts help you understand what you are like as a person. What makes you angry, what frightens you, what is important to you, and how you tend to manage conflicts are all highlighted when you are in conflict with someone. From being aware of what you are willing to argue about, you can learn a lot about yourself. From being aware of how you act in conflicts, you can learn a lot about yourself.

9. Conflicts can be fun when they are not taken too seriously.

Telling the Good from the Bad

How do you tell when a conflict has had helpful or harmful results? There are four things to look for:

1. If the two of you can work better together, the conflict has been beneficial.

2. If both you and the other person feel better about each other and your jobs, the conflict has been beneficial.

3. If both you and the other person are satisfied with the results of the conflict, the conflict has been beneficial.

4. If the ability of you and the other person to resolve future conflicts with each other has been improved, the conflict has been beneficial.

Your Style of Managing Conflicts

Conflicts always occur, and you can profit from them if you have the necessary skills. It is important, therefore, that you master the skills necessary for resolving conflicts in beneficial ways.

The first step in learning how to resolve conflicts beneficially is to become more aware of your style of managing conflicts. Your *conflict style* is how you most frequently act in conflict situations. Your present style may be to avoid conflicts. It may be to smooth conflicts over and pretend they are not there. It may be to meet your conflicts head on and to smash your way to victory. Your style may be to stick up for your rights while you feel anxious inside. Your style may be to try to persuade the other person that you are right. Or your style may be to give in and be as nice as you can to the person you have the conflict with. Whatever your style is now, your skills in managing conflicts begin with being aware of it.

To be more aware of your conflict style, you need to be aware of how you usually act in conflict situations. Be aware of your own behavior and your attitudes. Become conscious of your personal ideas about how to act in conflicts. Be aware of your feelings during and after conflicts. And think about the assumptions you make about how conflicts should be managed.

IS THE CUSTOMER ALWAYS RIGHT?

"The customer is always right!" is one style of managing conflicts with customers. Is the customer always right? Are there advantages to assuming that the customer is always right? Many people are careful never to disagree with their customers. Most persons who have steady customers are careful never to disagree with them. Sam Mature (Terkel, 1972) is a barber. He notes that a barber has to be able to talk about everything a customer may be interested in. But he is careful about disagreeing with what a customer believes. He states that it is all right to disagree on sports, but not on politics or religion. He tries to keep his customers by never disagreeing with them on a serious topic of conversation. What do you think of this style of managing conflicts?

Reviewing Your Conflict Style

To prepare for the following exercises, think back over the conflicts you have been involved in during the last few years. These conflicts could be with your parents or your brothers and sisters, with your boss or your coworkers, or with your teachers or with fellow students. They could even be with your friends.

On a sheet of paper, list the five largest and most important conflicts you can remember. Then describe your actions and feelings in dealing with the conflicts. Write down a complete description of each conflict.

EXERCISE 9.1   **Disagreeing**

PURPOSE

We all have different opinions about many issues. Because we have different opinions, we often get into disagreements and arguments. How we act and feel in arguing with another person is an important aspect of our conflict style. If you actively participate in this exercise, you will become more aware of how you act and feel during disagreements. You will also be able to give feedback to other group members about how they act during disagreements.

PROCEDURE

1. In your group, each member reads "The Fallout Shelter."
2. Working as a group, decide on the six people who are to go into the fallout shelter. You have twenty minutes to make the decision. During this exercise, argue strongly for your ideas and opinions. The future of the human species may depend on your group's decision. Make sure your group makes a good decision by arguing strongly for your opinions. Agree with the other group members only if they convince you that their ideas are better than yours.
3. Working by yourself, write the answers to the following questions:
   a. What were my feelings when I disagreed with someone?
   b. What were my feelings when someone disagreed with me?
   c. How did I act when I wanted to convince someone to change their ideas?
   d. How did I act when someone was trying to convince me to change my ideas?
   e. How would my conflict style be described during this group discussion?

4. Draw numbers to see who is going to be first. Then go around the group in a clockwise direction. Focusing on the member who is first, describe very briefly how you saw her actions during the group discussion. Make sure everyone in the group receives feedback before the lesson is over.

The Fallout Shelter

Your group is in charge of experimental stations in the far outposts of civilization. You work in an important department in Washington, D.C. Suddenly World War III breaks out. Nuclear bombs begin dropping. Places all across the world are being destroyed. People are getting into the available fallout shelters. Your group receives a desperate call from one of your experimental stations. They ask for your help. There are ten people at this station, but their fallout shelter only holds six. They cannot decide which six persons should enter the fallout shelter. They have agreed that they will obey your group's decision as to which six persons will go into the fallout shelter. Your group has only superficial information about the ten people and twenty minutes to make the decision. Your group realizes that the six people chosen may be the only six persons left to start the human species over again. Your group's decision, therefore, is very important. If your group does not make the decision within the twenty minutes allowed, all ten persons will die. Here is what you know about the ten people:

Bookkeeper, male, thirty-one years old

His wife, six months pregnant

Second-year medical student, male, militant black American

Famous historian and author, forty-two years old, male

Hollywood actress, a singer and dancer

Biochemist, female

Rabbi, fifty-four years old

Olympic athlete, all sports, male

College student, female

Policeman with gun (they cannot be separated)

Disagreeing: What's It Like?

While your group was deciding who was to enter the fallout shelter and who was not, there were some disagreements. It's impossible not to disagree, at least a little. Some members may have been silent during the whole discussion. Some members of your group may have agreed very quickly to what most of the other members wanted. Other members may have tried to overpower everyone else in order to get their opinions accepted. You may have noticed some members trying to seek compromises that everyone could agree to, while others kept trying to find out what made the most sense to do. They would keep going over the reasons why one person should be saved or not saved.

There are many ways to disagree. Some disagreements are so slight that they are never noticed. Other disagreements result in spirited arguments that can be heard for miles. The purpose of the Fallout Shelter exercise was to help you become more aware of how you feel and act during a disagreement. Did you learn anything new about yourself?

EXERCISE 9.2   **Dividing Up the Money**

PURPOSE

Some conflicts begin because there is only so much of something several people want, and no one can have as much as he would like. Salaries, promotions, office space, and supplies are often the source of such conflicts. When there is only so much money for raises, not everyone can get as large a raise as he wants. When there is only one manager's job open, only one person can get it. This exercise focuses on such a conflict. A group of three people have to decide how to divide some money two ways. If you actively participate in this exercise, you will become more aware of how you manage such conflicts. You will also be able to give other group members feedback on how they act during such conflicts.

PROCEDURE

1. Divide into groups of three. Each person contributes one dollar. The money is placed in the center of the group.

2. The group is to decide how to divide the money between *two* of their members. Only *two* people can receive money. The group has fifteen minutes to make this decision. The group cannot use any sort of "chance" procedure (such as drawing lots or flipping a coin) to decide which two persons get what amounts of money. Side agreements, such as buying a soda for the person left out, are not allowed. It is all right for one person to end up with all the money. A clear decision must be reached as to how the money is to be divided up between not more than two people.

3. Your object is to get as much money for yourself as you can. Try to convince the other two members of your triad that you should receive all the money. Tell them you are broke, poor, smarter than they are, or more deserving of the money. Tell them you will put it to better use or will give it to charity. If the other two people make an agreement to divide the money between themselves, offer one of them a better deal. For example, if they agree to split the money 50/50, tell one person that you will let her have a bigger share if she will agree to split the money with you.

4. A majority rules. Whenever two people make a firm agreement to split the money a certain way, the decision is made. Be sure, however, to give the third person a chance to make one of the two a better deal.

5. As soon as a decision is made, write your answers to the following questions. Work by yourself.
    a. What were my feelings during the decision making?
    b. How did I act during the decision making? What are the ways I handled the situation? Did I give up? Did I try to persuade others to my point of view? Did I try to take the money by force?
    c. How would my conflict style be described during the decision making?

6. In your group of three, give each other feedback. Draw a name to see who is going to be first. Then go around the group in a clockwise direction. Describe how you saw each other's actions during the decision making. Make sure all members of your group receive feedback.

7. In your six-member groups, discuss the following questions:
    a. What feelings were present in each small group during the decision making?
    b. How did members act in each small group during the decision making?
    c. What conflict styles were present in each small group during the decision making?
    d. What did we learn about conflict from the exercise?

Negotiating What's It Like?

The lesson on dividing up the money let you experience the process of negotiating. What is it like to negotiate? Did you:

_____ Stay silent during the whole thing and let the other two people divide the money?

_____ Try to force the other two people to let you have at least half the money?

_____ Try to give the money away to the two other people to make sure they didn't feel bad or get angry?

_____ Seek a compromise where somehow everyone would get their money back, even if it meant violating the rules for the exercise?

_____ Try to think of a logical reason as to which person (or persons) should get the money?

EXERCISE 9.3   **My Conflict Style**

PURPOSE

Different people learn different styles of managing conflicts. Your style of managing conflicts may be quite different from your best friend's style. The purpose of this exercise is to increase your awareness of your conflict style, and give you a chance to compare your conlfict style with the styles of the other members of your group.

PROCEDURE

1. Working by yourself, complete the Conflict Questionnaire on page 227.

2. Working by yourself, read the following text section entitled "Conflict Styles: What Are You Like?" Then take five slips of paper. Write the names of the other five members of your group on the slips of paper—one name only per slip.

3. Take one of the slips of paper and read the name on the slip. Then write on the slip the conflict style most like the person's actions in a conflict. Repeat this procedure until you have described the conflict style of each of the group members.

4. After all group members are finished, pass out your slips of paper. You should end up with five slips of paper, each containing a description of your conflict style as seen by the other group members. Each member of your group should end up with five slips of paper describing his or her conflict style.

5. Score your Conflict Questionnaire according to instructions given in Appendix B (see page 321). Rank the five conflict styles from most to least frequently used. This will give you an indication of how you see your own conflict style. The second most frequently used style represents your backup style to be used if your first one fails.

6. Draw names to see who is first. Then proceed around the group in a clockwise direction. The first person describes the results of her questionnaire. This is one view of her conflict style. Then she reads each of the five slips of paper on which the views of the group members as to her conflict style are written. Then she asks the group to give specific examples of how they have seen her act in conflicts. Repeat this procedure for every member of the group.

7. In your group, discuss the strengths and weaknesses of each of the conflict styles.

8. If there is time, your instructor will lead a discussion in which each group will give their conclusions as to the strengths and weaknesses of each conflict style.

*Conflict Questionnaire**

Proverbs state traditional wisdom. Below is a list of 20 proverbs and statements that reflect traditional wisdom for resolving conflicts. Read each carefully. Using the following scale, indicate how typical each proverb or statement is of your actions in a conflict.

> 5 = Very typical of the way I act in a conflict.
>
> 4 = Frequently typical of the way I act in a conflict.
>
> 3 = Sometimes typical of the way I act in a conflict.
>
> 2 = Seldom typical of the way I act in a conflict.
>
> 1 = Never typical of the way I act in a conflict.

1. Soft words win hard hearts.
2. Come now and let us reason together.
3. The arguments of the strongest always have the most weight.
4. You scratch my back, I'll scratch yours.
5. The best way of handling conflicts is to avoid them.
6. When one hits you with a stone, hit him with a piece of cotton.
7. A question must be decided by knowledge and not by numbers if it is to have a right decision.
8. If you cannot make a person think as you do, make him do as you think.
9. Better half a loaf than no bread at all.
10. If someone is ready to quarrel with you, he isn't worth knowing.
11. Smooth words make smooth ways.
12. By digging and digging, the truth is discovered.
13. He who fights and runs away lives to run another day.
14. A fair exchange brings no quarrel.
15. There is nothing so important that you have to fight for it.
16. Kill your enemies with kindness.
17. Seek till you find, and you'll not lose your labor.
18. Might overcomes right.
19. Tit for tat is fair play.
20. Avoid quarrelsome people—they will only make your life miserable.

*Adapted from Lawrence and Lorsh (1967).

Conflict Styles: What Are You Like?

Different people have different styles of handling conflicts. These styles are learned, usually when you are a child. And they seem to function automatically. Usually we are not aware of how we act in conflict situations. We just do whatever seems to come naturally. But we do have a personal style, and because it was learned, we can always change it by learning new and more effective ways of handling conflicts.

There are two major concerns in a conflict. *The first concern is achieving your personal goals.* You are in conflict because you have a goal that conflicts with another person's goal. Your goal may be highly important to you, or it may be of little importance. *The second concern is keeping a good working relationship with the other person.* You need to be able to work effectively with the person in the future. The relationship may be very important to you, or it may be of little importance. How important your personal goals are to you and how important the relationship is to you affects how you act in a conflict. Given these two concerns, five styles of managing conflicts can be identified.

1. ***The Turtle.*** Turtles withdraw into their shells to avoid conflicts. They give up their personal goals and relationships. They stay away from the issues over which the conflict is taking place and from the people they are in conflict with. Turtles believe it is hopeless to try to resolve conflicts. They feel helpless. They believe it is easier to withdraw (physically and psychologically) from a conflict than to face it.

2. ***The Shark.*** Sharks try to overpower opponents by forcing them to accept their solution to the conflict. Their goals are highly important to them and the relationship is of minor importance. They seek to achieve their goals at all costs. They are not concerned with the needs of other persons. They do not care if other persons like or accept them. Sharks assume that conflicts are settled by one person winning and one person losing. They want to be the winner. Winning gives sharks a sense of pride and achievement. Losing gives them a sense of weakness, inadequacy, and failure. They try to win by attacking, overpowering, overwhelming and intimidating other persons.

3. ***The Teddy Bear.*** To Teddy Bears, the relationship is of great importance, while their own goals are of little importance. Teddy Bears want to be accepted and liked by other people. They think that conflict should be avoided in favor of harmony and believe that conflicts cannot be discussed without damaging relationships. They are afraid that if the conflict continues someone will get hurt, and that would ruin the relationship. They give up their goals to preserve the relationship. Teddy Bears say, "I'll give up my goals, and let you have what you want, in order for you to like me." Teddy Bears try to smooth over the conflict in fear of harming the relationship.

4. ***The Fox.*** Foxes are moderately concerned with their own goals and about their relationships with other people. Foxes seek a compromise. They give up part of their goals and persuade the other person in a conflict to give up part of his goals. They seek a solution to conflicts where both sides gain something, the middle ground between two extreme positions. They are willing to sacrifice part of their goals and relationships in order to find agreement for the common good.

5. **The Owl.** Owls highly value their own goals and relationships. They view conflicts as problems to be solved and seek a solution that achieves both their own goals and the goals of the other person in the conflict. Owls see conflicts as improving relationships by reducing tension between two people. They try to begin a discussion that identifies the conflict as a problem. By seeking solutions that satisfy both themselves and the other person, owls maintain the relationship. Owls are not satisfied until a solution is found that achieves their own goals and the other person's goals. And they are not satisfied until the tensions and negative feelings have been fully resolved.

What Should I Be?

The exercises in this chapter may have made you more aware of your conflict style. In the last one, you gained both the results of the questionnaire and the feedback from fellow group members. This may have helped you become more aware of both your most frequently used and backup conflict styles. Your backup style is as important as your dominant style when your dominant has failed or when the conflict is causing a lot of stress. You may have found a lot of agreement between how you see yourself and how your group members see you. Or you may have found that you see yourself quite differently from the way your fellow group members see you. You may be wondering why other people do not see your actions the same way you do. If so, you may be planning changes in your actions to make them more clearly understandable by other people.

You may also be wondering what is the best conflict style. Is it better to be a turtle, shark, teddy bear, fox, or owl? And is it always a good idea to have the same conflict style? Maybe you should act differently in different conflicts? In Chapter 10 you will find out more about each conflict style, and when to use it.

Personality Conflicts: Handling Rejection

On every job you always encounter some personality conflicts. Not everyone will like everyone else. Some coworkers may not care for you.

But some of us may at times work someplace where almost everyone seems to reject us. How can we handle this rejection? What can we do when our fellow employees do not like us? The following advice may help.

1. Do not make the irrational assumption that you must be loved, liked, and approved of by everyone all the time or you will be absolutely miserable and will feel totally worthless.

2. Make the rational assumption that it would be nice if you were liked by everyone, but you can survive very well without the approval of some people. It is only the liking and approval of close friends and people with actual power over you (such as your boss) that you have to be concerned with.

3. Pay close attention to the feedback you receive from fellow employees. You need to find out why they do not like you.

4. Remember, you cannot force people to change how they interpret your actions and how they feel about you. What you can change is yourself. After changing yourself, you can try to influence people to change their interpretations and feelings.

5. Identify what actions your fellow employees do not like. Identify the conflicts you are having with them. How you define the conflicts is of great importance.

6. Try to see yourself from the standpoint of other people.

7. Change yourself. Try to behave in ways that do not trigger the situations in which you receive rejection. Avoid certain people if you have to. Behave in different ways.

8. Do not insult and anger your fellow employees. The more you reject them back, the harder it will be to change their opinion of you.

9. Be patient. It takes time for people to change. It takes time for your fellow employees to notice the changes in your behavior.

10. Do your work well. Take your responsibilities seriously and do a good job. Be dependable. Your fellow employees will respect you for this.

11. Like yourself. You cannot expect other employees to value you if you do not value yourself.

10

Resolving Conflicts Through Discussion

After completing the Questionnaire that follows, you should be able to define and give examples of:

- Negotiation
- Confrontation
- Hit-and-run
- Conflict strategy

The answers are given on the right side of the page. Work with a partner and keep the answers covered until you have agreed on your response. Remember to check each answer before going on to the next item, as explained on page 1.

1. *Negotiation* is a process of resolving a conflict by coming to a mutual agreement. Settling a dispute between you and a coworker so that you may get along together is the purpose of a _____.

   negotiation

2. A *confrontation* is engaging the other person in a conversation about the conflict directly, giving your definition of the conflict, sharing your feelings, and encouraging the other person to share his definition and feelings. When you tell another person how you see the conflict and feel about it, and ask him to do the same, you are engaging in a _____.

   confrontation

3. "I think we should talk about the disagreement we had last week. I'm uncomfortable with the way we have been avoiding each other since. How do you feel about it?" This is an example of a _____.

   confrontation

4. Confrontation is the opening step in a *negotiation*. When you confront another person, you are starting to _____.

   negotiate

5. We call it a "*hit-and-run*" when someone confronts a person about a conflict, gives her definition and feelings, and then takes off before the other person has a chance to respond. When a person gives her view of the conflict and her feelings about it and then leaves before the other person can say anything, a _____ has taken place.

   hit-and-run

6. "I'll never forgive you for not inviting me to your party. You have really made me feel rejected. There's my bus, goodby!" This is an example of a _____.

   hit-and-run

7. Choosing a *conflict strategy* means deciding which conflict style to adopt in a particular situation. Your goals and how important it is to maintain a good working relationship with the other person are the two things you need to consider in choosing a _____ _____.

   conflict strategy

8. In negotiating a conflict, it is helpful to be able to use whatever _____ _____ will work best.

   conflict strategy

It Takes Two to Tangle, It Takes Two to Untangle

It takes two people to create a conflict, and it takes two people to resolve a conflict. Conflicts are resolved through negotiation. ***Negotiation*** is a process by which persons who want to come to an agreement try to work out a settlement. Whenever two or more people get together to change their relationship, negotiations take place. Negotiation is an ever-present activity in human existence. We are all negotiators, from the first time we first cry for our mother's attention. We live in a world of constant negotiations, whether these be with coworkers, clients, superiors, suppliers, subordinates, friends, or family members. Not enough attention is paid to the role of negotiation in the work place, and not enough people know how to negotiate well.

Negotiations are rarely formal. Most negotiating occurs informally as an ongoing procedure to influence others and resolve disputes between you and your coworkers. The ultimate goal of negotiating is not to create winners and losers but to gain benefits for everyone involved. What works are solutions that meet the needs of all participants, otherwise you have to be careful when you go around dark corners. One-sided settlements imposed by the person with the most power at the moment are rarely stable or long lasting.

The purpose of negotiations is to reach an agreement as to how you and your coworkers will act toward each other in the future. You want to make sure that you and your coworkers have increased your ability to work together cooperatively. You want to make sure that you and your coworkers feel more friendly toward each other than before. By agreeing on how to act toward each other in the future, you can decrease the chances that the conflict will continue or reappear. The steps in negotiating to resolve a conflict with a coworker are:

1. Confronting the coworker.
2. Setting a time for discussion.
3. Jointly defining the conflict.
4. Communicating positions and feelings.
5. Communicating cooperative intentions.
6. Taking the opponent's perspective.
7. Coordinating motivation to negotiate in good faith.
8. Reaching an agreement.

Each of these steps will be discussed in this chapter.

To Talk or to Button Your Lips

If you want to resolve a conflict, you and the other person must discuss the conflict. If you do not discuss the conflict, it cannot be settled. But just any old discussion won't do. To derive benefits from the conflict, you have to discuss the conflict with some skill. And how you initiate the discussion of the conflict affects how beneficial or harmful the discussion of the conflict turns out to be . To confront the other person and begin a beneficial discussion of the conflict, you:

1. Start a direct conversation with the other person about the conflict.
2. Give your definition of the conflict.
3. Share your feelings about and reactions to the conflict.
4. Encourage the other person to do the same.

An open discussion is not always a helpful thing to have. It is a mistake to assume that you can *always* be open and discuss a conflict with a fellow employee. It is also a mistake to assume that you can *never* be open and discuss a conflict with a fellow employee. Whether you decide to open your mouth or button your lips depends on the other person and on the situation.

When you are trying to decide whether or not to begin a discussion about the conflict with the other person, you should ask yourself two questions:

1. What is your relationship with the other person like? How open is it? How strong is the relationship? Generally, the stronger the relationship, the more direct and powerful your discussion can be.

2. How able is the other person to discuss the conflict? If his anxiety level is high, the person may not be able to discuss the conflict in a helpful way. If the person's motivation to change his actions is low, he may not be able to discuss the conflict in a helpful way. If the person's ability to change is low, he may not be able to discuss the conflict helpfully.

If you do not think the relationship is strong enough, do not start a discussion about the conflict with the other person. If you do not think the other person is able to discuss the conflict in a helpful way, do not start a discussion.

Making a Date: Don't Hit and Run

Beginning the discussion of the conflict with your coworker does not mean that the conflict will be quickly resolved. It is a start, not the end. Be prepared to spend some time in negotiations before the conflict is fully resolved. You need to time your discussion so that you do not simply hit-and-run. *A hit-and-run* occurs when you start a conversation about the conflict, give your definition and feelings, and then take off before your coworker has a chance to respond. The hit-and-run approach creates resentment and anger. It does not lead to a constructive resolution of the dispute.

One of the most important aspects of confronting a coworker is the timing. Unconstructive fights often begin because the initiator confronts a coworker who is not ready. There are times when your coworkers will not be in the right frame of mind to face a confrontation. They might be too tired, in too great a hurry to take the necessary time, upset over another problem, or not feeling well. Starting a discussion when there is not enough time at least to define the conflict is a sure way of making the discussion destructive. Five minutes before the end of the work-

ing day is usually not a good time to confront a coworker. Calling a coworker late at night is usually not good timing, nor is trying to start a discussion just after the coworker has had a fight with his or her spouse. At times like these it is unfair to "jump" a coworker without notice and expect to get full attention for your conflict. Instead, approach your coworker with a request to discuss the conflict. Say, for example: "Something has been bothering me. Can we talk about it?" If the answer is yes, then you are ready to go further. It it is not the right time to confront your coworker, find a time that is agreeable to both of you.

**EXERCISE
10.1**   **Conflicts with the Boss**

PURPOSE

To have beneficial results from a conflict with your boss, the two of you have to talk directly to each other. For such a conversation to occur, someone must begin it. The purpose of this exercise is to give three specific examples of conflicts with the boss. These conflicts have actually happened. The group is to discuss what they would do to make sure the conflicts are managed in a beneficial way.

PROCEDURE

1. Working alone, read all three examples of conflicts with the boss. Then rank the five alternatives from the best ("1") to the worst ("5") way to start a discussion with your boss. In deciding what is the best thing to do, take into account the following:
   a. What are the employee's goals?
   b. How important are the goals to him?
   c. How important to him is the relationship with the boss?
   d. What is the best way to:
      (1) Improve the ability of the two people to work together.
      (2) Make their attitudes toward each other and their jobs more positive.
      (3) Reach an agreement that both are satisfied with.
      (4) Improve their ability to resolve future conflicts with each other.
   e. What is the most realistic thing to do?
2. In your group, rank the five alternative courses of action for the first example from the best ("1") to the worst ("5") way to start a discussion with your boss. Take into account the questions listed in Item 1.
3. Working as a group, list the interpersonal skills the employees need to discuss the conflict in a way that has beneficial skills. You may wish to refer to the list of interpersonal skills on pages 305–6.

4. Repeat this procedure for the second and third examples.
5. Your teacher will ask each group to report to the entire class as follows:
   a. In what order did the group rank the five alternatives for each example?
   b. What reasons does the group have for their rankings?
   c. What interpersonal skills are needed for a beneficial discussion of the conflict?

Examples of Conflicts with the Boss

1. MR. SMITH

You are a salesperson for a tire company. You work under a highly emotional sales manager, with whom you have a formal relationship. He calls you by your first name, but you call him "Mr. Smith." When he gets upset, he becomes angry and abusive. He browbeats you and your coworkers, and makes insulting remarks and judgments. These rages occur approximately once a week and last for about an hour. Most of the time, Mr. Smith is distant and inoffensive. He will tolerate no "back-talk" at any time. So far you and your coworkers have suffered his outbursts in silence. Jobs are scarce, and you have a spouse and a seven-month-old son to support. But you feel like a doormat and really do not like what Mr. Smith says when he is angry. The situation is making you irritable. Your anger at Mr. Smith is causing you to lose your temper more and more with your coworkers and family. Today he starts in again, and you have had it!

Rank the following five courses of action "1" to "5." Put a "1" by the course of action that seems most likely to lead to beneficial results. Put a "2" by the next most constructive course of action and so forth. Be realistic.

—— I try to avoid Mr. Smith. I am silent whenever we are together. I show a lack of interest whenever we speak. I want nothing to do with him for the time being. I try to cool down while I stay away from him. I try never to mention anything that might get him angry.

—— I lay it on the line. I tell Mr. Smith I am fed up with his abuse. I tell him he is vicious and unfair. And I tell him he had better start controlling his feelings and statements, because I'm not going to take being insulted by him any more! Whether he likes it or not he has to shape up. I'm going to make him stop or else I'll quit.

—— I bite my tongue. I keep my feelings to myself. I hope that he will find out how his actions are hurting our department without my telling him. My anger toward him frightens me. So I force it out of my mind. I try to be friendly, and I try to do nice things for him so he won't treat me this way. If I tried to tell him how I feel, he would only be angry and abuse me more.

—— I try to bargain with him. I tell him that if he stops abusing me I will increase my sales effort. I seek a compromise that will stop his actions. I try to think of what I can do for him that will be worth it to him to change his actions. I tell him that other people get upset with his actions. I try to persuade him to agree to stop abusing me in return for something I can do for him.

—— I call attention to the conflict between us. I describe how I see his actions. I describe my angry and upset feelings. I try to begin a discussion in which we can look for a way to reduce (1) his rages and (2) my resentment. I try to see things from his viewpoint. I seek a solution that allows him to blow off steam without being abusive to me. I try to figure out what I'm telling myself about his actions that is causing me to feel angry and upset. I ask him how he feels about my giving him feedback.

2. MR. JONES

You are employed as a mechanic. Most of the people who have their cars serviced and repaired have no idea what the labor and material charges should be. Your boss, Mr. Jones, is a friendly person. He is always slapping you on the back and telling you a joke, but he never engages in a serious conversation with an employee. He expects to be well-liked and obeyed without question. Employees are supposed to laugh at his jokes and keep their mouths shut about everything else. You are unmarried, broke, and paying for new furniture for your apartment and a new car. One day you notice that your boss has recorded twice as many hours as you worked on a customer's car. Checking back on other work you have done, you find that Mr. Jones regularly charges customers for more hours of labor than you actually worked. This really upsets you. You are not sure you can go on working for a person who overcharges customers.

Rank the following five courses of action from "1" to "5." Put a "1" by the course of action that seems most likely to lead to beneficial results. Put a "2" by the next most constructive course of action, and so forth. Be realistic!

—— I try to avoid Mr. Jones. I am silent whenever we are together. I show a lack of interest whenever we speak. I want nothing to do with him for the time being. I try to cool down while I stay away from him. I try never to mention anything that might make him angry at me.

—— I lay it on the line. I tell Mr. Jones I am fed up by his dishonesty. I tell him he is a crook. And I tell him he had better stop overcharging customers, because I'm not going to allow him to do it any more! Whether he likes it or not, he has to shape up. I'm going to make him stop, or else I'll quit.

—— I bite my tongue. I keep my feelings to myself. I hope that he will realize that honesty is the best policy without my having to tell him so. My anger toward him frightens me. So I force it out of my mind. I try to be friendly. I try to do nice things for him in the hope that he will voluntarily stop overcharging for my work. If I tried to tell him how I feel, he would only be angry at me. He wouldn't stop overcharging.

—— I try to bargain with him. I tell him that if he stops overcharging customers I will work harder. I seek a compromise that will stop his actions. I try to think of what I can do for him that will be worth it to him to change his actions. I tell him that other people are shocked and upset by his actions. I try to persuade him to agree to stop overcharging in return for something I can do for him.

—— I call attention to the conflict between us. I describe how I see his actions. I describe my angry and upset feelings. I try to begin a discussion in which we can look for a way to reduce his overcharging and my anger. I try to see things from his viewpoint. I seek a solution that allows him to look good to his boss without his overcharging customers. I try to figure out what I'm telling myself about his actions that is causing me to feel angry and upset. I ask him how he feels about my giving him feedback.

3. MS. BROWN

You are working as a bookkeeper in a large accounting firm. Your boss, Ms. Brown, is a highly skilled accountant. She is very much locked into doing things the way she has always done them. You have only worked for the firm one year. But within the first few weeks you started having ideas about how things could be done better. Ms. Brown is well liked among your coworkers, and she treats employees well as long as things get done the way she wants. She is friendly but impersonal. Even though she calls employees by their first name, there is a feeling of distance in her relationships. You have tried to make a good impression on her by making suggestions all year about how the work should be reorganized and changed. She has listened politely, made no comments, and has made no changes. This is your first job. You are ambitious and want to be promoted as fast as possible. You are using part of your salary to study accounting. You plan to be a certified public accountant in the future. When you received your annual evaluation, you found that Ms. Brown gave you a low rating. There is no explanation why. You think your work has been excellent. You know of no major mistakes you have made. Your impression is that you are always on time and very reliable in your work habits. You think you have worked as quickly and accurately as any other bookkeeper. You are furious at and hurt by the low evaluation. You do not know whether to quit, file a formal grievance, or ignore it.

Rank the following five courses of action from "1" to "5." Put a "1" by the course of action that seems most likely to lead to beneficial results. Put a "2" by the next most constructive course of action, and so forth. Be realistic!

—— I try to avoid Ms. Brown. I am silent whenever we are together. I show a lack of interest whenever we speak. I want nothing to do with her for the time being. I try to cool down while I stay away from her. I try never to mention anything that might make her angry at me.

—— I lay it on the line. I tell Ms. Brown I am fed up with her negative evaluation. I tell her she is biased and unfair. And I tell her she had better change it, or I will file a formal grievance against her. Whether she likes it or not, the evaluation has to be changed. I'm going to get a just evaluation, or else I'll quit.

——— I bite my tongue. I keep my feelings to myself. I hope that she will realize her evaluation has been unfair without my having to tell her so. My anger toward her frightens me, so I force it out of my mind. I try to be friendly, and I try to do nice things for her in hopes she will voluntarily change her evaluation of my work. If I tried to tell her how I feel, she would only be angry at me. Then she would give me a worse evaluation next year.

——— I try to bargain with her. I tell her that if she changes her evaluation of me I will do extra work. I seek a compromise that will change her opinion of my work. I try to think of what I can do for her that will be worth it to her to change her evaluation. I tell her that other people are shocked and upset by her evaluation of my work. I try to persuade her to agree to change her evaluation of my work in return for something I can do for her.

——— I call attention to the conflict between us. I describe how I see her actions. I describe my angry and upset feelings. I try to begin a discussion in which we can look for a way to change her evaluation of my work and my anger. I try to see things from her viewpoint. I seek a solution that allows her to give me more direct feedback about my work without her filing a negative evaluation. I try to figure out what I'm telling myself about her actions that is causing me to feel angry and upset. I ask her how she feels about my giving her feedback.

EXERCISE 10.2   **Role-Playing Conflicts with the Boss**

PURPOSE

Now that you have discussed the three examples of conflicts with the boss, it may be helpful to role-play them. Starting a discussion of a conflict is just the beginning. The conflict then has to be discussed in a way that leads to beneficial results. The purpose of this exercise is to role-play the entire discussion of the conflict between the employee and the boss.

PROCEDURE

1. In your group, take the first example from the previous exercise. One member should volunteer to play the role of the boss, Mr. Smith. Another member should volunteer to play the role of the employee. Every group member is to role play either the employee or the boss for one of three conflicts. The other four members observe to discuss the effectiveness of the employee's actions in discussing the conflict with her boss.

2. Spend up to ten minutes role-playing the discussion of the conflict.
3. In your group, discuss the role-playing:
    a. What were the approaches used to manage the conflict beneficially?
    b. What interpersonal skills were used?
    c. What interpersonal skills were not used, but might have been helpful?
    d. What changes in approaches would you make if you actually were in this situation?
4. Repeat this procedure for the second and third examples (Mr. Jones, Ms. Brown).
5. What conclusions can your group make about managing conflicts on the basis of your role-playing?
6. The instructor will ask each group to share their conclusions with the entire class.

EXERCISE 10.3   **Conflicts with Coworkers**

PURPOSE

To have beneficial results from a conflict with a coworker, the two of you have to talk to each other directly. For such a conversation to occur, some-one must begin it. The purpose of this lesson is to give three specific exam-ples of conflicts with a coworker. These conflicts have actually happened. The group is to discuss what they would do to make sure the conflicts are managed in a beneficial way.

PROCEDURE

1. Working alone, read all three examples of conflicts with a coworker. Then rank the five alternatives from the best ("1") to the worst ("5") way to start a discussion with the coworker. In deciding what is the best thing to do, take into account the following:
    a. What are the employee's goals?
    b. How important are the goals to him?
    c. How important to him is the relationship with the coworker?
    d. What is the best way to:
        (1) Improve the ability of the two people to work together.
        (2) Make their attitudes toward each other and their jobs more positive.

(3) Reach an agreement that both are satisfied with.

(4) Improve their ability to resolve future conflicts with each other.

e. What is the most realistic thing to do?

2. In your group, take the first example. As a group, rank the five alternative courses of action from best ("1") to worst ("5"). Take into account the questions listed in Item 1.

3. Working as a group, list the interpersonal skills the employee would need to discuss the conflict in a way that has beneficial results. You may wish to refer to the list of interpersonal skills on pages 305–6.

4. Repeat this procedure for the second and third examples.

5. Your teacher will ask each group to report to the entire class on the following:

a. In what order did the group rank the five alternatives for each example?

b. What reasons does the group have for their ranking?

c. What interpersonal skills are needed for a beneficial discussion of the conflict?

Conflicts with a Coworker

1. RALPH OVERTRAIN

You are working as a computer technician repairing computers. You make service calls to the customers of your company. Ralph Overtrain is one of your closest coworkers. He does the same type of work that you do. The two of you are often assigned to work together on large repair projects. You are married and have two children. Ralph is single and often has trouble with his girl friend. For the past several weeks, he has asked you to do part of his repair work because he feels too depressed and upset to concentrate on his work. You have agreed to such requests. Your wife is sick now, and you want to take some time off to visit her in the hospital. You ask Ralph if he would do part of your repair work so you can slip away and visit your wife. He refuses, saying that he is too busy and that it is your work, so you should do it. He says he sees no reason why he should do work you are getting paid for. You get more and more angry at Ralph. You see his actions as being completely selfish and ungrateful!

Rank the following five courses of action from "1" to "5." Put a "1" by the course of action that seems most likely to lead to beneficial results. Put a "2" by the next most constructive course of action, and so forth. Be realistic!

—— I try to avoid Ralph. I am silent whenever we are together. I show a lack of interest whenever we speak. I want nothing to do with him for the time being. I try to cool down while I stay away from him. I try never to mention anything that might make him angry or remind me of his ungratefulness.

—— I lay it on the line. I tell Ralph that I am fed up with his ungratefulness. I tell him he is selfish and a deadbeat. And I tell him he had better start paying back the favors I have done for him, because I am not going to help him if he will not help me. Whether he likes it or not he is going to do part of my work so I can visit my wife. I'm going to make him pay his debts to me, or else I'll quit.

—— I bite my tongue. I keep my feelings to myself. I hope he will find out his behavior is wrong without my having to tell him. My anger toward him frightens me. So I force it out of my mind and try to be friendly. I try to do nice things for him so he will be willing to do a favor for me in the future when I need him to. If I tried to tell him how I feel, he would only be angry. Then he would be less likely to do me favors when I need him to in the future.

—— I try to bargain with him. I tell him that if he does my work this time I will do part of his work tomorrow. I seek a compromise that will allow me to visit my wife. I try to think of what I can do for him that will be worth it to him to take part of my work today. I tell him that other people don't see him as being reasonable and friendly. I try to persuade him to agree to take part of my work today in return for something I can do for him.

—— I call attention to the conflict between us. I describe how I see his actions. I describe my angry and upset feelings. I try to begin a discussion in which we can look for a way to be more cooperative with each other's needs and to reduce my anger. I try to see things from his viewpoint. I seek a solution that allows him to feel he is only doing his work while at the same time allowing me to visit my wife in the hospital. I try to figure out what I'm telling myself about his actions that is causing me to feel angry and upset. I ask him how he feels about my giving him feedback.

2. SUSAN SPRING

You have been working as a keypunch operator in a large computer company for the past two years. You are friends with most of the other keypunch operators who work in your department. A couple of months ago, Susan Spring was hired as a keypunch operator. She is getting to know several of your friends. One of your friends has confided in you that Susan has been saying rather nasty things about your looks, the way you dress, the way you talk, and your personal character. For some reason you do not understand, she has taken an intense dislike to you. She is trying to get all the other keypunch operators also to dislike you. From what you hear, there is nothing too nasty for her to say about you. You are afraid that some people believe her and that most of your coworkers now dislike you. You are terribly upset and angry at Susan. Since you have a good job record and are quite skilled at keypunching, it would be easy for you to get a job elsewhere.

Rank the following five courses of action from "1" to "5." Put a "1" by the course of action that seems most likely to lead to beneficial results. Put a "2" by the next most constructive course of action, and so forth. Be realistic!

—— I try to avoid Susan. I am silent whenever we are together. I show a lack of interest whenever we speak. I want nothing to do with her for the time being. I try to cool down while I stay away from her. I try never to mention anything that might make her angry or remind me of her viciousness.

—— I lay it on the line. I tell Susan I am fed up with her gossiping. I tell her she is mean and vicious. And I tell her she had better stop talking about me behind my back, because I am not going to stand for it. Whether she likes it or not, she is going to stop her gossiping. I'm going to make her stop, or else I'll quit.

—— I bite my tongue. I keep my feelings to myself. I hope she will find out her behavior is wrong without my having to tell her. My anger toward her frightens me. So I force it out of my mind. I try to be friendly. I try to do nice things for her so she will stop gossiping about me. If I tried to tell her how I feel, she would only be angry. Then she would say even worse things about me.

—— I try to bargain with her. I tell her that if she will stop gossiping about me I will include her in everything my friends and I do at work. I seek a compromise that will stop her gossiping. I try to think of what I can do for her that will be worth it to her to stop gossiping. I tell her that other people are angry about her gossiping. I try to persuade her to agree to stop gossiping in return for something I can do for her.

—— I call attention to the conflict between us. I describe how I see her actions. I describe my angry and upset feelings. I try to begin a discussion in which we can look for a way for her to stop gossiping about me and for me to be less angry. I try to see things from her viewpoint. I seek a solution that allows her to feel accepted and liked and at the same time ends her gossiping about me. I try to figure out what I am telling myself about her actions that is causing me to feel angry and upset. I ask her how she feels about my giving her feedback.

3. SALLY OAKWORTH

You are working as a research analyst for a company that sells stocks and bonds. You are new in the company and have not yet learned all the ropes about how things are done around the office. You have been paired to do a series of research reports with Sally Oakworth. She has been working for the company for the past three years. Sally is a very friendly person. She has introduced you to many of the people in the company. She is always glad to eat lunch with you, and she has even invited you to her apartment for dinner. You feel you owe her a great deal. She is your best friend on the job. She is, however, very sloppy in her work. She often quickly writes down impressions without doing the needed research to back up her statements. She is consistently late with her part of the reports you are doing together. For two of the last three writing sessions you have scheduled with her, she has not shown up. She always seems to be talking to friends. Whenever you approach her to ask her about the reports the two of you are supposed to be writing, she introduces you to someone new. She then gets you engaged in a friendly and interesting conversation. Your boss has just asked you for the reports. He seems irritated when you tell him that they are not done. You are torn between your liking for Sally and your wanting to do a good job on the reports. You appreciate her help in getting to know people at work, but you are angry about her sloppy work and general nonproductiveness. Since she is so well-liked and since you are new, you are afraid you will be blamed for the sloppiness and lateness of the reports. This is your first job, and you do not want to blow it.

Rank the following five courses of action from "1" to "5." Put a "1" by the course of action that seems most likely to lead to beneficial results. Put a "2" by the next most constructive course of action, and so forth. Be realistic!

—— I try to avoid Sally. I am silent whenever we are together. I show a lack of interest whenever we speak. I want nothing to do with her for the time being. I try to cool down while I stay away from her. I try never to mention the reports, as that might make her angry. And the reports remind me of her sloppiness and failure to act responsibly.

—— I lay it on the line. I tell Sally I am fed up with her lack of work. I tell her she is lazy and irresponsible. And I tell her she had better start working, because I am not going to stand for her present lack of work. Whether she likes it or not, she is going to start doing her part on the reports. I'm going to make her do her share or else I'll quit.

—— I bite my tongue. I keep my feelings to myself. I hope she will find out her behavior is wrong without my having to tell her. My anger toward her frightens me. So I force it out of my mind. I try to be friendly, and I try to do nice things for her so she will start working more. If I tried to tell her how I feel, she would only be angry. Then she would do even less work on the reports.

—— I try to bargain with her. I tell her that if she will start doing more work I will have a series of parties and invite her. I seek a compromise that will increase the amount of time she spends working. I try to think of what I can do for her that will be worth it to her to work more on the reports. I tell her other people are angry at her sloppy work. I try to persuade her to work more in return for something I can do for her.

—— I call attention to the conflict between us. I describe how I see her actions. I describe my angry and upset feelings. I try to begin a discussion in which we can look for a way for her to work more and to reduce my anger. I try to see things from her viewpoint. I seek a solution that allows her to be friendly with other people while at the same time increases the quality of her work. I try to figure out what I am telling myself about her actions that is causing me to feel angry and upset. I ask her how she feels about my giving her feedback.

EXERCISE 10.4   **Role-Playing Conflicts with a Coworker**

PURPOSE

Now that you have discussed the three examples of conflicts with a coworker, it may be helpful to role-play them. Starting a discussion of a conflict is just the beginning. The conflict then has to be discussed in a way that leads to beneficial results. The purpose of this exercise is to role-play the entire discussion of the conflict between the employee and a coworker.

PROCEDURE

1. In your group, take the first example. One member should volunteer to play the role of the coworker. Another member should volunteer to play the role of the employee. Every group member is to role-play either the employee or the coworker for one of the three examples. The other four members observe to discuss the effectiveness of the employee's actions in discussing the conflict with her coworker.

2. Spend up to ten minutes role-playing the discussion of the conflict.

3. In your group, discuss the role-playing:
   a. What were the approaches used to manage the conflict beneficially?
   b. What interpersonal skills were used?
   c. What interpersonal skills were not used, but might have been helpful?
   d. What changes in approaches would you make if you actually were in this situation?

4. Repeat this procedure for the second and third examples.

5. What conclusions can your group make about managing conflicts on the basis of your role-playing?

6. The instructor will ask each group to share their conclusions with the entire class.

Putting Each Conflict Strategy in Its Place

Beginning a conversation about a conflict is like going swimming in a cold lake. Some people like to test the water, stick their foot in, and enter slowly. Such people want to get used to the cold gradually. Other people like to take a running start and leap in. They want to get the cold shock over quickly. Whether you go slowly or leap in, you have to discuss a conflict in order to resolve it. How you begin such a discussion depends on what conflict style you want to use.

The conflict style you adopt will depend on how important it is to you to:

1. Achieve your personal goals.
2. Keep a good working relationship with the other person.

Each of the conflict styles has its place. You need to be able to act like a Turtle, Shark, Teddy Bear, Fox, or Owl, depending on your goals and the relationship. It is not good to act the same in every conflict. In some conflicts, you will want to act one way; in other conflicts, you will want to act another way. To be effective in resolving conflicts, you have to vary your actions according to what will work best in the situation. You do not want to be an overspecialized dinosaur who can deal with conflict in only one way. You need to be able to switch actions according to what will work best.

When should you use each conflict style? Here are some helpful guidelines:

1. When the goal is not important and you do not need to keep a relationship with the other person, you may want to act like a *Turtle*. Avoiding a hostile stranger in the lunchroom or a bar may be the best thing to do.

2. When the goal is very important but the relationship is not, you may want to act like a *Shark*. When buying a used car or trying to get into a crowded restaurant, you may want to imitate a shark.

3. When the goal is of no importance to you but the relationship is of high importance, you may want to act like a *Teddy Bear*. When a fellow employee feels strongly about something, and you could care less, being a Teddy Bear is a good idea.

4. When both the goal and the relationship are moderately important to you and it appears that both you and the other person cannot get what you want, you may want to bargain like a *Fox*. When there is a limited amount of money, and both you and a fellow employee want a large raise, negotiating a compromise may be the best way to resolve the conflict.

5. When both the goal and the relationship are highly important to you, you may want to act like an *Owl*. When your boss is treating you unfairly or when you and a fellow employee disagree on how the work should be done, acting like an owl is the best thing to do.

Most of the time, you will want to act like an Owl or a Teddy Bear. In most conflicts on the job, these are the two styles that work best. When the goal is important, be an Owl. When it is not, be a Teddy Bear. Because you almost always need to keep good relationships at work, you will rarely want to act like a Shark or Turtle. Being a Fox is usually only helpful if being an Owl has failed or when there is not enough time to resolve the conflict like an Owl. Ideally, you will be able to use any of the five conflict styles, depending on the situation. It is important that you use each style skillfully and at the right time.

In the previous lessons in this chapter, you discussed how several conflicts should be managed. And you role-played each conflict. One of the purposes of those lessons was to give you a chance to discuss which conflict style should be used in each. For each of the conflicts discussed, you could choose to manage the conflict like a Turtle, Shark, Teddy Bear, Fox, or Owl. In what order did your group rank the five conflict styles for each conflict? What conflict styles did your group use most often? Did you emphasize the Owl and Teddy bear styles? Or did you use the Fox, Turtle, and Shark styles with some of the conflicts?

Agreeing on a Definition of the Conflict

Agreeing on the definition of a conflict is like putting gas in an airplane. Without it, conflict resolution will never get off the ground. After you begin a discussion about the conflict, you and the other person have to agree on a definition of the conflict. How you define the conflict together will influence how easily the conflict is to be resolved.

It is important that the conflict is defined in a way that does *not* make either you or the other person defensive. When people are defensive they feel attacked and defend their own point of view. Defensive people believe they are in a "win-lose" conflict and must prove that they are right and you are wrong. Defensiveness interferes with discussing a conflict in a helpful way. Making the other person defensive makes it more difficult to resolve the conflict.

When you begin the discussion of the conflict, you will have already arrived at your personal definition. The definition of the conflict you and the other person agree to, like your own personal definition, needs to:

1. Describe each other's actions without labeling or insulting each other.
2. Define the conflict as a mutual problem to be solved, not as a "win-lose" struggle.
3. Define the conflict in the smallest and most specific way possible.
4. Describe both your feelings and the other person's feelings.
5. Describe the actions of both you and the other person that help create and continue the conflict.

Once two people have agreed on a definition of a conflict, the conflict is usually easy to resolve.

Communicating Positions and Feelings

Be clear. Be flexible. Throughout negotiations, positions and feelings will change. Thus, the communication skills for presenting and listening to information and feelings will continually be necessary. Conflicts cannot be resolved if negotiators do not understand what they are disagreeing about. There are three major helpful hints to follow. Fight over issues, not personalities—find out about your differences before exploring your similarities, and manage your feelings constructively.

Fight Over Issues, Not Personalities

Never define a conflict as being caused by the other person's personality. It is easy to reject the other person when you disagree with him. It is easy to label, accuse, and insult the other person when you disagree with him. Instead of saying, "I disagree with your ideas," people often say, "You're stupid!" Instead of saying, "I think I work harder than you do," people often say, "You're lazy!" One of the first things to learn about helpful conflict is never to label, accuse, or insult the other person. *Make it clear it is ideas or actions you disagree with, not him as a person!* Do not criticize a person's personality when you disagree with his ideas or actions.

It is also important that you do not take criticism of your ideas and actions as rejection of you as a person. Do not let yourself feel rejected when someone disagrees with your ideas or actions. Do not take criticism of your ideas and actions personally. *An important conflict skill is being able to accept criticism of your ideas and actions without feeling rejected as a person.*

Find Out About Your Differences Before Exploring Your Similarities

Conflicts cannot be resolved unless you understand what you are disagreeing about. If you do not know what you are disagreeing about, you cannot find a way to reach an agreement. You must understand the differences between you and the other person. Only then will you be able to think of ways to combine ideas so that the conflict is resolved. *Only if you understand the differences can you think of a way to resolve the conflict helpfully.* Your ability to come up with satisfactory solutions de-

pends on how the other person's thoughts, feelings, and needs are different from yours. Thus, in discussing a conflict you try to find the answers to these questions:

1. What are the disagreements and differences between myself and the other person?
2. What do we agree on?
3. What actions of the other person do I find unacceptable?
4. What actions of mine does the other person find unacceptable?
5. What are possible solutions that satisfy both myself and the other person?

6. What are the things I need to do to resolve the conflict?
7. What are the things the other person needs to do to resolve the conflict?

○   ○   ○

I get angry when I'm at work. All the time people watching me, on my back, telling me to work harder. But who you gonna smash? You can't smash a company. You can't hit Washington. You can't take a swing at a system. I work so damn hard. I want to come home and sit down and lay around. But I gotta get it out. I want to be able to turn around and tell somebody to get lost. All day long I've wanted to tell the supervisor to get lost, but I can't. So I find a guy in a bar. I tell him to get lost. And he tells me too. I've been in brawls. He's hitting me and I'm socking him, because we both want to be punching someone else. The most that'll happen is being thrown out of the bar. But at work, you'll lose your job.

Ralph Adams, Factory Worker

○   ○   ○

Manage Your Feelings

Expressing and controlling your feelings is one of the most difficult aspects of resolving conflicts. There are negative feelings in conflicts that are hard to express and hard to control. Anger, rejection, and mistrust are three examples. There is a risk in expressing feelings such as anger. When you express anger, you have to worry about alienating the other person. Expressing anger could lead to losing the relationship or even losing your job. And you have to worry whether the other person will also get angry at you. Being exposed to the anger of others is painful.

Yet keeping anger buried is usually harmful. Repeated failure to express anger in words sometimes produces the appearance of apathy. The concealed anger is often displaced onto other persons. Not expressing anger in words at work can lead to being angry at your friends, family, or some stranger in a bar. Hidden anger does not vanish, but often suddenly erupts in physical violence and assaults on both people and property. In the long run, keeping anger to yourself will only hurt you and your relationships.

There is a need to express anger constructively in conflicts. To express anger constructively, it must be controlled. Uncontained anger often takes the form of verbal or physical threats. Threats make the conflict harder to resolve. The problem is to control your anger enough so it can be expressed helpfully.

There are several advantages to expressing anger in a conflict. Anger conveys to other people what your commitments are and which commitments must be respected or changed. Expressing anger can clear the air so that positive feelings can once again be felt and expressed. And it saves your family, friends, and other people with whom you come into contact much needless pain. *The key to expressing anger in a conflict is to say it directly in words, focusing it on the issue the conflict is about.* You may want to review the discussion of anger in Chapter 7.

Besides expressing negative feelings, it is important to express positive feelings while discussing a conflict. There are positive feelings, such as liking, appreciation, and respect, that strengthen your relationship with the other person. Both positive and negative feelings have to be communicated with skill in a conflict. Some general rules to follow are:

1. When the other person expresses a feeling toward you, use the communication skills of paraphrasing and checking perceptions to show you understand how she is feeling.
2. Always describe your feelings.
3. Always describe without evaluation the actions of the other person that influenced your feelings.
4. Avoid irrational assumptions that lead to negative feelings.
5. When a person expresses a feeling toward you, always respond with a feeling. Feelings need to be answered by feelings, not by silence, uninvolved understanding, or ridicule.
6. When it can be done in a helpful way, express your feelings. Hidden feelings usually cause problems in the future.
7. Review the suggestions about expressing feelings on pages 154–58.

Once you have expressed your anger constructively, you need to "let it go" and free yourself from it. A number of problems can result if you hold on to your anger. First, it adds to your frustrations. This is not sensible. Getting angry over a frustration does not usually remove the frustration and always adds to your discomfort. Second, anger prevents you from solving problems. Being hateful simply fills your thoughts with ways of getting even with others, not with how to get others to behave differently toward you. The net result is that things get worse and worse as you become angrier and angrier. Third, anger can make you physically sick. Headaches, high blood pressure, and physical pains are not helpful when you are trying to resolve a conflict.

Long-term anger is based on two irrational beliefs. The first is that you must have your way and that it is awful not to get everything you want. This is known as catastrophizing. The second is that people are bad and should be severely dealt with if they have behaved wrongly. They are wicked for frustrating you and deserve to be punished. This blame orientation distracts you from finding a solution to your frustration. The worst result of blaming others is the anger that you must then carry around inside your body. When you blame others, they become much more hostile and angry with you. *Blame* occurs when you find fault with someone's behavior and with that person at the same time. Be problem-oriented, not blame- or fault-oriented. Never blame anyone. Always separate the person from his actions. People behave badly for three reasons: stupidity, ignorance, and disturbance. Forgive everything. Sooner or later we forgive those we disagree with. Since you will eventually forgive the other person, the sooner you do so the better for you.

Communicating Cooperative Intentions

○   ○   ○

I hold it to be a proof of great prudence for men to abstain from threats and insulting words toward anyone, for neither . . . diminishes the strength of the enemy; but the one makes him more cautious, and the other increases his hatred of you and makes him more persevering in his efforts to injure you.

NICCOLO MACHIAVELLI,
16th Century Adviser to Florentine Princes

○   ○   ○

One of the most constructive things you can do in resolving a conflict with a coworker is to communicate clearly that you are motivated by a desire to work out a better relationship so the two of you can work more effectively together in the future. Make sure your intentions are cooperative, not competitive. One way to do this is to make it clear that you want the coworker's needs to be met as well as your own.

Successful negotiation lies in finding out what the other side really wants and showing it a way to get it while you get what you want. If you want to deal effectively with people, if you want to convince them, if you want to negotiate, if you want to persuade them, then you have to approach people based on their needs. The heart of negotiation is showing coworkers how their needs and your needs can be met simultaneously. This means that you need to find out what the needs of your coworkers are and propose solutions that take their needs into consideration.

Humor is one of the most important aspects of keeping conflicts constructive. Keep your sense of humor during the negotiations. The use of humor in relationships is discussed in detail in Chapter 12.

From the Other Person's Perspective

It is common to misunderstand the motivations behind an opponent's actions. In order to understand a coworker's actions and position, you will have to see the conflict from his perspective. And this will require that you be detached from your position sufficiently to see the conflict from new perspectives. Negotiation requires a realistic assessment of common and opposing interests. It requires the sacrifice of some of the opposing interests so that the common benefits, concerns, advantages, and needs may be built on. In order to settle a conflict, it is necessary to have a clear understanding of all sides of the issues and an accurate assessment of their validity and relative merits.

Resolving conflicts means that you have to understand the other person's thoughts, feelings, and needs. To do this, you use good listening skills. One of the most important communication skills in resolving conflicts is being able to view the conflict from the other person's shoes. To understand fully the other person's thoughts, feelings, and needs in the conflict, you need to be able to see it from her perspective. Different people have different perspectives. No two people will see a conflict in exactly the same way. Each person will interpret identical events slightly differently. Your boss will have one perspective. You will have another perspective. You will conclude one thing from someone's actions. Another person may conclude something entirely different. For example, your coworker may insult you. You may conclude he does not like you, but he may conclude that because he likes you he is teasing you. From your perspective, an insult means dislike. From his perspective, an insult means teasing, which means liking. To be able to resolve a conflict helpfully, you need to keep in mind both your own perspective and the perspective of the other person.

Role-playing is an easy way to increase your understanding of another person's perspective. By trying to present your opponent's thoughts, feelings, and needs as if you were he, you can gain insight into his perspective. When you and a fellow employee are having a conflict, try presenting her position as if you *were* she. Then have her present your position as if she were you. The more involved you get in arguing each other's positions, the more you will understand how the conflict appears from the other person's viewpoint. Role-playing as if you were your opponent will help you to find solutions that are mutually acceptable.

There is nothing more important in resolving conflicts helpfully than to understand how the conflict looks from the other person's perspective. Once you can view the conflict both from your perspective and the other person's perspective, you can find solutions that satisfy both you and the other person. You can also communicate to the other person that you really understand her thoughts, feelings, and needs. It is usually much easier to resolve a conflict when the other person feels understood. The more skilled you are in seeing things from other people's shoes, the more skilled you will be in resolving conflicts helpfully.

Coordinating Motivation to Resolve the Conflict

There are often differences in motivation to resolve a conflict. You may want to resolve a conflict but your fellow employee could care less. Your boss may be very concerned about resolving a conflict with you, but you may want to avoid the whole thing. Today you may want to resolve the conflict but your fellow employee does not. Tomorrow the situation may be reversed. Usually, conflict cannot be resolved until both persons are motivated to resolve it at the same time.

The motivation to resolve a conflict is based on the costs and gains of continuing the conflict for each person. The *costs* of continuing a conflict may be the loss of a friendship, loss of enjoyment from work, the loss of job productivity, the loss of the cooperation on the job, the loss of salary or promotions, or sometimes even the loss of your job. The *gains* for continuing the conflict may be satisfaction in expressing your anger or resentment and the protection of the status quo. By pro-

tecting the status quo, you avoid the possibility that things will get worse when the conflict is resolved. Answering the following questions will often help you clarify your motivation and the other person's motivation to resolve the conflict.

1. What do I gain from continuing the conflict?
2. What does the other person gain from continuing the conflict?
3. What do I lose from continuing the conflict?
4. What does the other person lose from continuing the conflict?

A person's motivation to resolve a conflict can be changed. By increasing the costs of continuing the conflict or by increasing the gains for resolving it, the other person's motivation to resolve it can be increased. Through changing costs and gains, you can change both your and the other person's motivation to resolve the conflict.

Success in negotiations is based on believing you have the power to influence your coworkers, seeing a number of optional agreements, and being willing to take risks during the negotiations. *Power* is the ability to influence another person. During negotiations you want both yourself and your coworker to believe that one of you has the power to influence the other. In many cases your power is based on your belief that you have it. If you think you are powerless and cannot influence your coworker, you will be powerless. If you think you can, often you can. Typically, you will have more power than you think. And it is important to you that your coworker believes that power is fairly equal between the two of you. When people are powerless, it is bad for everyone. Either they become hostile and try to tear down the system or they become apathetic and throw in the towel. You do not want either one.

Reaching an Agreement

The conflict ends when you and the other person reach an agreement. You seek an agreement that both you and the other person can be satisfied with. You look for a way to meet the needs of both persons. In reaching an agreement, the following points should be clearly understood.

1. The conflict is to end.
2. The ways in which you will act differently in the future are clear.
3. The ways in which the other person will act differently in the future are clear.
4. The ways in which cooperation will be restored if one person slips and acts inappropriately are clear.
5. The times the two of you will meet to discuss your relationship and to see if further steps can be taken to improve your cooperation with each other are spelled out.

It is important that both you and the other person understand which actions trigger anger and resentment in the other. Criticism, put downs, sarcasm, belittling, and other actions often trigger a conflict. If the two of you understand what *not* to do as well as what to do, the conflict will be resolved much more easily.

One way to understand how constructive agreements may be reached is to look at a few examples.

Example 1. Roger was a coin collector; his wife, Ann, loved to raise and show championship rabbits. Their income did not leave enough money for both to practice their hobbies, and splitting the cash they did have would not have left enough for either. SOLUTION: Put all the first year's money into the rabbits, and then after they were grown use the income from their litters and show prizes to pay for Roger's coins.

Example 2. Edythe and Buddy shared an office but had different work habits. Edythe liked to do her work in silence while Buddy liked to socialize in the office and have the radio on. SOLUTION: Mondays and Wednesdays Buddy would help keep silence in the office while on Tuesdays and Thursdays Edythe would work in a conference room that was free. On Fridays the two worked together on joint projects.

Example 3. Keith loved to spend his evenings talking to people all over the world on his ham radio set. His wife, Simone, felt cheated out of the few hours of each day they could spend together. Keith did not want to give up his radio time and Simone was not willing to forego the time they had together. SOLUTION: Four nights each week Keith stayed up late and talked to his ham radio friends after spending the evening with Simone. On the following mornings Simone drove Keith to work instead of having him go with a carpool. This arrangement allowed him to sleep later and gave them more time together.

You can not be sure the agreement will work until you try it out. After you have tested it for a while, it is a good idea to set aside some time to talk over how things are going. You may find that you need to make some changes or even re-think the whole problem. The idea is to keep on top of the problem so that the two of you may solve it creatively.

EXERCISE 10.5   **Starting an Argument***

PURPOSE

The purpose of this exercise is to start a safe argument and allow the release of anger without hurting someone.

PROCEDURE

1. Hold up either your thumb or your small finger in the air. Pair up with another person who is doing the same thing you are.
2. The basic procedure is to contradict every statement made by your partner. Say the opposite very forcefully. Start softly, get louder and louder, and then bring it back on down to soft again. Decide who is to make the first statement. The other states the opposite. The only rule is you cannot use either the words "I" or "you." Remember, start soft, work your way louder, and then back to softer again. The "nay-sayer" argues at exactly the same volume as the initiator. Use hand motions to emphasize your word or phrase. Coordinate your hand motions with the volume of your voice.
3. Switch roles and repeat the procedure.
4. Make up with your partner. Tell your partner you did not really mean it. Apologize and forgive.

---

*This exercise is taken from the book, *Playfair,* by Weinstein and Goodman (1980).

From My Shoes, Then from Your Shoes

PURPOSE

How well you understand your opponent's thoughts, feelings, and needs in-fluences how easily the conflict is resolved. The more the understanding be-tween two persons, the easier it is to resolve a conflict. The less the understanding between two persons, the harder it is to resolve a conflict. To understand fully the thoughts, feelings, and needs of your opponent you have to see the conflict from your opponent's shoes, and vice versa. The pur-poses of this exercise are to give you some practice in (1) presenting your position to an opponent and (2) seeing the conflict from your opponent's viewpoint.

PROCEDURE

1. In your group, decide on a topic of current interest on which there are differences of opinion. The topic could be women's rights, racial relations, abortion, drug use, corruption in politics, or any other con-troversial topic.

2. Divide your group into two subgroups of about three members each. The subgroups are to take opposite sides on the issue to be discussed.

3. The subgroups meet separately for fifteen minutes. They prepare their arguments to support their side of the issue. Think of all the arguments you can to support your position. Gather all the informa-tion you can to support your arguments. Plan how you will disprove the arguments of the other subgroup.

4. Each member of a subgroup is paired with a person from the other subgroup. This results in three pairs. Each pair is made up of one per-son from each subgroup.

5. Each person in the pair has up to five minutes to present his subgroup's position. All the skills for effective sending and receiving should be used. As the other person presents his subgroup's position, take notes to help you remember what he is saying.

6. Each person next has up to five minutes to present his opponent's position as if he were his opponent. Try to get into your opponent's shoes in presenting his position. Be as involved as you can.

7. In your group of about six, discuss the following questions.
   a. How did it feel to present your opponent's position?
   b. What did you learn from presenting your opponent's position?
   c. Have your attitudes been modified by presenting your opponent's position?
   d. Did anything stand in your way when you presented your opponent's position as if you were he? Was it hard to do?

e. How did it feel to hear your opponent presenting your position?

f. Did you learn anything from hearing your opponent present your position?

g. Were your attitudes modified by hearing your opponent present your position?

EXERCISE 10.7   **Feelings In Conflicts***

PURPOSE

A basic aspect of any conflict are the feelings a person has while the conflict is taking place. Two common feelings are rejection and mistrust. Many people are afraid of conflicts because they are afraid they will be rejected. And many people avoid conflicts because they do not trust the other person. The purposes of this exercise are to experience the feelings of rejection and mistrust and to discuss how they influence your actions in conflicts.

PROCEDURE, PART 1: Feelings of Rejection

1. The first half of the exercise deals with feelings of rejection. Divide the whole class into groups of four.

2. The instructor will pass out instructions (from Appendix B) to each person in each group. The groups have ten minutes to select one person to be rejected and excluded from the group.

3. In your regular group of about six, discuss the following questions:
   a. Did you feel rejected by the other members in your group of four?
   b. What is it like to feel rejected? What other feelings result from being rejected?
   c. How do you act when someone is rejecting you?
   d. When you are in a conflict, how can you act to minimize feelings of rejection on both your part and on the part of the other person?

PROCEDURE, PART 2: Feelings of Mistrust

1. The second half of this lesson deals with feelings of mistrust. In your groups of six, divide into pairs.

2. The instructor will give each member of the pair a set of instructions (from Appendix B). Your pair has five minutes to interact after you have both read the instructions.

*Instructions for this exercise are in Appendix B.

3. In your group, discuss the following questions:
   a. Did you feel mistrusted by the other member of the pair?
   b. Did you mistrust the other member of the pair?
   c. How do you act when someone mistrusts you?
   d. What is it like to feel mistrusted? What other feelings result from being mistrusted?
   e. When you are in a conflict, how can you minimize the feelings of mistrust on both your part and on the part of the other person?
4. Your instructor will ask each group to present their conclusions about how to minimize rejection and mistrust in conflicts.

HOW TO MAKE FRIENDS ON THE JOB

1. Whenever possible, manage conflicts like an Owl. View conflicts as problems to be solved. Be aware of their potential value. And seek a solution that achieves both your goals and the goals of the other person. Try to improve your relationship with the other person by resolving the conflict.
2. Define conflicts skillfully. Describe the other person's actions without insulting her. Make sure the conflict is over issues and actions, not personalities. Define the conflict as a mutual problem to be solved, not as a win-lose struggle. Define the conflict in the smallest and most specific way possible. Describe your feelings about the other person's actions. And describe your actions that help create and continue the conflict.
3. Begin open conversations about the conflict. Define the conflict jointly with the other person. Find out how you and the other person differ before trying to resolve the conflict. See the conflict from the other person's viewpoint. Manage your feelings so they do not make the conflict worse.

SUMMARY AND REVIEW: CHAPTERS 9 AND 10

Setting Learning Contracts

You are to make a learning contract with your group. The learning contract should summarize the most important things you have learned from Chapters 9 and 10. It should include a plan as to how you will use what you have learned. Chapters 9 and 10 focus on resolving conflicts. It is time to reflect, with your group's help, on what you have learned about resolving conflicts and on how you can use what you have learned.

Be as specific as you can in stating what you have learned and how you will apply what you have learned. The following procedure is to be used in setting your learning contract with your group.

Procedure

1. Working by yourself, make a list of the more important things you have learned about resolving conflicts. List at least five things you have learned.

2. Select the five most important things you have learned. For each one, plan an action you can take in the next two weeks to apply that learning. In making your action plans, be specific and practical. Do not try to do either too much or too little.

3. Copy the Learning Contract on page 59 and fill it out, but do not sign it.

4. In your group, draw numbers to see who is going to go first. The member selected reviews her learning and action plans with the group. The group helps the member be more clear about learnings. Some members' learnings may be too vague. Or a member may have achieved an insight about her career plans that she has not listed. The group also helps the member make better action plans. Some members may plan to do more than is possible; other members may not plan to do enough. You may be able to think of a better way to put the learning into action.

5. The member's learning contract is modified until both she and the rest of the group are satisfied with it. She then signs the contract, and then the rest of the group signs the contract. The member is now committed to the group to carry out her action plans.

6. The whole process is repeated until every member of the group has a learning contract with the group.

7. The instructor will set a date for the group to review each member's progress in completing his action plans. Two weeks from signing would be a good time.

8. Working alone, keep a record of your progress in completing your action plans. Fill out a copy of the Learning Contract Progress Report form on page 60, and use it to help you give a progress report to your group.

9. In the progress review session, give the day and date of the actions taken. You will be asked to describe what you did, what success you had, and what problems you encountered.

Reviewing Learning Contracts

At the end of Section IV, you made a contract with your group. Your contract dealt with what you learned from the exercises in Section IV and how you are going to apply those learnings. In this session you are to review your contract dealing with Section IV.

Procedure

1. Draw numbers to see who will go first. Then go around the group clockwise. Each person is to review what tasks and activities she was to engage in to apply learnings from Section IV. She then is to give the day and date on which the tasks and activities were completed, tell what success she experienced, and state what problems she encountered. Group members are to praise a person's successes and provide helpful suggestions to overcome any problems a person is having in completing a learning contract.

2. When a learning contract has been completed, it is considered fulfilled. If a member has not fulfilled her learning contract, she is expected to do so in the near future. An unfinished contract will be discussed again at the next session set aside for that purpose.

11

Identity, Career, and Life Goals

After completing the Questionnaire that follows, you should be able to define, discuss, and give examples of

- Identity
- Social roles
- Career identity

The answers are given on the right side of the page. Work with a partner and keep the answers covered until you have agreed on your response. Remember to check each answer before going on to the next item, as explained on page 1.

1. Your *identity* is a set of attitudes that defines who you are and how you are similar to and uniquely different from other people. Your view of who you are, how you are different from others, and how you are similar to certain people is your _____.

   identity

2. "I am a rather serious person, hard working, persistent, quiet, somewhat shy, intense, and emotional" is an example of one person's view of his _____.

   identity

3. Your *social role* is the set of actions that people expect of you and that define your identity in the eyes of other people. Some examples of _____ _____ are student, friend, parent, sibling, spouse, and citizen.

   social roles

4. The *career* you choose will affect the social roles you will play. Your career is an important influence on your *identity*. When you say "I am a lab technician," or "I am a salesperson," you are defining your _____ in terms of your _____.

   identity
   career

My Work Defines Me

Ralph Waldo Emerson once said, "We are what we do." Of all the things you do, your work probably defines you, your life goals, and your relationships with other people most clearly. Adult lives center around work. Your career determines where you live, where your children go to school, and with whom you come into contact. It establishes you in a network of relationships. It makes you part of a cooperative effort to create a product or service that is needed by others—an effort to contribute something of value to the lives of others. Your career helps put your past, present, and future in harmony. And your career gives your life meaning.

At the beginning of this book we reviewed your goals, needs, assets, and credentials. In this chapter we review how you see yourself as a person, how you now view your goals, how you see your career efforts as fitting in with those of other people, and how your past, present, and future are all tied together by your career.

Who I Am

How you describe yourself as a person is your identity. Your **identity** is a consistent set of attitudes that defines who you are. These attitudes contain both a view of how you are similar to other people and a view of how you are unique as a person.

The world can change. Other people can change. Your career can change. But there is something about yourself that stays the same. And that something is your identity.

○   ○   ○

I enjoy it, actually. I think any kind of work, after a while, . . . has an intensity of its own. You start out doing something for a reason, and if you do it long enough, even though the reason may have altered, you continue to do it, because it gives you its own satisfaction.

John Fortune, Advertising Department
in STUDS TERKEL, *Working*

○   ○   ○

I've been helping build cars for over twenty years. Sometimes I wonder if cars are worth all the pain and sweat that goes into them. But when I see them on the highway I think of all the good people I've known who spent their lives building cars. I think of the people who make the steel we shape into cars. I know that lots of people just like me put their work into building those cars. When I see a car go by, I feel proud.

Jake Garinger, Factory Worker
in STUDS TERKEL, *Working*

○   ○   ○

There are three ways you build your identity. The first is by comparing yourself with other people. The second is by trying to be like people you admire. And the third is by taking on social roles.

Being part of a cooperative effort allows you to compare yourself with others. It is within cooperative relationships that you increase your self-awareness (by finding out how other people see you). Through cooperating with people, you become aware of how you are similar to and different from others. The better you know other people, the clearer you will be about your identity. The more feedback you receive from other people, the better you will know yourself as a person. It is from your cooperative relationships that you find out whether you are an emotional or unemotional person, whether you are diplomatic or blunt, or whether you are sensitive or nonsensitive as a person. From hearing about other people's attitudes, you become more aware of your own attitudes. By sharing experiences and feelings, you become more self-aware. Cooperation promotes the type of relationships in which you can get to know other people and yourself.

A second way you build your identity is by deciding who you want to be like. Everyone has people they like, admire, and see as unusually competent or powerful. You will want to be like such people. So you will adopt their attitudes and actions. One of the interesting things about wanting to be like other people whom you admire is that the people do not have to be real. They can be fictional or fantasy persons! You may decide that you want to be like a character in a movie. You may decide that you want to be like a person in a book. Most of the people you will want to be like, however, will be people you cooperate with. Your parents, older brothers and sisters, older friends, and even teachers are all people you may wish to be like in certain ways. You can strengthen your identity by choosing people with positive qualities and trying to develop the same qualities in yourself.

A third way you build your identity is by taking on a stable set of social roles. A *social role* is a set of actions that other people expect of you. Examples of social roles are the roles of student, friend, spouse, sibling, child, parent, and citizen. Every social role has a set of expected actions. The social roles you take on help tell you who you are as a person. The more stable your social roles, the more stable your identity will be.

Your career provides you with one of the most important and stable social roles for your identity. Most people describe themselves in terms of their career: "I am a dental lab technician"; "I am a grocery store manager"; "I am a cosmetologist"; or "I am a salesperson." When you accept a job, you accept a certain role in an organization. This role affects your entire life. In most cases, the life of an electromechanical technician is different from the life of an accountant. Each career carries with it different skills, attitudes, ways of spending your time, and people to associate with. How you define yourself will be greatly affected by the career you choose. And the longer you have the same career, the more it will affect your identity.

The role you adopt as part of your career is not the only influence your career has on your identity. Depending on your career, you will have different types of people to compare yourself with. Depending on your career, you will be in different types of situations in which to be aware of yourself and other people. And depending on your career, you will want to be like different people. Your career is an important influence on your identity.

Where I Am Going

There are many people who agonize over what they should do with their lives. Sam, for example, is a sixteen-year-old who ran away from home at age fourteen. He hitchhiked around the country, looking for something to give his life meaning and direction. "There is nothing I want to do with my life," he explains. "I see no reason to go to school. I won't do anything with what I learn. I don't want to work. What sense does it make to make friends when I may leave town tomorrow? I just wish that something good would happen to me." Sam is lost in a sea of meaninglessness.

A meaningful purpose and direction in life, a sense of "Where I am going," is a requirement for a productive and fulfilling life. Everybody needs a meaningful purpose and direction in life, a purpose that is valued by others and that is similar to the goals of the significant other people in his or her life. Your sense of direction in life promotes both feelings of commitment, involvement, meaning, and the belief that life is worthwhile, challenging, meaningful, and has purpose.

People without a sense of direction flounder from one tentative activity to another. They search for experiences to give their lives meaning. They refuse to assume responsibility for their choices, make little effort to achieve their goals, fail to use their assets, and have low aspirations.

There are many aspects to having direction in your life. How would you rate yourself on the following ones?

_____ I direct my attention toward goals I want to achieve.

_____ I am aware of the choices I make among my desired goals.

_____ I am motivated to achieve my goals.

_____ I can achieve my goals if I apply my assets and work hard enough.

_____ I feel satisfaction and pride when I achieve one of my goals.

_____ I take the initiative in trying to achieve my goals.

_____ I try to develop and use my assets.

How My Efforts Fit in with the Efforts of Others

I once had a friend named David. "I want to build a house out in the woods," he would say, "I want to live so far away from civilization that I will never see another person. The only way I can feel happy is to get away from other people totally." David had no sense of meaningful and cooperative interdependence with other people. He saw work as an arbitrary attempt to destroy his personality. He saw no need to combine his efforts with the efforts of other people. "Why should I help them?" he would say. David was not a very happy person.

Your career depends not only on your efforts, but also on the efforts of many other people. You cannot be successful by yourself. You can only be successful as part of a joint effort by many different people, by acting in harmony with other people. All through your career, you will find yourself interdependent with other people. They may be fellow employees, customers, or people who supply you with the materials you need to do your job. But you will find that you cannot achieve your goals alone, because you need other people's help and resources. You will find that you have to coordinate your actions with the actions of other people if you are to be successful.

Your goals are related to the goals, actions, and efforts of other people. All aspects of your career are interdependent with aspects of other people's careers. The more aware you are of your interdependence with other people, the more successful your career will be.

In thinking about your career, do you think that:

_____ Both myself and my fellow employees are working toward the same overall goals. We get the same overall benefits from our efforts.

_____ My assets are needed by the organization I work for.

_____ The assets of other people are needed by the organization I work for.

_____ I am dependent on other people for their efforts, help, and assets if I am to do my job well and achieve my goals.

_____ Other people are dependent on my efforts, help, and assets if they are to do their job well and achieve their goals.

_____ Both my efforts and the efforts of my fellow employees are needed and must be coordinated if we are to achieve our goals.

_____ The long-term benefits of my work for myself and others are just as important as the short-term benefits.

There is nothing quite so personally rewarding and satisfying as being part of a joint effort to achieve important goals. Through your interdependence with other people, you find friendship and an emotional bond that adds a great deal to the overall quality of your life. Working for and with people gives you some of the most important emotional experiences and friendships of your life.

Building Your Career

Some people act as though the future is something that happens to them. They do not believe that the future is something they create every day. It is true that you cannot change your past, but your future is influenced greatly by the way you act today. You can take charge of your life. You can build a career that will be meaningful and fulfilling. By setting realistic goals and working to achieve them, you can influence your future.

In planning your career, it is important to tie the past, present, and future together. There is a great deal to learn from your past. And in reviewing your past, it is important not to be burdened by guilts, regrets, and resentments. You learn from the past when you examine where you have been and use your experiences to help plan the present and future. There is a great deal to be gained from planning the future. In thinking about the future, it is important to be realistic. The future should not be viewed unrealistically or with anxiety and fear. Your future goals, influenced by what you have learned from your past, determine how you act in the present. And it is your present actions that create your future. By understanding your past and being aware of your present, you can build a future that has meaning for you.

Your career goals must take into account your ability to work cooperatively with other people. Technical skills are of little use to you if you cannot get along with other people on the job. It is the interpersonal skills that are most important for your future career success.

The following exercises are aimed at helping you think about your past, present, and future. They are aimed at helping you become more aware of who you are, where you are going, and how your efforts fit in with the efforts of other people. After reviewing your career plans and the interpersonal skills you need to be successful, begin action! Get busy and create your future!

**EXERCISE
11.1**   **My Life Line**

PURPOSE

You can choose how you will spend the rest of your life. You can have a great deal of influence over what your future is like. By the choices you make today, your future is created. In making career choices, it is helpful to be aware of where you are in your life. It is helpful to review what your past has been like and what your future goals are. The purpose of this exercise is to help you review your past and your future goals.

PROCEDURE

1. Working alone, on a sheet of paper draw a line from left to right that stands for your life. The line can be straight, slanted, curved, jagged, or any other shape that represents to you the course of your life. The line stands for your entire past, present, and future.

2. Place a dot at each end of the line. Over the left dot, put the number zero. This dot represents your birth. Write your birth date under this dot. The dot on the right represents your ultimate death. How long do you believe you will live? Over the right dot, put a number that is your best guess as to how many years you will live. Under the right dot write the guesstimated date of your death.

3. Place a dot that stands for where you are right now on the line between your birth and your death. Write today's date under this dot.

4. Note on your life line the most significant events of your past life. Put the approximate dates and a brief description of these events on your life line.

5. Think about the future part of the life line, from today to the day of your death. Note on the life line the things you would like to see happen in your life before it ends. List as specifically as possible the things you want to do, try, become, and experience before the end of your life line. Put estimates of dates by which you want each of the significant future events of your life to happen.

6. In your group, discuss each member's life line. Share with your group the key events you put on your life line and explain their significance to you. When other members share their life lines, help them to make clear why certain events are significant for them. And help them clarify where they see themselves in their life.

EXERCISE 11.2   **Who Am I?**

PURPOSE

In planning how you will spend the rest of your life, it helps to review what you are now like as a person. The purpose of this exercise is to summarize who you are as a person at this time of your life.

PROCEDURE

1. Working alone, on 3 × 5 cards, write ten answers to the question, "Who am I?" You may wish to answer in terms of your social roles, the things you believe in, your qualities as a person, and your needs and feelings. Try to list things that make a big difference to your sense of self.

2. Look at each card separately. Try to imagine how it would be if that item were no longer true of you. After reviewing each item in this way, rank order the items on the basis of how big the adjustment would be if you lost that item. The item that is hardest to give up is ranked "1." The item that is easiest to give up is ranked "10."

3. In your group, review each member's cards and her rank order. Discuss whether the other group members would list the same ten items for the person. Discuss what the group thinks would be the hardest items for the person to give up.

EXERCISE 11.3 **Whom I Most Want to Be Like**

PURPOSE

We read about many people who seem so competent or admirable that we want to be like them. We may imitate our parents and older brothers and sisters, people we see on television, and people we read about. We may want to be as honest as Abe Lincoln, as ambitious as Henry Ford, as powerful as the king of Saudi Arabia, as rich as John D. Rockefeller, or as compassionate as Mother Theresa. The purpose of this exercise is to review the role models in your life—the people you especially like, admire, and respect and who you want to be like.

PROCEDURE

1. Working alone, on ten 3 × 5 cards, write ten different answers to these two questions:
    a. Whom do I most want to be like?
    b. What aspect of this person do I want to make part of myself? The people may be real, or they may be fictional or imaginary. You may want to mention their life-styles, their personal qualities, the things they do well. Try to think of people who are really important to your sense of self. Try to think of people who have qualities you really want to have yourself.
2. Consider each card separately. Then rank order them from most important to you ("1") to least important to you ("10").
3. In your group, review each member's cards and their ranking. Discuss whether the other group members would list the same ten people. Discuss what qualities the other group members think the person should develop in order to have a successful career.

An Inventory of My Life

PURPOSE

Your plans are part of your life goals, as are your skills. The things you would like to do better are important to know. Things that give you pleasure must be recognized. The purpose of this exercise is to take an inventory of your life, to help you be more aware of your life goals.

PROCEDURE

1. In your group, discuss each of the following questions. Make sure all members give their answers.
2. Working alone, write down your answers to the following questions. Be serious. Try to write down the most meaningful answers you can think of.

Life Inventory Questions

1. When do I feel fully alive? What events, things, activities, and experiences make me feel that life is really worth living? When do I feel it is great to be me and to be alive?
2. What do I do well? What assets can I contribute to cooperative efforts? What skills have I mastered?
3. What would I like to do better?
4. What would I like to try that I have not yet done?
5. Given my opportunities and my ambitions, what do I need to learn to do well?
6. What wishes should I be turning into plans? Do I have any dreams I've thrown out as unrealistic that I should start dreaming again?
7. What underdeveloped or misused assets do I have?
8. What should I start doing *now* in order to achieve my goals?
9. What should I stop doing *now* in order to achieve my goals?

**EXERCISE
11.5**

Beginning My Future

PURPOSE

It is one thing to discuss what you want out of life. It is another thing to do something about getting it. In this exercise, you will make a contract with yourself dealing with how you will begin working to achieve your goals. The purpose of the exercise is to make your plans about the future more concrete. Another objective is to review the people in your life who influence you.

PROCEDURE

1. Working alone, write down the projects you will have to begin right away if you hope to achieve your goals for the next five years.

2. List all the people who can help you achieve the things you want to in the next five years.

3. In your group, help each member plan what she will have to get done in the next six months to begin working on her life goals. Help each member be specific and concrete.

4. Working by yourself, write yourself a letter. In this letter, list your goals for the next five years. Then list your plan for the next six months to begin working to achieve your goals. Seal the letter in an envelope addressed to yourself. Open it six months from today.

Will You Be a Sue or a Sally?

Sue goes to work every day because she has to. She works as a bookkeeper for a construction company. Sue generally dislikes her work. She sees it as unimportant and boring. All day she enters figures into books while trying to keep herself awake by drinking coffee. She daydreams about what life would be like if she were rich. If she did not need the money, she would quit her job instantly. She is depressed and unhappy about her work. Since she does not like her job, she gets angry at her boss for thinking that she should work hard and be accurate. Her coworkers often get on her nerves because they interrupt her daydreams. And they seem upset by her negative attitudes and careless work. She is not sure what she is like as a person. Her goals in life are rather vague notions of being a world-famous playgirl. Since she has few friends and does not pay much attention to her fellow employees, she has little notion of how her career relates to others.

Sally also works as a bookkeeper for the same construction company. She goes to work every day, and she enjoys it, because she believes her work is an important part of her life. She carefully enters figures into books, and she takes pride in being accurate. She sees her work as an important contribution to the company. Her coworkers are her friends. She enjoys seeing fellow employees from all parts of the company. She enjoys finding out what other employees are doing and how her work relates to their work. She gets along well with her boss because they both believe her work is important and should be taken seriously. Her coworkers respect her for her ability as a bookkeeper and for being an easy person to work with. Her career is a central part of her self-image. She takes pride in knowing that she is building a meaningful and satisfying life.

12

Getting a Job and Keeping It

After completing the Questionnaire, you will be ready to find out more about

- the job interview
- interpersonal skills

The answers are given on the right side of the page. Work with a partner and keep the answers covered until you have agreed on your response. Remember to check each answer before going on to the next item, as explained on page 1.

QUESTIONNAIRE: Main Concepts in Chapter 12

1. The *job interview* is a formal conversation in which two people exchange information about each other to determine whether they wish to enter into an employer-employee relationship. The results of the _____ usually determine whether or not you are hired.

   job interview

2. An important asset to emphasize during the job interview are your *interpersonal skills*. During the interview you should be prepared to talk about and demonstrate your _____.

   interpersonal skills

○   ○   ○

We pay a heavy price for our fear of failure. It is a powerful obstacle to growth. It assures the progressive narrowing of the personality and prevents exploration and experimentation. There is no learning without some difficulty and fumbling. If you want to keep on learning, you must keep on risking failure—all your life. It's as simple as that.

JOHN GARDNER, *Self-Renewal*

○   ○   ○

Interpersonal Skills Determine Career Success

The success of your career depends largely on your interpersonal skills. Finding and holding a job depend largely on how well you can present yourself and relate to other people. Recognition and raises depend on your ability to work cooperatively with fellow employees. Being promoted depends largely on your effectiveness in collaborating with others.

To be employable, to be successful at your work, and to progress within your chosen career you must have interpersonal, organizational, and technical skills and competencies. Having the technical skills needed to do your job, however, is not enough to ensure your career success. Likewise, having necessary organizational skills, such as reliability (arriving on time, consistently coming to work) and responsibility (having good work habits and following through on assigned tasks), are important, but they are not enough to make you successful. *The most important skills for ensuring a successful career cycle are the interpersonal skills needed for cooperating with your fellow employees.* People who can not cooperate, be a contributing team member, provide leadership, communicate, build meaningful relationships, learn from others, solve problems, make decisions, and manage conflicts constructively are not promoted or otherwise rewarded in an organization, and they may find it hard to keep their job.

The interpersonal skills essential for career success are not inherited. They do not magically appear when needed nor are they a gift of fate. They are learned. Some interpersonal skills are learned from parents and other adults; other interpersonal skills are learned from peers. Some of your interpersonal skills you learned as a child and others you learned as a teenager. Still others you will learn during your adult years. All of your life, you will be learning new interpersonal skills and perfecting the ones you already have. You acquire new interpersonal skills as you would acquire any other skill. And you keep on acquiring them all your life.

Every career requires you to work for and with other people. To complete your work and to achieve your organization's goals, you have to interact with other people. Coworkers, supervisors, suppliers, subordinates, and customers cannot be avoided. To get a job, be successful in your work, and progress in your career, and to progress to jobs with greater responsibility, you must learn the interpersonal skills needed for cooperating with your fellow employees. If you are not interpersonally skilled, responsible, dependable, and willing to learn, technical abilities are of little value. To be a success, you have to be able to build and maintain good relationships. Interpersonal skills are an absolute necessity for a successful career.

How to Utilize Interpersonal Skills

Now that you have mastered the basic interpersonal skills in this book, there are two important issues to consider:

1. What are the ways to use the skills to enhance your career success?
2. How may you overcome the barriers to using your skills effectively?

There has been recent research on the nature of "excellent" companies and the characteristics of their employees that lead to continual organizational and personal success. The findings indicate that utilizing your interpersonal skills to maximize your career success depends on your *willingness to take risks, build support networks, use humor, be a good team member, and engage in the basic steps to obtain a job* (applying, interviewing, meeting basic expectations for dress and speech). Each of these factors will be discussed in this chapter.

Taking Risks, Tolerating Failure, Persisting, Celebrating Success

○   ○   ○

Even if the breath of hope which blows on us from that new continent were fainter than it is and harder to perceive, yet the trial (if we would not bear a spirit altogether abject) must by all means be made. For there is no comparison between that which we may lose by not trying and that by not succeeding.

SIR FRANCIS BACON, On Settling the New World

○   ○   ○

To be successful in interacting with other people, you must take risks. You must leave the beaten track and wander through the jungle of creative interaction, flirting with the not-yet-mastered and the unknown. For effective and successful people, risk-taking is a way of life. To live a creative, interesting, challenging, and successful life, you have to gamble, take some risks, and experiment.

Special attributes of successful people are:

1. A willingness to take risks.
2. A substantial tolerance for failure.
3. Persistence.
4. The personal celebration of success.

Growth demands commitment. To change your life even in small ways requires energy, participation, and enthusiasm. You cannot grow while you are inert. Overcoming the barriers to interpersonal effectiveness requires that you take risks. It is your first step to increased interpersonal competence. The essential advice for risk-taking is:

1. Take risks often.
2. Start small. Small risks, with small penalties for failure, may be attempted

first. If successful, you will increase in both self-confidence and knowledge and therefore be able to take on bigger risks.

3. The most appropriate risk is one in which there is a 50/50 chance of success or failure. This means that on the average, you will fail half of the time and succeed half of the time.

4. Prepare for your risks. Do not try to swim the English Channel without studying how it is done, practicing, getting into shape physically, and obtaining the proper equipment and support systems. The more experienced and better equipped you are, the more likely that your risk will succeed. You can control the outcome of your risks by being prepared and well-informed.

After taking a planned risk, you then accept failure gracefully, reflect on and learn from it, and persist in your efforts until you succeed. Once you have succeeded, celebrate! You have earned it.

○   ○   ○

With the good people, you can see the learning juices churning around every mistake. You learn from mistakes. When I look back, my life seems to be an endless chain of mistakes.

EDWARD JOHNSON, Millionaire Businessman

○   ○   ○

A basic tenet of all individuals who wish to become more effective interpersonally is, "I have to be willing to fail." You cannot learn, you cannot improve your interpersonal effectiveness, you cannot build better relationships, and you cannot try new procedures and approaches unless you are willing to accept mistakes. You need the ability to fail. Tolerance for failure, and the ability to learn from it, are very specific characteristics of any highly successful person. The important things to remember about failure are:

1. See failure as a positive indication that you are in the process of becoming more competent and effective.

2. Analyze your failure, reflect on it, and learn from it. Use it to plan your next attempt to do the same thing.

3. Give failure its due, but no more. Do not see it as catastrophic. Do not see it as the perfect indicator of your personal worth.

4. Do not make the penalty for failure worse than the reward for success. The worse penalty should be reserved for doing nothing at all.

Failure and success are intimate relatives. If you want to dine on success you must occasionally "sit down" to failure.

○   ○   ○

A bright and energetic self-starter can make all the mistakes in this business in five years. With fools and sluggards, it may take a lifetime.

Unknown Stockbroker

○   ○   ○

The third step to successful growth is persistence. Try and try again. Keep practicing. Never (or almost never, depending on the circumstances) give up.

○   ○   ○

Do what you can, with what you have, where you are.

TEDDY ROOSEVELT

○   ○   ○

Finally, when you are successful, celebrate! Reward yourself. Tell all your friends. Make sure the rewards you give yourself for success are far greater than the punishment you give yourself for any failure along the way.

℞ Humor for a Sound Mind and Body

Humor can change everything—from calming our anger, easing our embarrassment, relaxing our tensions, freeing us from boredom, disolving our fears, establishing rapport with strangers, to dramatically building more positive relationships. Like a sudden ray of sunshine that creates a rainbow in a thunderstorm, humor transforms our emotions from negative to positive, our perspective from egocentric to objective, and our relationships from cold to warm. Humor, when used appropriately, is a valuable tool for increasing the success of your career.

Laughter is just plain good for you and your relationships. And it should be taken seriously as a means for building and maintaining both effective working relationships and friendships. Humor is a valuable business and personal success asset to anyone who applies it. You may use humor to:

1. **Improve your personal health, well-being, and longevity.** On a personal level, hearty laughter results in heart and blood circulation rates being elevated, muscles vibrating in a relaxing internal massage, and the brain emitting hormones that trigger the release of endorphins, the body's natural painkillers. Humor can release tensions, ease pain, and promote healing and health. Laughter provides relief for mental, nervous, and psychic energy, and thus restores balance and calm after struggle, tension, or strain. Laughing keeps you from cracking up or breaking down, vents your negative feelings, and promotes healthy self-acceptance. Learning to get more laughter

from life enhances your motivation and morale. Laughter is a wonderful way of making today better and heading off stress and problems. Humor can help you keep life in perspective. Humor can expand awareness and broaden your perspective, thereby improving your ability to solve problems and relate effectively to others. The ability to find the humor in situations can go a long way toward helping you avoid job burnout. The good health and relaxation achieved through laughing every day will tend to lengthen your life. Through humor you learn to accept yourself as a mortal, prone to failure and living with anxiety, yet always capable of coping anew.

2. **Improve your relationships with coworkers.** Victor Borge once said, "Humor is the shortest distance between two people." Interpersonally, humor livens up your own and your associates' lives. Generally, the more humor you bring to relationships, the more positive and constructive they will be. People are perceived to be more attractive, friendly, and desirable as friends when they offer others a chance for positive interactions. People tend to enjoy being around a person who creates an atmosphere that is optimistic, constructive, and happy.

3. **Relieve stress and improve your problem-solving capabilities.** In laughing or joking you separate yourself from annoying incidents. The Roman philosopher Epictetus stated, "Men are disturbed not by things but by the view that they take of things." By choosing to react to anxiety-provoking events with humor, you can reduce your stress and preoccupation, thereby inducing creativity, alertness, and problem-solving ability. Learning to think funny when it's necessary to think straight—thereby relieving your mind of the grip of stress—can make the difference over the course of a career between retiring as a department manager or less and retiring as a corporate vice president or more. Remember, "allow nonsense and sense is not far behind!"

4. **Resolve interpersonal conflicts.** Humor is an important tool for managing conflicts. First, humor can blunt your anger and calm the anxiety that you will often have when you are in conflict with coworkers. It is hard to be angry, to be afraid, or to carry a grudge when you are laughing. When a coworker is angry at you, disagrees with you, or is rejecting of you, you can transform your negative reactions into laughter. Second, you may use humor to defuse the anger, hostility, and opposition of coworkers. By the skillful use of humor you may redirect coworkers away from potentially hostile, aggressive, or tense reactions. When coworkers face each other in a competitive or hostile situation, humor may lessen the tension and allow them to make concessions without appearing weak or appeasing. Humor is often used as a tool of diplomacy to create a more relaxed and frank atmosphere in discussions. In direct negotiations, humor has been found to produce more concessions and less resentment and anger on the part of opponents.

5. **Motivate yourself and your coworkers.** Humor energizes, freeing you from anger, resentment, hostility, disappointment, and other negative mood states so that you have more energy to work productively. Humor boosts enthusiasm and energy, which are stepping stones to greater motivation and productivity.

6. **Gain attention.** People remember more of what you say when you are humorous. Your communications will have greater impact when they include humor. Although humor does not increase your success in persuading others, it does get other people's attention and goodwill.

7. **Adjust to the insoluble problems in life.** A sense of humor helps you survive until conditions change and problems can be solved. In the words of William Makepeace Thackeray (a nineteenth-century English novelist): "A good laugh is sunshine in a house." Trying to view one's problems with a sense of humor and to laugh off setbacks and hurts are widely used means of dealing with problems that are currently beyond your power to solve.

Many people must relearn the humorous approach to life because it was squelched when they were children. "Wipe that smile off your face." "Don't laugh in church." "Don't be silly." "Settle down and get serious." Children often hear statements like these from their parents and other adults. Here is some good advice for you as an adult: "Put a smile on your face," "laugh often and deeply," "be silly whenever it is appropriate," and "be less serious." Relearn how to approach life with a sense of humor.

Humor is a skill that you can learn and use to your benefit. "There are three things that are real," wrote John F. Kennedy. "God, human folly, and laughter. The first two are beyond our comprehension. So we must do what we can with the third." To become skillful in being humorous try the following:

1. Look for humor everywhere, in signs, newspapers, and daily events. Most of all, learn to guide your reaction to the events around you into a humorous outcome.

2. Set a goal of having fifteen laughs a day. Joke books, a tape of your favorite comedian, or a phone call to a friend may help. Carry a small notebook with your favorite jokes and cartoons in it. At any time during the day when a laugh may help, take out the notebook and look at it until you laugh.

3. Learn to be an "inverse paranoid." Believe that the world is out to do you good.

4. You can use humor to control your anger and to maintain at least a working relationship with people you must deal with regularly—even though you resent their attitude, disdain their ability, and dislike their looks. Do it this way: List their obnoxious traits in a notebook. Then match each trait with an expression of humor. Whenever you interact with them, think of the humor connected with them. You will find it much easier to relate to them in a relaxed and natural way.

5. Give each member of your family or workgroup a coupon book imprinted with messages such as: "Good for 10 minutes of silence—no matter how much I want to keep arguing." or "Hand me this and I won't say 'I told you so'."*

*If you are interested in learning more about the productive uses of humor, write to Joel Goodman, Director of the Humor Project, 110 Spring Street, Saratoga Springs, NY 12866.

NEW SICK LEAVE POLICY

SICKNESS: No excuse. We will no longer accept your doctor's statement as proof, as we believe that if you are able to go to the doctor, you are able to come to work.

LEAVE OF ABSENCE (FOR AN OPERATION): We are no longer allowing this practice. We wish to discourage any thought that you may have about needing an operation. We believe that as long as you are employed here, you will need all of whatever you have and should not consider having anything removed. We hired you as you are, and to have anything removed would certainly make you less than we bargained for.

DEATH (YOUR OWN): This will be accepted as an excuse, but we would like two weeks' notice, as we feel it is your duty to teach someone else your job.

Being a Good Team Member

We require other people to meet many of our needs. Being isolated, lonely, unloved, unknown, alienated from others can result in sickness and unhappiness. You require people on whom you can rely for assistance, encouragement, acceptance, and caring. So do your coworkers. Your coworkers are an important source of social support for you, and you are an important source of social support for your coworkers. Your relationships with others provide the most powerful forces either increasing or decreasing the stress you feel. Arguments with a coworker, troublesome colleagues, problems getting along with your boss, and hassles from your subordinates are all sources of stress. Everyone, no matter how well-adjusted and skilled, at times experiences high levels of stress and a need for social support.

Knowing that there are other employees you can rely on for assistance, encouragement, acceptance, and caring can affect your well-being in three ways. First, social support can directly increase your competence, productivity, and self-esteem. Second, social support can indirectly benefit you by buffering you from stress by increasing your psychological and physical health. Third, social support may increase your defenses for dealing with stress. Friends may provide reassurrance that you are a worthwhile person who is coping as well as others who have the same problem.

One of the secrets for being a good team member is to provide social support for the other members of your team. The more supportive you are of coworkers who are experiencing stress and dealing with problems, the more you will be liked, respected, and appreciated.

Hunting for a Job

In building your career you will need to find a job, establish career goals and a career path, select and implement relevant career-advancement strategies, and switch careers if the need or opportunity arises. In hunting for a job you need to:

1. Clarify what types of jobs you want.
2. Identify your potential contribution to companies that have job openings you are interested in.
3. Use the insider system. Most jobs are filled by the recommendation of someone in the company. Ask friends and relatives if they know of openings for which you are qualified.

4. Use multiple approaches. Try everything that may lead to a job.

5. Enlarge your number of business contacts. The more contacts you make, the better your chances are of being suggested for a job.

6. Persist. Try companies over and over again. People quit all the time. New openings may appear any day.

7. Expect some rejection. Do not take rejection personally; it is part of job hunting.

The Resumé and Cover Letter

Write a good job resumé and cover letter. The purpose of a resumé is to help you obtain an interview. Your resumé must therefore attract enough attention for an employer to invite you for an interview. Make sure your resumé contains complete and only useful information, is well organized (avoid repeating the same information under different headings), is typed perfectly with correct grammar and spelling. Your resumé should present the basic facts about your education, skills, job experiences, and any relevant accomplishments. Usually your resumé should be accompanied by a cover letter explaining who you are and why you are applying for this particular job.

The Job Interview

Your career begins with a job interview. An interview is an opportunity that may open a gate to a job. It is during the interview that a potential employer may judge your ability to get along with your fellow employees. And it is during the job interview that you can demonstrate your interpersonal skills to a potential employer.

The job interview is a formal conversation in which two people seek to learn more about each other. The job interview has two objectives:

1. To give the employer information about you.

2. To give you information about the employer and the organization.

As the applicant, you both give and seek information. You prepare for the interview by reviewing what you need to share with the interviewer and by reviewing what you wish to find out about the organization.

"This person has the skills for the job, but can he get along?" This question is in the mind of every employer who interviews you. And it is the answer to this question that this book focuses on specifically. There are other aspects of the job interview that are discussed in other courses. In this book, we concentrate on the part of the job interview that focuses on the question. "Can you get along with others? Do you fit in with the other people in our organization?"

The average job interview lasts from ten to fifteen minutes. Most employment interviewers agree that they usually make their decision to hire a person within the first five minutes of the interview. Since the results of the interview will determine whether or not you are hired, you need to be able to create an immediate positive impression. How do you do this? Here are some helpful hints.

The most important information about yourself relates to your goals, assets, and credentials. This information should be presented in the first five minutes of the interview. An important asset to be emphasized are your interpersonal skills. You should be prepared both to talk about your interpersonal skills and to demonstrate them during the interview. It is important that you know your credentials and assets so thoroughly that you can discuss them without having to stop and think about what to say or how to say it. Throughout this book, the discussion of your assets with your fellow group members has been emphasized, to help you prepare a short statement about your goals, credentials, and assets for your job interviews. During the job interview, you have to see yourself as a good worker and as a competent and skilled person. Be proud of yourself. Be proud of what you can offer the employer. You should be ready to answer such questions as, "Why do you believe you should be hired by this company?" and "Where do you expect to be in this company in ten years?" Do not undersell yourself. The interviewer wants to know what assets you can contribute to the organization. And she wants to know about your goals and credentials. You need to be able to discuss yourself without fake modesty. If you cannot discuss your assets, credentials, and goals realistically, review the second chapter of this book.

During the job interview, remember that when you are hired to do a job you are hired to be part of a cooperative effort to achieve organizational goals. The interviewer is looking for a person who can fit in with the other employees and for a person who can contribute to the overall effort to achieve the organization's goals. Your ability to cooperate is important. And your ability to provide leadership to help the organization achieve its goals and maintain good relationships among employees is also important. During your interview, use words such as *cooperation* and *teamwork*. Let the interviewer know that you see yourself as being part of a cooperative effort, as helping to achieve the organization's goals. And let the interviewer know you see yourself as helping maintain good working relationships among employees.

Your communication skills are of great importance during the interview. Review the communication skills discussed in this book, and be sure to use them during the interview. Both sending and listening skills are of great importance during the job interview. The more skilled in communicating you are during the interview, the more likely you will be to get the job.

The first impression you make is the most important part of the interview. First impressions do count, no matter what your qualifications are. Plan the communication of a favorable first impression. This includes your greeting, your actions during the interview, your appearance, and your exit from the interview.

Your Greeting

When you enter the interview, walk in briskly. Shake hands firmly. Say "thank you" when the interviewer indicates where you should sit. When the interviewer says "How are you?" you should reply "Fine, thank you," even if you have a bad headache.

Your Actions During the Interview

Sit in your chair in such a way that you look alert. Look the interviewer in the eye without staring. Do not chew gum. Speak clearly without hiding your mouth with your hand. Use complete sentences, and avoid slang. Do not interrupt the interviewer, but *do* allow yourself to be interrupted. Avoid disagreeing with the interviewer. Do not smoke during the interview. (If you are a smoker you may want to find out what the employer's policy is with regard to smoking in the workplace. More and more organizations and states are restricting or banning smoking.) Good posture is important, so do not slump carelessly in the chair. Show that you are interested in the job—look and sound enthusiastic. You can do this by having done some research on the organization before the interview. For example, read their annual report. Find out things about the organization and mention them in the interview. By mentioning what you know about the organization, you communicate interest and enthusiasm.

Your Appearance

Your personal appearance and dress communicate a great deal about you. Be sure your fingernails are clean, shoes are shined, and breath is fresh (no smoking or drinking before the interview). Use a deodorant. In deciding how to dress, consider the job you are applying for. If you are applying for a sales position in a department store, dress fashionably. If you are seeking a managerial job, dress conservatively. If you are seeking a job as a mechanic, dress in clean work clothes. Carefully choose the most appropriate clothes you have. If you are not sure what to wear, observe the persons working for the organization. Note what they are wearing. Then wear something similar. Do not wear clothing that requires your attention, such as a dress that looks good only if you stand or sit in a certain way, a shirt that will not stay tucked into your trousers if you move about, or garments with zippers that come open if you forget to hold your breath. Choose clothing that is comfortable, that you can forget about, so you can concentrate on the interview. Take your appearance seriously. It is an important nonverbal communication about you as a person. And it greatly influences the first impression you make on the interviewer.

Your Message

During the interview, you must convey your ability to get along with fellow employees and customers. This means communicating your interpersonal skills and your commitment to form and maintain good relationships. During the interview, you should also communicate that you are able to fit in with what the organization wants from its employees. Communicate your organizational skills of dependability and reliability. Communicate that you have few personal problems that could interfere with your work. And communicate your knowledge of the job and your ability to do the job.

Since the interview takes place between you and another person, your interpersonal skills will greatly influence its outcome. Before going into a job interview, practice demonstrating the interpersonal skills covered in this book. They will help you get the job you want.

Your Exit

Thank the interviewer. Leave promptly when the interview is over. Walk out briskly.

EXERCISE 12.1   **The Job Interview**

PURPOSE

Interviewing for employment is frequently a traumatic experience. Interviewers often ask questions that are hard to answer, such as, "Why do you want to work for our company?" and "What are your life goals?" Before going for a job interview you need to prepare, so the interviewer will not catch you by surprise. The purpose of this exercise is to give you practice in answering difficult questions during an employment interview.

PROCEDURE

1. In your group, list the twelve hardest questions you might be asked in a job interview. Pick questions you would find threatening or difficult to answer honestly in a job interview. Each member should make a copy of the group's list.

2. Divide into triads and decide which role each person will play in a mock interview. Person A plays the interviewer. Person B plays the interviewee, and Person C the observer. A asks B a question from her list. B tries to answer the question as truthfully and honestly as he can. C observes the good aspects of how B handles the question and the ways in which B could improve in handling the question. At the end of the interview, the three group members discuss how B's answers could be strengthened.

3. The same procedure is repeated, with B as the interviewer, C the interviewee, and A the observer.

4. The same procedure is repeated, with C as the interviewer, A the interviewee, and B the observer.

5. Continue this rotation until all the questions on the list have been asked.

6. Working alone, write your answers to the following questions:
    a. What were the good aspects of how I handled the questions?
    b. What were the weak aspects of how I handled the questions?
    c. What job interview questions are difficult for me to answer competently?

Advancing Your Career

Career advancement begins with setting your personal goals. Most of your career goals should be realistic in terms of your capabilities and job opportunities. As you achieve each goal, you can continue to raise your sights. Yet you should also have some fantasies about extraordinary accomplishments. Someday they may become realistic goals.

Career advancement may depend on your making an accurate self-appraisal of your strengths, preferences, and areas of improvement, sticking with what you do best, identifying growth fields and growth companies, and finding the right organization for you (in terms of fitting your style with its climate). Good performance is the bedrock on which you build your career. Develop your interpersonal, organizational, and technical skills. Obtain broad experience to strengthen your credentials. Find a mentor who teaches and coaches you and finds opportunities for you. Network with other competent and ambitious individuals. Document your accomplishments. Keeping an accurate record of what you have accomplished can be valuable when you are in an annual review or are being considered for promotion.

Developing Proper Attitudes and Values

Success on your job sometimes depends on having the organizational skills needed to impress your boss with your reliability and responsibility. Make sure you value good attendance and punctuality, avoid perfectionism (recognize that you will make mistakes and that the world does not come to an end when you do), avoid schmoozing (doing so much socializing that no work gets done), learn to say no to others so that you take care of your own priorities, strive for both quantity and quality of work, ask yourself "What is the best use of my time right now," and avoid working so hard that your ability to function is impaired.

Job success can be influenced by the extent to which you are clear about your priorities, concentrate on achieving the important tasks, stay in control of your paperwork, work at a steady pace, maximize your efficiency by scheduling similar tasks together, making use of odd bits of time, break projects down into manageable units, remember where you put things, capitalize on your natural energy cycles (you may be more productive in the morning or in the afternoon), set a time limit for certain tasks, keep your work area or desk orderly, minimize interruptions, use the telephone efficiently, and be decisive.

Breaking Through Your Barriers

There are a number of barriers to engaging in effective interpersonal interaction that have their origins in interpersonal relationships. When you are troubled by these barriers your interpersonal effectiveness is seriously impaired. The barriers are:

1. Procrastination.
2. Fear and anxiety.
3. Shyness.
4. Self-blame.

Unproductive people are often procrastinators. Procrastination can be an enormous problem and needs to be minimized. Fear and anxiety, more than any other emotion, incapacitates interpersonal interaction. It creates avoidance of the anxiety-provoking situation and an immobilization of interpersonal interaction within the situation. And fears can persist year after year, interfering with constructive relationships and effective interaction chronically. Learning to overcome fear and anxiety is an essential ingredient of being effective interpersonally. One specific type of problem arising from fear and anxiety is shyness. The excessive caution and self-consciousness in interpersonal relationships produced by shyness can stand as a major barrier to developing and maintaining friendships and effective working relationships. When interpersonal interaction is inhibited, interpersonal skills either never appear or are underutilized. Finally, self-blame, the directing of anger towards yourself for not living up to your expectations and hopes, results in depression that interferes with effectively relating to other people. This chapter focuses on overcoming the inhibition and avoidance created by these three barriers.

Coping with Procrastination

A major cause of procrastination is an inner fear of the consequences of your actions. You may be apprehensive that your boss will evaluate your work negatively. You may wish to delay bad news. You may wish to avoid an uncomfortable or difficult task. Whatever the reason for procrastination, it may be lessened by:

1. Calculating the price you pay for your procrastination.
2. Reinforcing yourself with a pleasant reward soon after you accomplish an arduous task. Or penalize yourself and do something you abhor immediately after you procrastinate.
3. Arousing your enthusiasm for doing the job.
4. Cutting a large project into small pieces that seem more manageable.
5. Making finishing the project imperative. Making a commitment to other people is one way of doing so.
6. Removing all temptations that may interfere with your work.

Managing Anxiety and Fear

Of all the emotions humans experience, fear is perhaps the most chronic and troublesome (Johnson, 1986). All of us, many times during our lives, are afflicted with fear, anxiety, nervousness, phobia, or worry. Anger can quickly flare up and quickly die down. Depression may hang on, but sooner or later it will be replaced with a neutral feeling or even a positive one. A fear of failure, however, can influence practically everything you do every day of your life. It may not hurt as much as depression, or flare up like anger, but it will be there all the time, ready to disturb, year in and year out. It is fear that has the unique power of preventing you from fulfilling your potential. It is fear that can suppress talents and prevent genius from being actualized. Stage fright can prevent a great singer from being recognized, fear of failure can prevent an Einstein from entering a doctoral program or beginning a research project, fear of humiliation can prevent a young inventor from submitting his or her ideas to a potential manufacturer. Fear can be devastating in a special way that anger and depression cannot.

Fear exists when a person is afraid and knows what he or she is afraid of. *Anxiety* exists when a person is afraid but does not know what he or she is afraid of. The fears and anxieties that most rule our lives are not spectacular ones. Most of us do not chronically fear having to fight a great white shark with a letter opener. What we do fear is being rejected and failing. We all experience anxiety at times— a troubled uneasiness of mind mixed with uncertainty and doubt. But when the feeling is persistent, with an intensity out of proportion to the object or situation that caused it, the anxiety is called a *phobia*. Phobias can develop in at least three ways. They can result from anxiety attacks, as people associate their feelings of panic with the places and situations in which they occur. A panic attack that occurs while you are driving your car, for example, may result in a phobia about driving. Phobias can also grow out of specific experiences. If you were bitten by a dog when you were a young child, for example, you may develop a phobia around dogs. Finally, phobias can be learned from others, such as by observing parents who fear lightning or bugs. In some cases the fear involved in a phobia is displaced from its original source to a different place or situation. A fear of falling in social status, for example, may be repressed and displaced into a fear of falling an elevator.

Fear and anxiety usually involve two kinds of pain. One type of pain comes from doing what you are afraid of. The other type of pain comes from avoiding what you are afraid of. Either way you experience pain. The pain connected with doing an activity is generally less in the long run than the pain connected with avoiding an activity. Replacing the unpleasantness of rejection with the pain of loneliness usually is not a good bargain. Simply avoiding anxiety-provoking situations does not remove discomfort. There is discomfort in combatting the fear and there is discomfort in giving into the fear. The discomfort connected with overcoming your fears has an ending, whereas the annoyance connected with not changing your fears can go on as long as you live.

The procedures for managing and overcoming your fears and anxieties include:

1. Do not fear anxiety. Once you become afraid that your anxiety may come back, it will. Fearing that you may become anxious creates anxiety. The more you worry about the possibility of experiencing an anxiety attack, the more likely it is that you will have one. Generally, the more you worry about something, the worse it gets.

2. Accept yourself as you are. Rejection from others cannot hurt unless you reject yourself as a result. Failing cannot hurt unless you reject yourself as a result. Being an anxious person or a person who has anxiety attacks does not make you a horrible outcast. You do not have to be loved and accepted by others to like yourself, you do not have to be perfect in order to respect yourself, and you do not have to be in perfect control of your feelings in order to feel worthwhile.

3. Challenge the idea that you must worry over something unpleasant just because it "might" happen to you. Do not "what-if." Avoid the neurotic idea that it is important to think about a danger. Fight the idea that you should constantly think of, dwell upon, and worry over a frightening situation. Do not dwell upon "a grain of truth" and magnify it out of proportion. Vigorously attack the mental nonsense (neurotic misconceptions) that:
   a. You ought to be terribly upset about something.
   b. Worrying helps.
   c. The more you focus on the dreaded event, the better it is, i.e., it is important to think about potential danger just because it "might" happen.
   d. Outside events can upset you. Remember that it is your thinking about things that disturbs you, not the things themselves.

4. Avoid catastrophizing. The moment you tell yourself that something is awful or terrible, or that you are facing a catastrophe, you are going to become disturbed. The two things you can do are to:
   a. Convince yourself that the situation is not a catastrophe after all. Accept your fear as being a minor, not a major, inconvenience.
   b. Convince yourself that even if the situation is a catastrophe there is really no need to become terribly upset over it, since it only makes your situation worse.

5. Remember that being afraid does not mean that you are crazy. Many people fear that experiencing an anxiety attack will drive them crazy. They are afraid that experiencing anxiety means that they are losing their minds. They see themselves as going out of control and running berserk down the street. Being afraid and being psychotic are two separate things entirely. An anxiety attack may feel strange and puzzling, but it does not mean you are going crazy.

6. Systematically densensitize yourself to the fearful situation by:
   a. Learn how to relax systematically. A relaxed person cannot be an anxious person.
   b. After you are relaxed, imagine yourself overcoming your fears by engaging in the behavior you are afraid of.

7. Flood yourself with actual experiences of doing what you are most afraid of. Such flooding involves at least three elements:
   a. Taking risks by repeatedly exposing yourself to the very thing you are most afraid of. You overcome your fear when you do the thing you are afraid to do and are willing to face the dangers involved. Those persons who do not take risks in facing their fears live in a constant state of anxiety and apprehension. If you are afraid of riding an elevator, you must do so anyway. People who have ridden in an elevator thousands of times do not have the same nervousness as the person who rarely takes an elevator.
   b. Not blaming yourself if you perform less than perfectly in the situation. Separate your actions and performance from yourself.
   c. Practicing facing the fearful situation and then practicing some more. Practice

makes you the master. If you have not mastered the situation you are afraid of, you have not practiced it enough. To master an activity you have to:

a. Practice it.

b. Examine the performance to find out where you can improve.

c. Change.

d. Practice it again.

In other words, stick your neck out and do the thing you are afraid of. Then, after you have done less than perfectly, sit back objectively and look over your mistakes so that you can improve next time. Progress is built on mistakes. The person who does not make mistakes does not learn.

8. Distract yourself when the anxiety becomes too high. It is impossible to be upset about something unless you are thinking about it. Anything that diverts you from your troubles will give you relief.

9. Work on developing a broad view of life and a wide variety of experiences. The more you know about the world, and the more you have experienced, the more comfortable you tend to be in any situation. The person with the most experiences is the person who can compare the next experience to those that he or she has already had.

10. Do not be afraid of being independent. Do not ask for sympathy from other people. There is a tendency to use one's fear and anxiety to control others by expecting them to feel sorry for you or to make excuses and exceptions for you, because you are terrified. People who are afraid and who lean upon others to help them with their fears are not always quick to give them up, because to do so means they have become independent, which they are sometimes reluctant to do.

11. Accept reality. Life is full of danger, heartache, and injustice. Every living creature has to go through some suffering and you are no different. If you are not facing some suffering today, you will be tomorrow. There is no need to be terrified or nervous or worried about these possibilities. Remind yourself that:

a. Most frustrations are really not as bad as you think they are.

b. Even if some are that bad, you do not have to lose your mind over them and thus make matters worse. If you focus on danger, heartache, and injustice unduly, you will create unnecessary additional suffering for yourself and for the people around you.

Breathing

Breathing is essential to life. Proper breathing is an antidote to stress. It is through proper breathing that your blood is purified of waste products, infused with oxygen, and purged of carbon dioxide. Poorly oxygenated blood contributes to anxiety states, depression, and fatigue, making it many times more difficult to cope with stressful situations. Proper breathing habits are essential for good mental and physical health and are a key to relaxing effectively. When you are faced with an anxiety-provoking situation, deep and proper breathing is one of your first lines of defense.

Breathing exercises have been found to be effective in reducing anxiety, depression, irritability, muscular tension, and fatigue.

**EXERCISE
12.2**   **Learning How to Breathe Deeply**

PURPOSE

The objective of this exercise is to help you relax systematically when you are anxious by controlling your breathing. The procedure for the exercise is:

1. Sit up straight in good posture in a hard-backed chair.

2. Slowly breathe inward through your nose counting from one to four as you do so.
   a. First fill the lower section of your lungs. Your diaphram will push your abdomen outward to make room for the air.
   b. Second, fill the middle part of your lungs. As you do so you will feel your lower ribs and chest move slightly forward to accomodate the air.
   c. Third, fill the upper part of your lungs. Raise your shoulders and collarbone slightly so that the very tops of your lungs are replenished with fresh air.

   Practice until these three steps are performed in one smooth, continuous inhalation.

3. Hold your breath for four seconds.

4. Exhale slowly counting to eight while you do so. Pull in your abdomen slightly and lift it slowly as the lungs empty. When you have completely exhaled, relax your abdomen and chest.

5. Continue deep breathing for about five to ten minutes at a time.

6. Scan your body for tension. Compare the tension you feel at this time with the tension you felt at the beginning.

7. Use this deep breathing procedure whenever you feel yourself getting tense.

The Problem of Shyness

○   ○   ○

Every person, experiencing as he does his own solitariness and aloneness, longs for union with another.

ROLLO MAY, *Love and Will*

○   ○   ○

○   ○   ○

There is no joy except in human relationships.

ANTOINE DE SAINT-EXUPERY *Wind, Sand, and Stars*

○   ○   ○

Answer the following questions yes or no

____ 1. I often become anxious when I am the center of attention.

____ 2. I am often concerned about being rejected by others.

____ 3. I tend to be very self-conscious in interacting with other people.

____ 4. When I am with people I do not know, I hesitate before expressing my thoughts and feelings.

____ 5. I am very conscious of whether people like me or not.

____ 6. I need to be more aggressive in forming relationships with other people.

If you answered yes to several of the above questions, you may be suffering from a very common problem, shyness. *Shyness* is an excessive caution in interpersonal relations (Johnson, D.W. 1986). Specifically, shy people tend to (1) be timid about expressing themselves, (2) be overly self-conscious about how others are reacting to them, (3) embarrass easily, and (4) experience physiological symptoms of their anxiety, such as a racing pulse, blushing, or an upset stomach (Zimbardo, 1977). Shyness involves excessive caution in social interaction and may include timidity, self-consciousness, anxiety, and sensitivity to embarrassment.

If you are shy, you are not alone. Most people have been shy during some stage of their lives and up to 40 percent of Americans report being troubled currently by shyness. Most people experience shyness only in certain situations, such as when asking someone for help, when interacting with a member of the opposite sex, or when attending large parties. Shyness has a number of undesirable consequences, such as contributing to difficulty in making friends, being lonely and depressed, and being sexually inhibited. It is no surprise, therefore, that the vast majority of shy people do not like being shy.

Shyness can be successfully overcome. Although shyness tends to be a deeply entrenched part of a person's personality, and it takes a great deal of hard work to overcome, most shy people believe that they have conquered their shyness. The three steps in doing so are (1) understanding your shyness, (2) building your self-esteem, and (3) improving your social skills.

Understanding Your Shyness

You should analyze your shyness to pinpoint exactly what social situations tend to elicit your shy behavior, and you should try to ascertain what *causes* your shyness in the identified situations. In his study on shyness Zimbardo (1977) found that the people who generated shyness (in decreasing order) were:

1. Strangers.
2. Members of the opposite sex.
3. Authorities by virtue of their knowledge.
4. Authorities by virtue of their role.
5. Relatives.
6. Elderly people.
7. Friends.
8. Children.
9. Parents.

The situations in which people tended to feel shy (in decreasing order) were being:

1. The focus of attention of a large group (such as when giving a speech).
2. A member of a large group.
3. Of lower status than the other people present.
4. In social situations in general.
5. In new situations in general.
6. In situations requiring assertiveness.
7. In situations where one was being evaluated.
8. The focus of attention of a small group.
9. In small social groups.
10. In one-to-one interactions with a member of the opposite sex.
11. Vulnerable (needing help).
12. In small task-oriented groups.
13. In one-to-one interactions with a member of the same sex.

Building Your Self-Esteem

Your shyness lies primarily within your evaluation of your self-worth. Increased self-confidence is an important aspect of combatting shyness. Some of the guidelines for building higher self-esteem are as follows:

1. **Control your self-esteem through how you see yourself.** Changing the way in which you think about yourself will change your self-esteem.
2. **Set your own standards for evaluating yourself.** Do not fall into the common trap of letting others set the standards by which you evaluate yourself. People with low self-esteem tend to be particularly susceptible to persuasion and too readily accept others' standards for their own.
3. **Set realistic goals.** Do not demand too much of yourself. Do not expect your-

self to perform always at your best. Compare your performance against that of average individuals, not superstars.

4. **Modify negative self-talk and attributions.** Individuals with low self-esteem tend to think in counterproductive ways and make negative statements to themselves. When they succeed, for example, they may attribute it to good luck rather than to their ability and effort. Make sure you take credit for your successes and consider seriously the possibility that failures may not be your fault. Make self-enhancing conclusions about the way in which you applied your abilities and effort and tell yourself what a competent and good person you are.

5. **Emphasize your strengths.** People with low self-esteem often derive little satisfaction from their accomplishments and virtues. They pay little heed to their good qualities while emphasizing their defeats and faults. Accept your personal shortcomings that you are powerless to change and work to change those that are changeable. At the same time, you should increase your awareness of your strengths and learn to appreciate them.

6. **Work to improve yourself.** Efforts at self-improvement can be used to boost your self-esteem. Many personal shortcomings can be conquered. Although it is important to reassess your goals and discard those that are unrealistic or are imposed by others, this book is an example of how you can improve your interpersonal skills and your confidence in relating to others.

7. **Approach others with a positive outlook.** Negativity towards yourself can result in negativity towards others. Fault-finding and criticism destroy relationships with others. It leads to tension, bitter exchanges, and rejection which, in turn, lower your self-esteem. When you approach people with a positive, supportive outlook, you will promote rewarding interactions and gain acceptance. Nothing enhances self-esteem more than acceptance and genuine affection from others.

EXERCISE 12.3   **Understanding Your Shyness**

PURPOSE

The objective of this exercise is to help you analyze the social situations in which you feel shy and the causes of your shyness. Without understanding your shyness you cannot build an effective strategy to overcome it.

PROCEDURE

1. Divide into pairs. Complete the following steps for both of you.
2. Specify your target behaviors.
   a. Examine the lists of Zimbrado's findings on which people and situations tend to generate shyness in others (see pages 299–300). List the ones that seem most characteristic of you.
   b. Which of the following may be reasons for your shyness?
      (1) Concern about negative evaluation.
      (2) Fear of rejection.
      (3) Lack of self-confidence.
      (4) Lack of specific interpersonal skills.
      (5) Fear of intimacy.
      (6) Preference for being alone.
      (7) Emphasis on and enjoyment of nonsocial activities.
      (8) Personal inadequacy or handicap.
   c. Which of the following negative thoughts are typical of you and help prevent you from pursuing relationships in an active and positive way? Each of these thoughts undermines or precludes productive interpersonal behavior.
      (1) I am undesirable.
      (2) I am dull and boring.
      (3) If I ever admitted this thought to anyone, he/she would reject or ridicule me.
      (4) Other people are not interested in my thoughts and feelings.
      (5) I can not relax, be spontaneous, and enjoy myself.
      (6) I can not seem to get what I want from this relationship.
      (7) If I said how I feel, he/she might leave me and I will be all alone.
      (8) I will not risk being hurt again.
      (9) There must be something wrong with me if he/she left me.
      (10) I do not know how to act around other people.
      (11) I will make a fool of myself.
   d. Generate a number of specific behaviors you wish to increase in frequency within the problem situations and with the problem people. Initiating a conversation, asking someone to dance, and paraphrasing a person's remarks are examples.

3. Gather the baseline data. The baseline period is a span of time, before the actual beginning of your efforts to change, during which you systematically observe your target behaviors. Gathering baseline data includes (a) measuring the specific frequency of the behaviors targeted to be increased, (b) noting the situations or events that precede the occurrence of the targeted behavior, and (c) noting the typical consequences of the targeted behavior.

   a. Place yourself in the situation in which you feel shy. Count how often you engage in the behavior targeted to be increased (such as initiating a conversation). You need to know the initial frequency of the target behavior in order to evaluate later how effectively you are increasing it. Because it is crucial that you have accurate data about the initial frequency of your behavior it is important that you be honest with yourself and count all instances of the targeted behavior. It may be necessary to carry a portable device for recording your behavior, which may be simply an index card. The information should then be transferred to a permanent, written record sheet or a graph. Do this for a week or for a minimum of five times.

   b. For each instance of the target behavior, note the situations, events, feelings, or thoughts that precede the occurrence of your targeted behavior. These questions may help:
      (1) What did I think or say to myself?
      (2) What behavior of other people occurred?
      (3) What were the physical circumstances of the past few minutes?

4. Based on your tentative conclusion as to the causes of your shyness and the data you have gathered about the frequency with which you naturally initiate and build a relationship, design a plan to increase the frequency of your targeted behavior. The plan should include:

   a. How you will reinforce or reward yourself for engaging in the desired behavior.

   b. The conditions you have to meet in order to earn the reward. Set a behavioral target and frequency that is both challenging and realistic.

5. Complete a Self-Change Contract for each member of the pair.

Avoiding Self-Blame

A major threat to self-acceptance and using your interpersonal skills is self-blame (Johnson, 1986). Self-blame exists when you say "bad me" to yourself or when you judge your basic self-worth on the basis of your inadequate or rotten behavior. Blame involves a double attack: one against your actions and the other against yourself as a person. If you spill coffee on your computer you can see your behavior as being uncoordinated, or you can see your behavior as clumsy and yourself

```
┌─────────────────────────────────────────────────────────┐
│                                                         │
│                  SELF-CHANGE CONTRACT                   │
│                                                         │
│                                                         │
│                                                         │
│     I, _____ do hereby agree │
│                                                         │
│  to initiate my action plan as of (date) _____ and to │
│                                                         │
│  continue it for a minimum period of _____ weeks or until │
│                                                         │
│  (date) _____.                           │
│                                                         │
│     My specific action plan is to _____ │
│                                                         │
│  _____ │
│                                                         │
│  _____ │
│                                                         │
│  _____ │
│                                                         │
│     I will do my utmost to complete this action plan to the best │
│  of my ability, and I will evaluate its effectiveness only after it has │
│  been honestly tried for the specified period of time.  │
│                                                         │
│     For every _____ times I successfully comply with my │
│                                                         │
│  action plan, I will reward myself with _____ │
│                                                         │
│  _____ │
│                                                         │
│     I hereby request that the witness who has signed below sup- │
│  port me in my action plan and encourage me to comply with the │
│  specifics of this contract.                            │
│                                                         │
│  Signed _____ Date _____      │
│                                                         │
│  Witness _____ Date _____      │
│                                                         │
└─────────────────────────────────────────────────────────┘
```

as rotten and no-good. Self-blame is similar to giving your basic self a grade on the basis of a behavior you do not like. It is based on the two beliefs that (1) you must be perfect and (2) bad people should be severely blamed and punished for their evil acts. When you blame yourself you see yourself as being imperfect and, therefore, being a bad person who should be severely punished. Blaming yourself is, in effect, being angry with yourself. You therefore have to carry the anger around inside you. Perhaps most important, blaming yourself distracts you from finding a solution to your problems. All the punishment in the world does not promote creative insight into how a situation may be managed more constructively.

You should never blame yourself for:

1. **Lacking intelligence.** If you don't have as much intellectual ability as you would like, it's not your fault. Intelligence is for the most part a genetic trait, and is determined greatly by your genes.

2. **Being ignorant.** Ignorance means that you have not yet learned a skill. You cannot blame yourself if you did not know better.

3. **Being in an emotionally disturbed state.** In such a state, irrational behavior can occur. You cannot blame yourself if your behavior was not under your control.

4. **Having behaved badly.** You should separate your behavior from your sense of self-worth. You are *not* your actions. Engaging in bad behavior does not make you a bad person.

5. **Not being perfect.** In perfectionism, you attempt to be all things, rather than who you are. A perfectionist never has developed an internal sense of how much is good enough. Only when you can stop trying to be all things do you ever become free to be who you are.

To combat self-blame you must first (a) change your basic assumptions about the need to be perfect and be punished when you fail to live up to your expectations, and (b) engage in an internal debate to replace your old assumptions with new, more constructive, ones. Secondly, you must forgive yourself for everything. The sooner you forgive yourself the better. Finally, be problem-oriented, not blame- or fault-oriented. Focus on the problem to be solved, not on your failure to live up to your expectations.

Growing on the Job

The longer you have the same job, the better you will do it. But your real growth on the job does not come from increasing your technical skills. Your real growth on the job comes from increasing your skills in working cooperatively with other people. You grow on the job as you improve your interpersonal skills—as you improve your relationships with your fellow employees.

Mastering interpersonal skills does not end when you finish this book, or your training. Your interpersonal skills will improve as long as you are alive.

No matter how old you are, no matter how long you have worked, your interpersonal skills can still be improved. As you meet more and more people within an organization, learn new ways to provide leadership and increase cooperation among fellow employees, you will grow on the job. You will grow on the job as you become more skillful in managing conflicts and as your relationships with your fellow employees deepen. Your growth depends on continuing to improve your interpersonal skills and on improving your relationships with your fellow employees.

Improving your technical and organizational skills is important. But do not forget that the organization you work for is a network of interpersonal relationships aimed at achieving goals. As you improve your interpersonal skills, you improve the organized efforts of the people you work with. Your organization is held together by the ability of employees to work with each other. Your organization survives by employees cooperating with each other. Therefore, as your interpersonal skills improve, so does your ability to contribute to the organization.

Basic Interpersonal Skills

Other people are a key factor in your success or failure on the job. They can help you do a good job, or they can make you do a bad job. Other people can make your job fun and interesting, challenging and rewarding. It is other people who make your career meaningful. If you like your fellow employees and they like you, going to work is something you look forward to. If you dislike your fellow employees and they dislike you, going to work is something you dread. In the long run, it is your interpersonal relationships at work that make your career satisfying and successful. Your interpersonal skills are the most important aspect of your career.

If your career is to be successful, it is essential to master the following set of interpersonal skills:

1. **Setting realistic goals.** You need to be aware of your goals, assets, and credentials. And you need to be able to communicate them to potential employers. Your goals need to be flexible so they can be modified to overlap with the goals of the organization you work for.

2. **Cooperating and leading.** Your career depends on your ability to work cooperatively with other people. The very nature of an organization demands cooperation among employees. And cooperation takes leadership. An essential part of cooperating is helping the organization achieve its goals and maintain good working relationships among employees.

3. **Communicating.** Sending and receiving messages is an essential aspect of any job. Managing your feelings is an essential aspect of any job. And communicating your feelings is an important interpersonal skill. The more skilled in communicating you are, the more successful your career will be.

4. **Forming good relationships.** Your self-awareness, self-acceptance, and ability to let yourself be known are essential aspects of forming good relationships on the job. You also need to be able to get to know others. You need to be skilled in building and maintaining trust. The ability to appreciate yourself and appreciate diversity among fellow employees is also important. Forming good relationships on the job is one of the most rewarding aspects of your career.

5. **Managing conflicts.** Being able to manage conflicts like an Owl is an important interpersonal skill. Conflicts will inevitably occur. You need to be able to define them constructively. You need to initiate helpful conversations about the conflict, arrive at joint definitions, disagree without rejecting the other person, accept disagreement without feeling rejected, see the conflict from the other person's viewpoint and arrive at a solution that leaves both you and the other person satisfied. Managing conflicts is probably the most difficult aspect of maintaining good relationships on the job. It takes all the interpersonal skills discussed in this book to manage conflicts successfully.

All these interpersonal skills have been discussed in this book. Experiences have been structured so you can learn the skills. You have practiced most of the skills. You may find you wish to repeat many of the exercises. You may want to reread many of the chapters of the book. You will want to keep practicing the skills until they are so automatic that they are your natural way of acting.

It is your relationships with other people that make your career seem worthwhile and enjoyable. Keep improving your interpersonal skills. And enjoy your relationships with the people you interact with during your career.

Interpersonal Skills: A Detailed Outline

1. Goals:
   a. Be aware of your goals.
   b. Be aware of your assets.
   c. Increase your credentials.
   d. Seek opportunities.
   e. Be ready to modify your goals so that they overlap the goals of the organization and your fellow employees.
2. Cooperating and Leading:
   a. Join with other people and work together toward goals both you and they want to achieve.
   b. Try to view the overall task to be achieved.
   c. Contribute reliably your part of the overall task to be done.
   d. Help others to complete their part of the overall task.
   e. Keep your actions within the expectations of your supervisor and fellow employees.
   f. Engage in actions that help achieve the task.

g. Engage in actions that help maintain good relationships among employees.

h. Be aware of what actions are needed to help achieve the task and maintain good relationships among employees.

i. Cheerfully follow the instructions of your supervisor.

3. Communicating:

a. Speak for yourself by using personal pronouns when expressing thoughts, feelings, and needs.

b. Describe other people's actions without making value judgments.

c. Use relationship statements when they are appropriate.

d. Take the receiver's perspective into account when sending your message.

e. Ask for feedback about the receiver's understanding of your message.

f. Make your nonverbal messages agree with your words.

g. Describe your feelings.

h. Describe what you think the other person is feeling and then ask if you are correct.

i. Paraphrase accurately without making value judgments about the sender's thoughts, feelings, and needs.

j. Understand what the message means from the sender's perspective.

k. Recognize your irrational assumptions that lead to negative feelings.

l. Build more rational assumptions.

m. Argue with yourself, replacing your irrational assumptions with your rational ones.

4. Forming Good Relationships:

   a. Be aware of and accept your thoughts, feelings, needs, and behavior.

   b. Express your thoughts, feelings, and needs to other people when it is appropriate; let other people know you as you really are.

   c. Listen to the thoughts, feelings, and needs of fellow employees. Get to know coworkers as well as possible.

   d. Seek out feedback from fellow employees.

   e. Give feedback to fellow employees when they request it.

   f. Build trust by taking small risks in relating to fellow employees and by being accepting and supportive of the risks taken by fellow employees.

   g. Appreciate yourself.

   h. Appreciate diversity among your fellow employees.

5. Conflicts:

   a. Be aware of your habitual conflict style. Modify your conflict style according to the situation and the person you are dealing with. Whenever possible, manage conflicts like an Owl. View conflicts as problems to be solved. Be aware of their potential value. And seek solutions that achieve both your goals and the goals of the other person. Try to improve your relationships with the other people by resolving the conflicts.

   b. Define conflicts:

      (1) Describe the other person's actions without labeling or insulting him.

      (2) Describe the conflict as a mutual problem to be solved, not as a "win-loss" struggle.

      (3) Describe the conflict as specifically as possible.

      (4) Describe *your* feelings and reactions to the other person's actions.

      (5) Describe *your* actions that help create and continue the conflict.

   c. Know when and how to confront—to begin open discussions of the conflict, aimed at resolving it constructively.

   d. Define the conflict jointly with the other person.

   e. Be sure to define the conflict. This should involve issues, not personalities. Make it clear that you disagree with the other person's ideas or actions, not with him as a person. Do not take criticism of your ideas and actions as criticism of you as a person.

   f. Find out how you and the other person differ before seeking to resolve the conflict.

   g. See the conflict from the other person's viewpoint.

   h. Increase both your motivation and the other person's motivation to resolve the conflict.

   i. Manage your feelings so that they do not make the conflict worse.

   j. Reach an agreement about how the conflict is to end and not recur.

SUMMARY AND REVIEW: Chapters 11 and 12

Setting Learning Contracts

You are to make a learning contract with your group. The learning contract should summarize the most important things you have learned from Chapters 11 and 12. It should include a plan as to how you will use what you have learned. Chapters 11 and 12 focus on career skills and surviving on the job. It is time to reflect, with your group's help, on what you have learned about career skills and how you can use what you have learned.

Be as specific as you can in stating what you have learned and how you will apply what you have learned. The following procedure is to be used in setting your learning contract with your group.

Procedure

1. Working by yourself, make a list of the more important things you have learned about career skills and job survival. List at least five things you have learned.

2. Select the five most important things you have learned. For each one, plan an action you can take in the next two weeks to apply that learning. In making your action plans, be specific and practical. Do not try to do either too much or too little.

3. Copy the sample learning contract on page 59 and fill it out, but do not sign it.

4. In your group, draw numbers to see who is to go first. The member selected reviews her learnings and action plans with the group. The group helps the member be more clear about learnings. Some members' learnings may be too vague. Or a member may have achieved an insight about her career plans that she has not listed. The group also helps the member make better action plans. Some members may plan to do more than is possible; other members may not plan to do enough. You may be able to think of a better way to put the learning into action.

5. The member's learning contract is modified until both she and the rest of the group are satisfied with it. She then signs the contract, and then the rest of the group signs the contract. The member is now committed to the group to carry out her action plans.

6. The whole process is repeated until every member of the group has a learning contract with the group.

7. The instructor will set a date—about two weeks after the contract was signed—for the group to review each member's progress in completing his action plans.

8. Working alone, keep a record of your progress in completing your action plans. Copy and fill out the Learning Contract Progress Report form on page 60. Use it when you give a progress report to your group.

9. In the progress review session, you will report to your group the day and date of the actions taken, describe what you did, what success you had, and what problems you encountered.

Reviewing Learning Contract

At the end of Section V, you made a contract with your group. Your contract dealt with what you learned from the exercises in Section V and how you were going to apply those learnings. At that time, you were told that in a progress review session you would be asked to give the day and date of the actions taken, describe what you did, and state what success you had and what problems you encountered. The purpose of this session is to review your contract dealing with Section V.

Procedure

1. Draw numbers to see who will go first. Then go around the group clockwise. Each person is to review what tasks and activities he was to engage in to apply learnings from Section V. He then is to give the day and date on which the tasks and activities were completed, tell what success he experienced, and state what problems he encountered. Group members are to praise a person's successes and are to provide helpful suggestions to overcome any problems a person is having in completing a learning contract.

2. When a learning contract has been completed, it is considered fulfilled. If a member has not fulfilled his learning contract, he is expected to do so in the near future. An unfinished contract will be discussed again at the next session set aside for that purpose.

Tournament Rules

When you have finished a section of the book, your class can hold a competitive tournament to see which group knows the material best. In this tournament, you will be a representative of your group and will compete with two other classmates from two other groups. The competition is run as follows:*

1. Sit at a table with two other students, both representing other groups.

2. The teacher places an answer sheet and a deck of cards face down in the middle of the table. Each card contains a question on the material in this section. Each player draws a card and tries to answer the question. The object is to see who can correctly answer the most cards. (The complete rules for the tournament are given below.)

3. After all the cards have been answered correctly (or when the teacher calls time), you count to see who has the most cards. The person with the most cards gets six points, the second highest gets four points, and the person in third place gets two points. If all three contestants have the same number of cards, they each get four points. If there is a tie for first and second, each person gets five points. If there is a tie for second and third, each person gets three points.

4. Return to your group and report how many points you won. Then the group adds up all the points its members received.

5. The teacher posts the total points of each group. The group with the most points is the winner.

Tournament Rules

Study the following rules, so that everyone in your group knows how to play in the tournament.

*Procedures and game rules are adapted from the work of David DeVries, Keith Edwards, and their colleagues at Johns Hopkins University.

A. To start the game shuffle the cards and place them face down on the table. Play is in a clock-wise rotation.

B. To play, each player in turn takes the top card from the deck, reads it aloud, and does one of two things:

1. Says he does not know or is not sure of the answer and asks if another player wants to answer. If no one wants to answer, the card is placed on the bottom of the deck. If a player answers, he follows the procedure below.

2. Answers the question immediately and asks if anyone wants to challenge the answer. The player to his right has the first chance to challenge. If he does not wish to challenge, then the player to his right may challenge.

   a. If there is no challenge, another player should check the answer:
      1. If correct, the player keeps the card.
      2. If incorrect, the player must place the card on the bottom of the deck.

   b. If there is a challenge and the challenger decides not to answer, the answer is checked. If the original answer is wrong, the player must place the card on the bottom of the deck.

   c. If there is a challenge and the challenger gives an answer, the answer is checked.
      1. If the challenger is correct, he receives the card.
      2. If the challenger is incorrect, and the original answer is correct, the challenger must give up one of the cards he has already won (if any) and place it on the bottom of the deck.
      3. If both answers are incorrect, the card is placed on the bottom of the deck.

C. The game ends when there are no more cards in the deck. The player who has the most cards is the winner.

B

Instructions
and Answers
for Selected Exercises*

CHAPTER 3: "Broken Squares Puzzle"

Instructor's Directions for Making a Set of Squares

Prepare a set of five envelopes containing pieces of cardboard that have been cut in different patterns and that, when properly arranged, will form five squares of equal size. You need one set for each group of five people.

To prepare a set, cut out five identical cardboard squares measuring 6 × 6 inches. Mark the squares as shown in the diagrams, and pencil in the letters a, b, c, etc. (lightly, so they can be erased later).

The lines should be so drawn that when cut out, all pieces marked a will be identical, all pieces marked c will be identical, and so on. By using multiples of 3 inches, several combinations are possible that will enable participants to form one or two squares, but only one combination is possible that will form five squares, 6 × 6 inches.

---

*For additional exercises that focus on the same skills and ideas, see D. W. Johnson, 4th edition (1990) and D. W. Johnson and F. P. Johnson, 4th edition (1991).

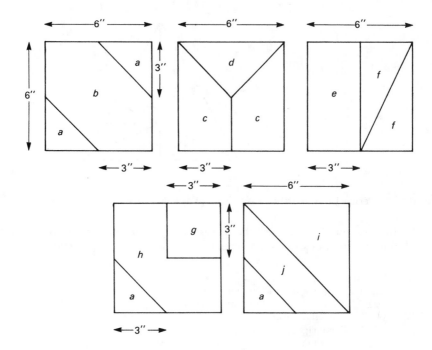

After drawing the lines and labeling the sections with lowercase letters, cut up each square as marked into smaller pieces to make the parts of the puzzle.

Mark each of five envelopes A, B, C, D, and E. Distribute the cardboard pieces in the five envelopes as follows:

Envelope A has pieces i, h, e.
Envelope B has pieces a, a, a, c.
Envelope C has pieces a, j.
Envelope D has pieces d, f.
Envelope E has pieces g, b, f, c.

Erase the small penciled letter from each piece and write, instead, the appropriate envelope letter—A, B, etc. This will make it easy to return the pieces to the proper envelope for reuse.

Chapter 3: "Triangles Exercise"

Instructor's Directions

Duplicate the triangle diagram below and distribute it with the following instructions:

Here is a triangle with several triangles inside of it. Working alone, try to find as many of the triangles as you can. Write your answer on a sheet to hand in. *No talking is allowed.* You will have fifteen minutes to do this exercise.

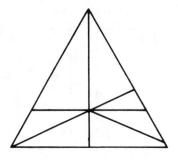

Chapter 4: "Your Leadership Behavior" (Task-Maintenance Style)

In the blanks below, insert the scores from your questionnaire: odd-numbered items go under task actions; even-numbered items under maintenance actions. Then total each list.

Task Actions

_____ 1. Information and Opinion Giver
_____ 3. Information and Opinion Seeker
_____ 5. Direction Giver
_____ 7. Summarizer
_____ 9. Coordinator
_____ 11. Energizer
_____ Total for Task Actions

Maintenance Actions

_____ 2. Encourager of Participation
_____ 4. Tension Reliever
_____ 6. Communication Helper
_____ 8. Evaluator of Emotional Climate
_____ 10. Process Observer
_____ 12. Active Listener
_____ Total for Maintenance Actions

Locate your position on the Task-Maintenance Grid on page 98 by finding your total score for Task Actions on the bottom, horizontal axis of the grid. Then move up the column corresponding to your Task score to the point of intersection with your score for Maintenance Actions. Place an "X" at the intersection that represents your two scores. Numbers in parentheses correspond to the major styles of Task-Maintenance leadership actions. The Key describes each behavior style.

Chapter 4: "Murder on the Amtrak Express"

Instructor's Directions for Preparing Clues

Put one clue each on a 3 × 5 card. You need a deck of 30 for each group.

☐ A bullet was found to have been fired from Edythe's gun.

- [ ] Frank, Helen, Roger, David, and Edythe refused steadfastly to eat any meals on the train.
- [ ] Edythe, a Texan by marriage, had brought along her gun.
- [ ] Edythe boarded the train in Taylor, Texas, at noon on the day of the murder.
- [ ] Frank went along for the ride.
- [ ] David and Roger Johnson were riding the Amtrak Express to Austin, Texas, to hold a workshop on cooperation.
- [ ] The Johnsons found out that Mr. Jones was getting twice as much money for his workshop as they were getting for theirs.
- [ ] Mr. Smith disappeared from the train soon after it left Taylor, Texas.
- [ ] Mr. Brown sometimes held workshops on competition.
- [ ] Keith and Dale Johnson were hired as cooks on the Amtrak Express, their first steady employment in years.
- [ ] Mr. Jones was going to Austin to hold a workshop on competition.
- [ ] Mr. Jones boasted loudly that his competitive goal structure was better than the Johnsons' cooperative goal structure.
- [ ] Frank reported that he had heard a loud noise about the time he was complaining to Helen about Edythe.
- [ ] All but two of the passengers boarded the train at Minneapolis.
- [ ] Frame Switch is a small community about eight miles out of Taylor, Texas.
- [ ] Frank, Helen, Roger, David, Keith and Dale all boarded the train together.
- [ ] A bullet was found lodged in Frank's guitar.
- [ ] Edythe went along to see that her brothers did not slander her.
- [ ] Mr. Jones complained of stomach pains soon after breakfast.
- [ ] Mr. Jones had talked several groups into hiring him to do workshops instead of Mr. Brown.
- [ ] Helen reported that someone had stolen the poison she always carried with her.
- [ ] Mr. Brown was a very competitive person.
- [ ] Mr. Jones, Mr. Smith, and Mr. Brown always ate their meals together.
- [ ] A shot was heard just before the body was found.
- [ ] The murderer did not board the train in Minneapolis.
- [ ] The victim died an hour after eating breakfast in the dining car.
- [ ] Breakfast on the train was always served at 8:00 A.M.
- [ ] Helen went along to supervise.
- [ ] Mr. Smith was found drinking Lone Star beer at Frame Switch, Texas.
- [ ] Mr. Jones and Mr. Smith boarded the train at the same time.

Answers to the Murder Mystery

Victim:	Mr. Jones
Murderer:	Mr. Brown
Weapon:	Poison
Time of Death:	9:00 A.M.
Place:	The train
Motive:	Revenge (competition)
The Moral:	Cooperation is healthier than competition.

Chapter 4: "Selecting a City"

Instructor's Directions for Preparing Envelope Instructions

The following instructions should be written on the large envelope, which contains all the other envelopes:

> Enclosed you will find three envelopes containing directions for the phases of this group session. You are to open the first one (labeled Envelope A) at once. Later instructions will tell you when to open the second (Envelope B) and third (Envelope C).

Envelope A contains the following directions:

> **Directions for Envelope A:**
>
> Time allowed: fifteen minutes.
>
> Special instructions: Each member is to take one of the enclosed envelopes and follow the individual role-playing instructions contained in it.
>
> Task: The group is to select a city
>
> DO NOT LET ANYONE ELSE SEE YOUR INSTRUCTIONS!
>
> *(After fifteen minutes, go on to the next envelope.)*

Envelope B contains the following directions:

> **Directions for Envelope B:**
>
> Time allowed: five minutes.
>
> Task: You are to choose a group chairperson.
>
> *(After five minutes, go on to the next envelope.)*

Envelope C contains the following directions:

> **Directions for Envelope C:**
>
> Time allowed: ten minutes.
>
> Task: You are to evaluate the first phase of this group session.
>
> Special instructions for the second phase: The newly selected chairperson will lead a discussion on the roles and actions of group members in the process of decision making and their feelings and reactions to that process. The discussion should begin with the report of the observers.
>
> *(After ten minutes return the directions to their respective envelopes and prepare for a general discussion of the exercise.)*

Students' Role-Playing Instruction Envelopes for Phase I

Here are the contents of the six individual-instruction envelopes to be used in the first phase of the exercise. Each envelope contains an assigned leadership action and a position concerning which city to select. Two of the envelopes also contain special knowledge concerning the selection process.

> 1. *Leadership Action:* Evaluator of Emotional Climate
>   *Position:* Introduce and support Albuquerque. Oppose San Diego.

2. *Leadership Action:* Encourager of Participation
   Position: Introduce and support San Diego. Oppose Albuquerque.
   Special Knowledge: The group is going to select a chairperson later in the exercise. You are to conduct yourself in such a manner that they will select you.

3. *Leadership Action:* Process Observer
   Position: Introduce and support New York City.

4. *Leadership Action:* Active Listener
   Position: Oppose New York City.

5. *Leadership Action:* Communication Facilitator
   Position: When there seems to be a clear polarity in the discussion, suggest a compromise city, such as Minneapolis or Frame Switch, Texas.

6. *Leadership Action:* Tension Reliever
   Position: Support San Diego.
   Special Knowledge: The group is going to select a chairperson later in the exercise. You are to conduct yourself in such a manner that they will select you.

7. (if needed) *Leadership Action:* Any
   Position: Any

Chapter 5: "Who Owns This?"

Answers

1. N	2. S	3. N	4. O	5. S	6. O	7. O	8. N
9. O	10. O	11. S	12. N	13. O	14. S	15. S	16. N
17. S	18. N						

Chapter 5: "Describing"

Answers

1. D	2. J	3. J	4. J	5. D	6. J	7. J	8. D
9. D	10. J	11. J	12. D	13. D	14. D		

Chapter 5: Relationship Statements

Scoring

1. "We really enjoyed ourselves last night." This is a poor relationship statement because it speaks for the other person as well as oneself. It should be marked O.

2. "Our relationship is really lousy!" This is a poor relationship statement because it judges the quality of the relationship rather than describing some aspect of the relationship. It should be marked J.

3. "For the past two days, you have not spoken to me once. Is something wrong with our relationship?" This is a good relationship statement because it describes how the speaker sees one aspect of the relationship. It describes the speaker's perceptions of how the two people are relating to one another. Label it R.

4. "You look sick today." This is a poor relationship statement because it focuses on a person, not on a relationship. It should be marked P. The person may look sick, but such a statement

does not describe how the two people are relating to each other. It could be reworded as a good relationship statement as follows: "For the past fifteen minutes you have been holding your head in your hands. Are you not feeling well or is what I'm saying giving you a head-ache?"

5. "You really make me feel appreciated and liked." This is a good relationship statement be-cause the speaker is describing one aspect of how she and the other person relate to each other. Label it R.

6. "You're angry again. You're always getting angry." This is a poor relationship statement be-cause it speaks for the other person. It should be marked O. A good relationship statement would be: "You look angry. You've frequently looked angry to me during the past two days. Is there a problem about our relationship that we need to discuss?"

7. "We are great at communicating!" This is a poor relationship statement because it makes a judgment about the quality of communication between the speaker and the listener. It should be marked J. It also speaks for both you and the other person and, therefore, may also be marked O.

8. "I think we need to talk about our disagreement yesterday." This statement describes an aspect of the relationship and is, therefore, a good relationship statement. It should be marked R.

9. "I think you can finish that job today." This statement focuses on the listener, not on the relationship. It should be marked P.

10. "I feel you're making nasty comments. Are you angry with me?" This is a good relationship statement as it describes one aspect of the interaction between the speaker and the listener. It should be marked R.

11. "You really are mean and vicious!" This statement focuses on the other person and makes a judgment. It therefore can be marked P and J.

12. "My older brother is going to beat you up if you don't stop doing that." This statement focuses on another person (both the older brother and the listener). It should be marked P.

13. "I'm concerned that when we go to lunch together we are often late for work in the after-noon." This is a relationship statement and should be marked R. It describes an aspect of the relationship in that the two people manage their lunches together in such a way that they end up being late for work in the afternoon.

14. "You really seem happy about your promotion." This statement focuses on the other person and should be marked P. It describes how the other person seems to be feeling. The state-ment could be rephrased as a good relationship statement in the following way: "Since I enjoy working with you, I'm really happy that you were promoted."

15. "This job stinks!" Definitely a judgment (J). To be a good relationship statement, it would have to be something like the following: "I get so angry and upset at the way you treat me that I dislike working here."

16. "I'm confused by you. Last week you were really friendly to me. This week you have not even said hello once." This is a description of how the two people are relating to each other and is, therefore, a good relationship statement (R).

Chapter 6: "Perception-Check"

Answers

1. Q	2. PC	3. O	4. J	5. O	6. Q	7. PC
8. PC	9. J	10. PC	11. Q	12. J	13. O	14. PC
15. PC						

Chapter 8: Group Climate Questionnaire

Scoring

Write in your answers to each question and then add the total number of points in each column. Items with starred (*) numbers are reversed in the scoring; subtract your answer from 6 before entering the score for each starred item.

HONESTY	UNDERSTANDING	VALUING	ACCEPTING
1. ____	2. ____	*3. ____	4. ____
5. ____	*6. ____	7. ____	8. ____
*9. ____	10. ____	11. ____	*12. ____
13. ____	14. ____	15. ____	*16. ____
____Total	____ Total	____ Total	____ Total

Chapter 9: Conflict Questionnaire

Scoring

Write in your answers to each question and then add the total number of points in each column. The higher the total score for each conflict style the more true that style is for you. The lower the total score for each conflict style, the less true that style is for you. Rank the five conflict styles from most to least frequently used.

TURTLE	SHARK	TEDDY BEAR	FOX	OWL
____ 5.	____ 3.	____ 1.	____ 4.	____ 2.
____ 10.	____ 8.	____ 6.	____ 9.	____ 7.
____ 15.	____ 13.	____ 11.	____ 14.	____ 12.
____ 20.	____ 18.	____ 16.	____ 19.	____ 17.
____ Total	____ Total	____ Total	____ Total	____ Total

Chapter 10: Instructions for "Feelings in Conflicts"

Part 1: Feelings of Rejection

Person No. 1

You are to try to get the person sitting opposite you in your circle (Person 3) rejected from your group. Use any reason you can think of—he has big feet, she's the only person with glasses, he's got chapped hands—anything you think of. Stick to this, and try to convince the other members of your group that this is the person who should be rejected. You can listen to the arguments of the other members in the group, but don't give in. Be sure to talk about the person and not about rules for rejecting.

Person No. 2

You are to try to get the person sitting opposite you in your circle (Person 4) rejected from your group. Use any reason you can think of—he has big hands, she's the only person in a dress, he's got chapped lips, anything you can think of. Stick to this, and try to convince the other members in your group that this is the person who should be rejected. Be sure to talk about the person and not about the rules for rejecting. You can listen to the arguments of other group members, but don't give in.

Person No. 3

You are to try to get the person sitting at your left (Person 2) rejected from your group. Use any reason you can think of—he has large ears, she has freckles, he has dandruff, anything you can think of. Stick to this, and try to convince the other members that this is the person who should be rejected. You can listen to the arguments of other members, but don't give in.

Person No. 4

You are to try to get the person sitting on your right (Person 1) rejected from the group. Use any reason you can think of—he misses too many meetings, she's the only one in the group wearing a sweater, she's the shortest person, anything you can think of. Stick to this, and try to convince the other group members that this is the person who should be rejected. You can listen to the arguments of other people in the group, but don't give in. Be sure you talk about the person and not about rules for rejecting.

Part 2: Feelings of Mistrust

Instructions A

Do not share these instructions with the other person in your pair. Your task for the next five minutes is to talk as positively and warmly as you can to the other person. Say only positive and friendly things, showing especially that you want to cooperate and work effectively with her in the future. Your conversation is to concentrate on her, about your impression of her, and the need for cooperation between the two of you. Don't talk about yourself. No matter what happens you say only positive things. Keep the conversation moving along quickly. You are to speak first.

Instructions B

Do not share these instructions with the other person in your pair. The other person will speak first. Your task for the next five minutes is to talk with the other person in a way that shows distrust of him. Whatever he says, say something in return that communicates suspicion, distrust, disinterest, defiance, disbelief, or contradiction. Talk only about the things the other person talks about, and avoid starting conversation or bringing up new topics. Try not to help the other person out in any way. As an example, should your partner comment "Say, I like the shirt you're wearing," you might respond "What do you say that for? It's ugly. I don't like it at all. What are you trying to accomplish by complimenting my shirt?"

References

CAMPBELL, D.   1974. *If you don't know where you're going, you'll probably end up somewhere else.* Niles, IL: Argus.

COVEY, S.   1989. Seven habits of highly effective people. New York: Simon and Schuster.

DEUTSCH, M.   1973. *The resolution of conflict.* New Haven, CT: Yale University Press.

JANIS, I., and MANN, L.   1977. *Decision-making: A Psychological analysis of conflict, choice and commitment. New York: Free Press.*

JOHNSON, D. W.   1986, 1990. *Reaching out: Interpersonal effectiveness and self-actualization,* (3rd and 4th eds.). Englewood Cliffs, NJ: Prentice Hall.

JOHNSON, D. W., and JOHNSON, F.   1987, 1991. *Joining together: Group theory and group skills,* (3rd and 4th eds.). Englewood Cliffs, NJ: Prentice Hall.

JOHNSON, D. W., and JOHNSON, R.   1987. *Creative conflict.* Edina, MN: Interaction Book Company.

JOHNSON, D. W., and JOHNSON, R.   1989a. *Leading the cooperative school.* Edina, MN: Interaction Book Company.

JOHNSON, D. W., and JOHNSON, R.   1989b. *Cooperation and competition: Theory and research.* Edina, MN: Interaction Book Company.

JOHNSON, D. W., JOHNSON, R., and HOLUBEC, E.   1986, 1990. *Circles of learning: Cooperation in the classroom.* (revised editions). Edina, MN: Interaction Book Company.

JOHNSON, D. W., JOHNSON, R., and HOLUBEC, E.   1988. *Cooperation in the classroom.* (revised edition). Edina, MN: Interaction Book Company.

KOUZES, J., and POSNER, B.   1987. *The leadership challenge.* San Francisco: Jossey-Bass.

KRAUSE, C.   1978. *Guyana massacre: The eyewitness account.* New York: The Washington Post.

LAWRENCE, P., and LORSCH, J.   1967. *Organization and environment: Managing differentiation and integration.* Cambridge, MA: Division of Research, Graduate School of Business Administration, Harvard University.

MAGER, R.   1962. *Preparing instructional objectives.* Palo Alto, CA: Fearon.

MANN, L., and JANIS, I.   1983. Decisional conflict in organizations, in D. Tjosvold and D. Johnson (Eds.), *Productive Conflict Management.* New York: Irvington Publishers.

MILLER, S., NUNNALLY, E., and WACKMAN, D.   1975. *Instructor's Manual: Groups: Theory and Experience.* Boston: Houghton Mifflin.

National Center for Manufacturing Sciences   1989. *Making the grade: Student perspectives on the state of manufacturing.* Ann Arbor, MI: Engineering Education in America.

STANFORD, G., and STANFORD, B.   1969. *Learning discussion skills through games.* New York: Citation Press.

TERKEL, S.   1974. *Working.* New York: Pantheon Books.

VON MISES, L.   1949. *Human action; A treatise on economics.* New Haven, CT: Yale University Press.

WEINSTEIN, M., and GOODMAN, J.   1980. *Playfair: Everybody's guide to noncompetitive play.* San Luis Obispo, CA: Impact Publishers.

ZIMBARDO, P.   1977. *Shyness.* Reading, MA: Addison-Wesley.

Index